T0214838

Communications in Computer and Information Science　　592

Commenced Publication in 2007
Founding and Former Series Editors:
Alfredo Cuzzocrea, Dominik Ślęzak, and Xiaokang Yang

More information about this series at http://www.springer.com/series/7899

Weixia Xu · Liquan Xiao
Jinwen Li · Chengyi Zhang (Eds.)

Computer Engineering and Technology

19th CCF Conference, NCCET 2015
Hefei, China, October 18–20, 2015
Revised Selected Papers

Springer

Editors
Weixia Xu
National University of Defense Technology
Changsha
China

Liquan Xiao
National University of Defense Technology
Changsha
China

Jinwen Li
School of Computer Science
National University of Defense Technology
Changsha
China

Chengyi Zhang
National University of Defense Technology
Changsha
China

ISSN 1865-0929   ISSN 1865-0937   (electronic)
Communications in Computer and Information Science
ISBN 978-3-662-49282-6   ISBN 978-3-662-49283-3   (eBook)
DOI 10.1007/978-3-662-49283-3

Library of Congress Control Number: 2015960230

Printed on acid-free paper

This Springer imprint is published by SpringerNature
The registered company is Springer-Verlag GmbH Berlin Heidelberg

Preface

We are pleased to present the proceedings of the 19th Annual Conference on Computer Engineering and Technology (NCCET 2015). Over its short 19-year history, NCCET has established itself as one of the major national conferences dedicated to important and emerging challenges in the field of computer engineering and technology. Following previous successful events, NCCET 2015 provided a forum for bringing together researchers and practitioners from academia and industry to discuss cutting-edge research on computer engineering and technology.

We are delighted that the conference continues to attract high-quality submissions from a diverse and national group of researchers. This year, we received 158 paper submissions, among which 18 papers were accepted. Each paper received three or four peer reviews from our Technical Program Committee (TPC) comprising a total of 61 TPC members from academia, government, and industry.

The pages of this volume represent only the end result of an enormous endeavor involving hundreds of people. Almost all this work is voluntary, with some individuals contributing hundreds of hours of their time to the effort. Together, the 61 members of the TPC, the 16 members of the External Review Committee (ERC), and the 13 other individual reviewers consulted for their expertise wrote nearly 500 reviews.

Every paper received at least two reviews and many had three or more. With the exception of submissions by the TPC, each paper had at least two reviews from the TPC and at least one review from an outside expert. For the second year running most of the outside reviews were done by the ERC, which was selected in advance, and additional outside reviews beyond the ERC were requested whenever appropriate or necessary. Reviewing was "first read double-blind," meaning that author identities were withheld from reviewers until they submitted a review. Revealing author names after the initial reviews were written allowed reviewers to find related and previous material by the same authors, which helped greatly in many cases in understanding the context of the work, and also ensured that the author feedback and discussions at the PC meeting could be frank and direct. For the first time in many years, we allowed PC members to submit papers to the conference. Submissions co-authored by a TPC member were reviewed exclusively by the ERC and other outside reviewers, and these same reviewers decided whether to accept the PC papers; no PC member reviewed a TPC paper, and no TPC papers were discussed at the TPC meeting.

After the reviewing was complete, the PC met at the National University of Defense Technology, Changsha, during May 25–28 to select the program. Separately, the ERC decided on the PC papers in e-mail and phone discussions. In the end, 18 of the 158 submissions (11 %) were accepted for the conference.

First of all, we would like to thank all researchers who submitted manuscripts. Without these submissions, it would be impossible to provide such an interesting technical program. We thank all PC members for helping to organize the conference program. We thank all TPC members for their tremendous time and efforts during the paper review and selection process. The efforts of these individuals were crucial in constructing our successful technical program. Last but not least, we would like to thank the organizations and sponsors that supported NCCET 2015. Finally, we thank all the participants of the conference.

December 2015

Weixia Xu
Huaguo Liang
Minxuan Zhang
Liquan Xiao

Organization

General Co-chairs

Xu Weixia   National University of Defense Technology, China
Liang Huaguo   HeFei University of Technology, China
Zhang Minxuan   National University of Defense Technology, China

Program Chair

Xiao Liquan   National University of Defense Technology, China

Publicity Co-chairs

Li Jinwen   National University of Defense Technology, China
Zhang Chengyi   National University of Defense Technology, China

Local Arrangements Co-chairs

Liang Huaguo   HeFei University of Technology, China
Li Jinwen   National University of Defense Technology, China
Du Gaoming   HeFei University of Technology, China

Registration and Finance Co-chairs

Du Gaoming   HeFei University of Technology, China
Wang Yongwen   National University of Defense Technology, China
Li Yuanshan   National University of Defense Technology, China
Zhang Junying   National University of Defense Technology, China

Program Committee

Han Wei   631 Institute of AVIC, China
Jin Lifeng   Jiangnan Institute of Computing Technology, China
Xiong Tinggang   709 Institute of China Shipbuilding Industry, China
Zhao Xiaofang   Institute of Computing Technology Chinese Academy of Sciences, China
Yang Yintang   Xi Dian University, China
Dou Qiang   National University of Defense Technology, China
Li Jinwen   National University of Defense Technology, China
Zhang Chengyi   National University of Defense Technology, China

Technical Program Committee

Chen Yueyue	Hunan Changsha DIGIT Company, China
Dou Qiang	National University of Defense Technology, China
Du Huimin	Xi'an University of Posts and Telecommunications, China
Fan Dongrui	Institute of Computing Technology Chinese Academy of Sciences, China
Fan Xiaoya	Northwestern Polytechnical University, China
Fang Xing	Jiangnan Institute of Computing Technology, China
Gu Tianlong	Guilin University of Electronic Technology, China
Guo Donghui	Xiamen University, China
Guo Wei	Tianjin University, China
Hou Jianru	Institute of Computing Technology Chinese academy of Sciences, China
Huang Jin	Xi Dian University, China
Ji Liqiang	Cesller Company, China
Jin Jie	Hunan Changsha Fusion Company, China
Li Ping	University of Electronic Science and Technology of China, China
Li Qiong	Inspur Information Technology Co. Ltd., China
Li Yuanshan	Inspur Information Technology Co. Ltd., China
Li Yun	Yangzhou University, China
Lin Kaizhi	Inspur Information Technology Co. Ltd., China
Li Zhenghao	Tongji University, China
Sun Haibo	Inspur Information Technology Co. Ltd., China
Sun Yongjie	Hunan Changsha DIGIT Company, China
Tian Ze	631 Institute of AVIC, China
Wang Dong	National University of Defense Technology, China
Wang Yaonan	Hunan University, China
Wang Yiwen	University of Electronic Science and Technology of China, China
Xing Zuocheng	Hunan Changsha DIGIT Company, China
Xue Chengqi	Southeast University, China
Yang Peihe	Jiangnan Institute of Computing Technology, China
Yang Xiaojun	Institute of Computing Technology Chinese Academy of Sciences, China
Yin Luosheng	Synopsys Company, China
Yu Mingyan	Harbin Institute of Technology, China
Yu Zongguang	China Electronics Technology Group Corporation No. 58 Research Institute, China
Zeng Tian	709 Institute of China Shipbuilding Industry, China
Zeng Xifang	Hunan Great Wall Information Technology Co. Ltd., China
Zeng Yu	Sugon Company, China
Zeng Yun	Hunan University, China
Zhang Jianyun	PLA Electronic Engineering Institute, China

Contents

Computer Application and Software Optimization

Technology on the Horizon

Processor Architecture

Modeling and Analyzing of 3D DRAM as L3 Cache Based on DRAMSim2

Litiao Qiu[✉], Lei Wang, Qiang Dou, and Zhenyu Zhao

School of Computer, National University of Defense Technology,
Changsha 410073, Hunan, China
qiulitiao@163.com, {leiwang, zyzhao}@nudt.edu.cn,
douq@vip.sina.com

Abstract. Cache memory system with a die-stacking DRAM L3 cache is a promising answer to break the Memory Wall and has a positive effect on performance. In order to further optimize the existing memory system, in this paper, a 3D DRAM as L3 Cache is modeled and analyzed based on DRAMSim2 simulator. In order to use an on-die DRAM as cache, tags and data are combined in one row in the DRAM, meanwhile, utilize the 3D DRAM with wider bus width and denser capacity. The cache memory modeling platform is evaluated by running traces which simulate the access behavior of core from spec2000 that generated by gem5. With DRAM L3 cache, all the test traces experience an improvement of performance. Read operation has an average speed-up of 1.82× over the baseline memory system, while write operation is 6.38×. The improvement of throughput in 3D DRAM cache compared to baseline system can reach to 1.45×'s speedup.

Keywords: DRAM cache · 3D · Die-stacking · Modeling

1 Introduction

In recent years, as the dramatic increase happened in microprocessor's frequency, DRAM access latencies have not live up to their expectations. Thus, it caused a huge frequency gap between core and the main memory. This problem is prevalently referred to as the Memory Wall [8]. In order to attack this wall, three-dimensional (3D) die-stacking has been promoted [9, 10]. In a 3D integrated IC chip, multiple device layers are stacked together. The layers could be connected with through-silicon-vias (TSV), which are low-latency, high-bandwidth and very dense vertical interconnects. Still, stacking DRAM directly on top of a processor is a natural way to solve the Memory Wall problem.

In a three-dimensional (3D) chip, vertical interconnects are used to connects multiple device layers. A conceptual 2-layer 3D integrated circuit [7] is showed in Fig. 1. The direct vertical interconnects are called die-to-die (d2d) vias. The advantages of a 3D chip over a traditional two-dimensional (2D) design include: (1) higher performance due to the reduction of average interconnect length; (2) lower interconnect power consumption due to reduced total wiring length; and (3) denser capacity due to the stacking fabrication.

© Springer-Verlag Berlin Heidelberg 2016
W. Xu et al. (Eds.): NCCET 2015, CCIS 592, pp. 3–12, 2016.
DOI: 10.1007/978-3-662-49283-3_1

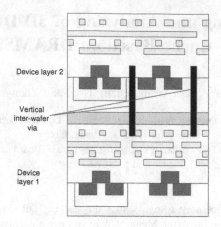

Fig. 1. A conceptual 3D IC: vertical interconnects across two stacking device layers [7].

3D integration is used to increase the storage capacity of on-chip memory. Some research promotes using large 3D DRAM caches to break the memory bandwidth wall. However, there are challenges for the utilization of 3D architectures. Few commercially available EDA tools and design methodologies are suitable for 3D implementation. Consequently, a 3D DRAM simulator need to be built as a platform to do further study on 3D memory system, to explore the space design of 3D architecture and power management.

In this paper, a DRAM cache simulator is implemented, which later be seen as a L3 cache in a processor's the memory system. To our knowledge, there is no existing platforms suitable for us to research the power dissipation, which is our future work. In this paper, Alloy Cache [12] is exploited as our basic DRAM caching structure. In addition, two experiments are carried out to compare the performance between a baseline system which is L1-L2-DRAM memory system and a L1-L2-L3 (DRAM cache)-DRAM (DRAM as main memory) memory system. According to the experimental results, compared to the baseline system, using DRAM cache as L3 cache achieves better performance. In our tests, on average, read operation has a speed-up of 1.82×, 6.38× of write operation and 1.45× of throughput.

To better illustrate our contributions of this work, our related work is discussed by elaborating the progress in memory systems in Sect. 2. Then our modeling methodology and implementation are described in Sects. 3 and 4. The comparison and evaluation are presented in Sect. 5. At last, the conclusion is made in Sect. 6.

2   Related Work

Due to SRAMs are faster than DRAMs, traditional processors usually utilize SRAMs [21] as last level cache. However, their six-transistor implementation makes the SRAM units have large size. Thus, don't mention SRAMs are more expensive than DRAMs, they have a relatively higher leakage current and lower density. With the utilization of

3D technology in processors, DRAMs can be stacked together to achieve short TSVs, thereby obtain fast access speed.

In the existing studies of 3D die-stacking technology, whether die-stacked DRAM should be utilized as a main memory [4], DRAM cache [11], or a software-managed extension to off-chip main memory, or any other functions is still not come into a final conclusion yet [9, 14, 16].

An Intel Core 2 with 3D-stacked L2 cache [14] is implemented by B. Black et al. Our memory architecture of using DRAM as Last Level cache is inspired by this work. Chiachen Chou et al. proposed a structure called CAMEO [5], a hardware-based Cache-like Memory Organization that makes stacked DRAM visible as part of the memory address space and utilizes data locality. Despite this proposal is a good way to fix the Memory Wall, we find that is pretty complex to modify or create a brand new OS, so it lacks wide applicability.

DRAMSim2 [1] is chosen as our memory system simulator, which is a cycle accurate system can be used in trace-based simulations. At the architecture level, a circle accurate main memory simulator is utilized to simulate non-volatile memories named NVMain [21]. It provides flexibility to perform different variations of organizations, interconnects, memory controllers, etc. However, the present status of non-volatile memory cannot be settled, so that is a researching tool for exploring the organization of main memory.

Using a DRAM cache, in order to decrease the overhead of finding tags in large, in 3D DRAM cache, existing works have considered integrates the tags directly in the DRAM array with the data. Therefore, in this paper, our caching structure is implemented using the Alloy Cache [12]. This 3D DRAM cache implementation is an early stage realization, a more complicated architecture will be implemented in the future.

3   Architecture of 3D DRAM Cache Simulator

This section shows the detail modeling procedure of our experimental platform.

The implemented infrastructure of memory system which is shown in Fig. 2 contains two major parts:

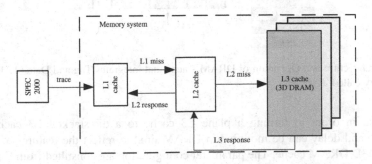

Fig. 2. Base Cache Infrastructure with Three Level Caches

- A two level on-chip cache: it models the basic Two Level Cache. It is implemented by C ++ and modeling the access behavior of cache memory system.
- L3 cache: it is implemented by a DRAM. The DRAM is simulated by a cycle-accurate simulator, DRAMSim2. See more details in Sect. 4 to find how to model a 3D die-stacked DRAM cache.

In L1 cache, when a request comes, the cache is checked according to the contents of memory location for its data. If it hits, return the data to processor immediately. But if not hits, read the required block from the next level (L2 cache) to L1 cache. If still miss, it will be searched in the main memory. The caches are include tags to identify which block of next level cache is in their last level cache slot.

N-way (N) set associative cache is used in L1/L2. The detailed configuration information about memory system will be demonstrated in Sect. 5.1. The address width from trace file is 64 bits. The replacement strategy in L1/L2 is LRU (Least Recently Used).

Caches save two kinds of information, tags and data. Alloy cache [12] is effective latency-optimized cache architecture. It alloys or combine the tag and data into one basic unit (Tag and Data, TAD), instead of separating cache constructions into two parts ("tag store" and "data store"). For Alloy cache stream tag and data in one burst, it can get rid off the delay because of tag serialization. It helps handle cache misses faster without wasting time to detect cache miss in the same situation.

In Fig. 3, each TAD represents one set of the direct-mapped Alloy cache. In our DRAM cache, every data line has a tag. The address is compared with the tags in DRAM cache. If it is the same, then hit. Or vice versa. In our paper, for a physical address space of 64 bits, 41 tag bits are needed. The minimum size of a TAD is thus 72 bytes (64 bytes for data line and 8 bytes for tag). There are 28 lines in a row of an alloy cache.

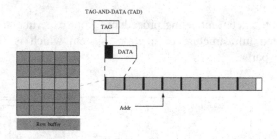

Fig. 3. Architecture and Operation of DRAM Cache that integrates Tag and Data (TAD) into a single entity called TAD [12].

At last, in order to turning a plane L3 cache to a die-stacked L3 cache. The bandwidth and delay can be modified in DRAMSim2 to reflect the features of a large and dense 3D DRAM cache. The parameter configuration are consulted from [5, 6, 18]. See detailed information in Sect. 5.1.

4   Implementation of 3D DRAM Cache Simulator

This section discusses the detail implementation of our simulator. The specific process of realizing a 3D DRAM cache is demonstrated as followed.

In our work, gem5 simulator [17] is exploited to generate test traces from benchmark SPEC 2000. Although gem5 and DRAMSim2 can connect together to simulate full system behavior, the running time of a slightly large program often costs one or two days, is really inefficient. While in our promoted memory system, only several minutes is needed to execute the programs.

4.1   Using DRAM as a L3 Cache

Due to DRAMSim2 has a very simple programming interface and it offers a robust visualization tool, DRAMvis, that can be used to compare and visualize the effects of memory system parameters like bandwidth, latency and power. It is an appropriate memory system simulator for us to do exploration on DRAM cache. Plus, in this paper, our L1 cache and L2 cache are implemented by C ++, so DRAMSim2 is chosen as our DRAM simulator.

About the interaction between L2 and L3 DRAM cache, we learn the connection between gem5 simulator and DRAMSim2, which can be connected together to perform full system simulations. Thus, we imitate the way DRAMSim2 and gem5 connect to link L2 cache and DRAM in a memory system.

After a 2D L1-L2-DRAM (original DRAMSim2) baseline memory system is built up, the architecture of Alloy cache is utilized that mentioned above to implement the DRAM cache. Every time when there comes a L2 cache miss, DRAMSim2 will not find the data directly, but compare the tag bits first, then get the corresponding dataline. Using DRAM as a L3 cache has an opposite effect on the access latency of L3 DRAM cache.

4.2   Implementing a 3D DRAM Cache

Compared to a plane DRAM cache which is implemented in baseline, a stacked DRAM cache has some obviously merits, such as wider bandwidth, more banks in a rank and more channels.

In DRAMSim2, there are several initial files to do configuration. The parameters can be changed to meet up the standard of 3D features. Check the table demonstrated in Sect. 5.1. In order to compare the performance of these two memory systems fairly, their capacity is the same, 2G. While due to 3D DRAM cache is die-stacked, it has more channels, here is 16 channels.

We learned the electrical parameter showed in Table 1 of DRAMs from Gabriel [4].

Table 1. Electrical parameter configuration of 2D and 3D DRAM cache [4]

	t_{RAS}	t_{RCD}	t_{CAS}	t_{WR}	t_{RP}
2D DRAM	36 ns	12 ns	12 ns	12 ns	12 ns
3D DRAM	24.3 ns	8.1 ns	8.1 ns	8.1 ns	8.1 ns

4.3 Interaction Between Caches

Our work is based on an open source cache simulator implemented by C ++ [19]. And the interactive behavior is described as follows.

In L1 Cache: There is a global tick in simulator that determines the run time of L1 cache, which is setup in trace file already. So long as the global tick arrives, no matter what happened in the following caches, L1 cache emissions an instruction. After an emission from L1, if the matching tag is found in L1, then hit. Returning to main function and waiting for another instruction. But if misses, then we should visit L2 cache and try to find the specified tag. In this cache simulator, L1 cache is made up by an instruction cache and data cache. The FETCH process happened in instruction cache, plus the READ and WRITE executed in data cache.

In L2 Cache: Not like the instruction of L1 cache having two parts of caches, L2 cache is a unified cache. All the access behaviors are all in one cache. This level of cache receive the address from L1 cache, just like L1 cache, check the index first to determine the set, then compare the tag to see if the data can be found in L2 cache. A hit in L2 cache can be considered if the tag is the same. Then a signal returned to L1 cache, and informed them the hit. But if it is a miss, compare the tags again in the next level cache.

In L3 Cache: Corresponding tags and data are placed on the same row in order to achieve row buffer locality in DRAM cache. When an access comes to the DRAM cache, the tag bits will be compared with the given line address. A cache hit happens when their tags are the same, then the data line in the TAD will be supplied. Once the operation has completed in DRAM cache, a response will be sent to the L2 cache and we know the process is done. Not like the traditional SRAM last level cache, usually between 2 and 8 MB, DRAM cache has bigger capacity. In this paper, DRAM cache offers a larger capacity to be used as a L3 cache between the largest SRAM cache (L2 cache) and main memory. Although the access time of die-stacked DRAM cache is longer than SRAM, it runs faster than main memory due to its smaller size and higher bandwidth. In our work, the state-of-art Alloy Cache optimizes the system performance by a reduction of hit latency.

5 Simulation

A set of experiments are conducted to demonstrate the advantages of the die-stacked L3 cache. First, the configuration of the baseline memory system (L1 cache-L2 cache-DRAM) and innovative memory system (L1 cache-L2 cache-3D L3 cache) are presented. Then, the performance optimization of die-stacked L3 cache is clarified.

5.1 Configuration

Two sets of simulations are executed in this paper; in the first set, a DRAM is followed after L2 cache. While the other set is a two-level-cache with a die-stacked L3 cache. For each simulation, there are 5 traces to show the different performance between these two memory systems. One of the traces, *mase_art.trc,* is the sample traces in DRAMSim2 folder. Other traces are generated by gem5 simulator. They are *164gzip, 175vpr, 181mcf,* and *255vortex,* which are programs from SPEC2000.

The gem5 simulator is modified to generate traces that originally from SPEC 2000 can be accepted by DRAMSim2. Maxinsts, the largest number of operation instructions, are showed in Table 2.

Table 2. The maxinsts of each program.

	164gzip	175vpr	181mcf	255vortex
maxinsts	10^4	10^8	10^7	10^6

The detail configuration of these two platforms is demonstrated in Table 3. These two platforms have the same L1 cache and L2 cache, the only difference is the characteristic of DRAM.

Table 3. The different configuration between Baseline Memory System and Memory System with Die-stacked L3 Cache

L1-I/D cache			
capacity		64KB	
blocksize		64B	
way		4	
set		128	
latency		2 cycle	
L2 cache (unified)			
capacity		4MB	
blocksize		64B	
way		16	
set		4096	
latency		12 cycle	
DRAM		**L3 cache (stacked DRAM cache)**	
bus frequency	0.67GHz	bus frequency	0.67GHz
capacity	2G	capacity	2G
channel	1	channel	16
bank	8	bank	16banks per rank
bus width	8 bytes	bus width	16 bytes
		way	32

5.2   Performance Evaluation

Figure 4 displays the average execution time of one read/write of 3D DRAM as L3 cache and the baseline memory system. Two simulations are executed: One based on using DRAMSim2 as DRAM and the other one is utilized as a 3D L3 cache. The measure of execution time is tick. 1 tick = 1/0.67 GHz = 1 clock cycle. The average tick format is presented as follow. Average tick = total tick/access number.

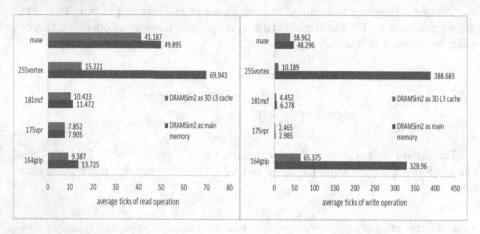

Fig. 4. The performance between two systems. The average ticks of read and write operation (Color figure online).

As it shows in the histogram, in all the cases, the performance of using DRAMSim2 as a 3D L3 cache gains performance lifting. Especially in *255vortex*, the read and write process both achieve a huge benefit over the baseline. So does *164gzip*, the reduced handling time contribute a lot to the performance of the memory system. Because of more channels, wider bandwidth and other 3D features, it is not surprise that the performance becomes better.

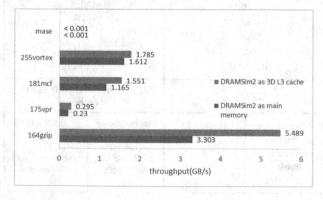

Fig. 5. The throughput in two platforms.

Besides read/write cycle time, the aggregate average throughput of our two memory systems depicted in Fig. 5. The average throughput in the 3D stacked DRAM cache experienced a boost. This is because under the 3D condition, the read/write operation running time becomes shorter. In a cycle time, more operations can be handled in the memory system. Thus, the throughput in 3D L3 DRAM cache increased to 1.45×.

6 Conclusion and Future Work

A die-stacked L3 DRAM cache is demonstrated which improves the performance of the memory system. It utilizes traces and output design constraints such as read/write average execution time and throughput. To clarify this idea, two kinds of cache memory system are presented in our work (a baseline system with 2 levels cache and DRAM; a three levels cache system) and model the L3 cache to a 3D configuration. To proceed the simulation, a sample trace is chosen that DRAMSim2 has and four real program traces (from SPEC2000) that generated by gem5. Plus, the feasibility of integrating tag and data in one unit is studied in this thesis.

The simulator in this paper is a base platform to do 3D architecture space exploration. In the future, our simulator will be become more configurable. Power management and efficiency study will be conducted on it in the near future.

Acknowledgments. This work was supported by the National Nature Science Foundation of China (61402501, 61272139).

References

1. Rosenfeld, P., Cooper-Balis, E., Jacob, B.: DRAMSim2: A cycle accurate memory system simulator. Comput. Archit. Lett. **10**(1), 16–19 (2011)
2. Sadri, M., Jung, M., Weis, C., et al.: Energy optimization in 3D MPSoCs with wide-I/O DRAM using temperature variation aware bank-wise refresh. In: Proceedings of the conference on Design, Automation & Test in Europe. European Design and Automation Association, p. 281(2014)
3. Woo, D.H., Seong, N.H., Lewis, D.L., et al.: An optimized 3D-stacked memory architecture by exploiting excessive, high-density TSV bandwidth. In: High 2010 IEEE 16th International Symposium on Performance Computer Architecture (HPCA), pp. 1–12. IEEE (2010)
4. Loh, G.H.: 3D-stacked memory architectures for multi-core processors ACM SIGARCH computer architecture news. IEEE Comput. Soc. **36**(3), 453–464 (2008)
5. Chou, C.C., Jaleel, A., Qureshi, M.K.: CAMEO: a two-level memory organization with capacity of main memory and flexibility of hardware-managed cache. In: 2014 47th Annual IEEE/ACM International Symposium on Micro-architecture (MICRO), 1–12. IEEE (2014)
6. Jevdjic, D., Volos, S., Falsafi, B.: Die-stacked DRAM caches for servers: hit ratio, latency, or bandwidth? have it all with footprint cache. ACM SIGARCH Comput. Archit. News **41**(3), 404–415 (2013)
7. Xie, Y., Loh, G.H., Black, B., et al.: Design space exploration for 3D architectures. ACM J. Emerg. Technol. Comput. Syst. (JETC) **2**(2), 65–103 (2006)

8. Wulf, W.A., McKee, S.A.: Hitting the memorywall: implications of the obvious. Comput. Archit. News **23**(1), 20–24 (1995)
9. Kgil, T.H., D'Souza, S., Saidi, A.G., Binkert, N., Dreslinski, R., Reinhardt, S., Flautner, K., Mudge, T.: Pico server: using 3D stacking technology to enable a compact energy efficient chip multiprocessor. In: Proceedings of the 12th Symposium on Architectural Support for Programming Languages and Operating Systems (2006)
10. Madan, N., Balasubramonian, R.: Leveraging 3D technology for improved reliability. In: Proceedings of the 40th International Symposium on Micro-architecture (2007)
11. Loh, G.H., Hill, M.D.: Efficiently enabling conventional block sizes for very large die-stacked DRAM caches. In: Proceedings of the 44th International Symposium on Micro-architecture, December 2011
12. Qureshi, M.K., et al.: Fundamental latency trade-off in architecting dram caches: Outperforming impractical SRAM-tags with a simple and practical design. In: MICRO-45 (2012)
13. N, Chatterjee., et al.: Leveraging heterogeneity in dram main memories to accelerate critical word access, In: MICRO-45 (2012)
14. Black, B., Annavaram, M., Brekelbaum, N., et al.: Die stacking (3D) micro-architecture. In: 2006 39th Annual IEEE/ACM International Symposium on Micro-architecture MICRO-39. (2006)
15. Henning, J.L.: SPEC CPU2000: Measuring CPU performance in the new millennium. Computer **33**(7), 28–35 (2000)
16. Kgil, T., D'Souza, S., Saidi, A., et al.: PicoServer: using 3D stacking technology to enable a compact energy efficient chip multiprocessor. ACM SIGARCH Comput. Archit. News **34** (5), 117–128 (2006)
17. Binkert, N., Beckmann, B., Black, G., et al.: The gem5 simulator. ACM SIGARCH Comput. Archit. News **39**(2), 1–7 (2011)
18. Qureshi, M.K., Loh, G.H.: Fundamental latency trade-off in architecting DRAM caches: Outperforming impractical SRAM-tags with a simple and practical design. In: 2012 Proceedings of the 45th Annual IEEE/ACM International Symposium on Micro-architecture. IEEE Computer Society (2012)
19. http://blog.csdn.net/gaoxiang__/article/details/41494189
20. Chen, K., Li, S., Muralimanohar, N, et al.: CACTI-3DD: Architecture-level modeling for 3D die-stacked DRAM main memory. In: Proceedings of the Conference on Design, Automation and Test in Europe, pp. 33–3. EDA Consortium (2012)
21. Poremba, M., Xie, Y.: Nvmain: an architectural-level main memory simulator for emerging non-volatile memories. In: 2012 IEEE Computer Society Annual Symposium on VLSI (ISVLSI), pp. 392–397. IEEE (2012)

Partitioning Methods for Multicast in Bufferless 3D Network on Chip

Chaoyun Yao[1]([⊠]), Chaochao Feng[1], Minxuan Zhang[1], Wei Guo[1],
Shouzhong Zhu[1], and Shaojun Wei[2]

[1] College of Computer, National University of Defense Technology,
Changsha 410073, People's Republic of China
ycy021417@163.com
[2] The Department of Electronic System, Tsinghua University,
Beijing 100083, People's Republic of China

Abstract. In this paper, we proposed two region partition multicast routing algorithms for the 3D mesh Interconnection Network to enhance the overall system performance. The proposed two algorithms shorten the network long path latency. Compared to the based multicast routing algorithm, our simulations with six different synthetic workloads reveal that our architecture acquires high system performance.

Keywords: NoC · 3D · Multicast

1 Introduction

The technology trends to scale with Moore's law, a single die can incorporate several hundreds of cores. When the number of core increases, interconnect becomes more and more complicated in System-on-chip design. The number of core on a single chip continues to increase to efficient utilize the process elements. Networks on chip were shown to be feasible and easy to scale for supporting a large number of cores and memory rather than shared buses or point-to-point interconnect wires [1]. However, with the increasing cores number in the 2D plane is not an efficient way due to its long wire interconnects [2,3]. The emerging of the 3D integrated circuit that stacks several dies to reduce the long wire delay, it results in lower power consumption and higher performance [4,5]. The 3D integrated circuit is also an attractive way for Network on chip design. The 3D NoC architecture is widely studied in the network topology [4,5], router architecture [6,7], and routing algorithms [8,9].

In order to run many kinds of communication applications in Multi-Processors System-on-Chip (MPSoC), collective communications must be supported. In an MPSoC system, the cache-coherent shared memory protocols (such as directory-based or token-based) require one-to-many or broadcast communications to

C. Yao—The research is supported by National Natural Science Foundation of China with Grant No. 61303066 and 61373032 and by Specialized Research Fund for the Doctor Program of Higher Education of China with Grant No. 20124307110016.

W. Xu et al. (Eds.): NCCET 2015, CCIS 592, pp. 13–22, 2016.
DOI: 10.1007/978-3-662-49283-3_2

obtain shared data or invalidate shared data on different cache blocks [10]. It has been proved that only percent 2–5 multicast traffic in the total network traffic will have a serious impact on system performance [10]. If multicast communication is supported in NoC can advance system performance significantly. Several recent research and industry products trend to support multicasting in hardware implementation.

There are three multicast mechanisms that can be classified as unicast-based, tree-based and path-based. In unicast-based multicast scheme [11], the multicast packet is partitioned into multiple unicast packets at the source node and transmits to the destinations separately. The advantage of this multicast scheme is which can be executed on the unicast routers, and the unicast routers did not require make any change. However, such a scheme is very inefficiency owe to the multiple copies of the same packet is injected into the network in turn. In path-based multicast scheme, the multicast packet selects a path to route the multicast packet to each destination sequentially until it arrives to the last node. Hence, path-based multicast routing does not block message along the path. So in path-based method is reducing the overall path length in the multi-packet [12] show that path-based routing is more beneficial in the wormhole switched network, yet in networks employing tree-based, store and forward routing is advantageous.

In this paper, we work on shorten multicast path length algorithm that is for 3D bufferless mesh architectures to enhance the overall system performance. The rest of paper is organized as follows. The related work is reviewed in Sect. 2. Section 3 proposes the general multicast schemes in bufferless 3D mesh architecture. In Sect. 4, Partition methods for is proposed. In Sect. 5, the simulation and experimental results are presented and analyzed, followed by the conclusion in Sect. 6.

2   Related Work

The fact is that the multicast communication is used to support several collective communication operations. There has been several multicast communication research in 2D NoCs. Low Distance multicast (LD) [13] algorithm is a path-based multicast communication method which optimized destination nodes order and utilized adaptive routing for multicast packets through the network. The Virtual Circuit Tree Multicasting (VCTM) [14] is a typical tree-based multicast routing method. This routing method first sends a setup packet to build a multicast tree, then sends multicast packet. Similar as VCTM multicast scheme, two phase multicast tree construct method is proposed in [15] which consume less power than VCTM algorithm. The Recursive Partitioning Multicast (RPM) [16] which supposes the network is divided into several partitions, the multicast packet selects intermediate nodes to replicate, minimizes the packet replication time. This scheme performs better than VCTM due to its more path diversities. However, it is not implemented in hardware. Feng [17] proposed bufferless multicast routing algorithms for 2D NoC architecture.

Recently, researches have considered on evaluating the performance metric of 3D NoCs. Feero [18] showed that 3D-NoC can reduce latency and the energy per packet by 40 % by decreasing the number of hopes. [5] is proved that 3D-NoC can decrease 62 % and 58 % power consumption compare to a traditional 2D-NoC topology for a network size of N = 128 and N = 256 nodes, respectively. The fact is that 3D mesh-based NoC architecture can reduction in the average wire length and wire delay resulting in better performance and lower power consumption [4].

In the open literature, there has been no work addressing bufferless multicasting for 3D NoCs systems. In this work, we first put forward a new idea of balanced partitioning in 3D bufferless mesh network for unicast/multicast traffic.

3   Preliminaries

The general path-based routing algorithm for buffer 3D mesh architecture is based on Hamiltonian path strategy. It is constructed two directed Hamiltonian Paths (high channel sub-network and low channel sub-network) [19]. However, this routing algorithm does not suit to the bufferless 3D mesh architecture. The algorithm in bufferless 3D mesh architecture is a non-deterministic path-based multicast scheme. The multicast packet is routed to every destination along a non-deterministic path. When a multicast packet arrives at a midway router, the router always selects a destination with the minimum manhattan distance to the current router from the destination address nodes. Owe to the packet would be deflected away from the shortest path to the destination, During the routing process the best destination nodes in the multicast will change dynamically. Table 1 is shown the pseudo code of the path-based bufferless 3D multicast routing algorithm. The algorithm first gains multicast destination node IDs in the packet to an array dst_id_array (Steps 1–7), then sets the first element of dst_id_array as the best candidate node ID and calculates the manhattan distance between the current node and the best candidate node (Steps 8–10). Third, acquires the minimum manhattan distance of the best candidate node to the current node (Steps 11–17). Finally, the optimal direction is based on the position of the best candidate node to the current node (Step 18).

4   Partitioning Methods for 3D Mesh Architecture

In this section, we put forward two partition methods for bufferless 3D mesh architecture. They are two block partition (TBP) and four block partition (FBP). This partition method is first applying for bufferless architecture.

4.1   Partitioning Methods

Two block partition, the network is partitioned into up block sub-network and down block sub-network. In up block sub-network contains all destination node IDs in this block. In down block sub-network contain all destination node IDs

Table 1. Path-based algorithm for bufferless 3D mesh architecture

Routing computation function *for path-based bufferless 3D multicast routing algorithm* **Input**: *Multicast destination address dst_add Coordinate of current node* (x_c, y_c, z_c) **Output**: *Optimal direction set (doptimal)*

```
1: i←0
2: for j in 0 to N-1 loop
3:   if dst_add[j] = 1 then
4:     dst_id_array[i]←j
5:     i←i+1
6:   end if
7: end loop
8: best_candidate_id← dst_id_array[0]
9: (x_d, y_d, z_d)← get_dst_coordinate(dst_id_array[0])
10: distance← get_manhattan_distance(x_d, y_d, z_d, x_c, y_c, z_c)
11: for j in 1 to i-1 loop
12:   (x_d, y_d, z_d) ← get_dst_coordinate( dst_id_array[j] )
13:   if distance ¿ get_manhattan_distance(x_d, y_d, z_d, x_c, y_c, z_c) then
14:     distance ← get_manhattan_distance(x_d, y_d, z_d, x_c, y_c, z_c)
15:     best_candidate_id ← dst_id_array[j]
16:   end if
17: end loop
18: doptimal ← get_optimal_direction (best_candidate_id, x_c, y_c, z_c )
```

in it. All destination nodes are split into two disjoint groups use this method. They are up group and down group.

Figure 1 shows an example of this partitioning policy and the portions of each partition which depends on the source node position. If the multicast packet can inject into the network, the multicast will deflection routing in the network. When the coordinate (x, y, z) of the current node is equal to the destination node coordinate (x, y, z), the multicast arrives to the current destination and modifies the multicast destination address. In the example, it is assumed that for 3D mesh NoC architecture, the source node is at node 25 where the destination set is D = 9, 16, 17, 24, 39, 44 and for FBP multicast algorithm using our proposed multicasting strategy, the source node and the destination set is the same as the TBP algorithm. For the TBP multicast routing scheme is shown in Fig. 1(a), First Node 25 is copied into two node and separate sends to different partitions if the source node have more than two empty ports. Node 24 and 39 are chosen at the first best candidate since it has the minimum manhattan distance to the source node 25. After the packet is sent to node 24 and 39, node 16 and 9 are chosen as the second best candidate. Without contention, the multicast minimum latency is equal to 9 hops. The path shown in Fig. 1(a) is not the only one path since the packet may be deflected due to contention.

For the FBP multicast routing strategy, there is a great improvement in terms of packet latency for the same source node and destination set. As illustrated in Fig. 1(b), the destination set is partition into four parts. In this case, the latency is equal to 5 hops. The reason for such a significant improvement is that multiple region partition way is shorten the long path.

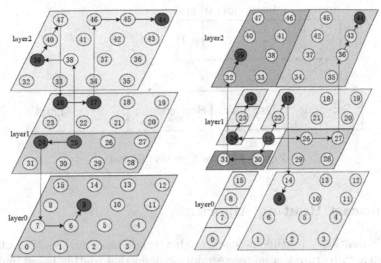

(a) 3D mesh NoC architecture us- (b) 3D NoC mesh architecture using
ing TBP multicast routing   FBP multicast routing

Fig. 1. Two multicast routing where the source is at node 25

4.2   Packet Format

The router supports two packet types: unicast and multicast. The format of
multicast packet type is shown in Fig. 2. The packet fields are explained as
follows:

Type field (2 bits): indicate the type of the packet (10: multicast packet; 0:
   unicast packet; 00/11: invalid packet).
Dst_addr field: it use bit string encoding. A bit of 1 in the string means the
   corresponding nodes is one of destinations.
Hop_counter field (11 bits): record the number of hops the packet has been
   routed and used it as packet priority to avoid livelock.
Src_addr field (18 bits): denote the relative address to the source node (6 bits
   for row addresses, 6 bits for column addresses and the other 6 bits for layer
   addresses).
Payload field: the payload can be extended to contain more bits for different
   application requirements.

In our multicast routing, When a multicast packet arrive to a destination,
the bit in the destination address corresponding to that destination node reset to
0, the message is copied and sent with its header to the next node in accordance
with our proposed routing algorithm which will be shown in the following subsection. The hop counter field of the packet will be added 1.

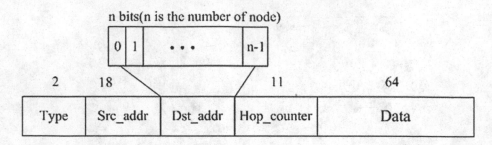

Fig. 2. Multicast packets format

5   Multicast Routing Algorithm

The TBP multicast routing of packets that takes place in the 3D bufferless NoC mesh architecture is a non-deterministic deflection routing based multicast algorithm. The pseudo code of the two block partition function for the routing scheme is shown in Table 2. The function judges the coordinate of current node and destination node, then collects multicast destination node IDs into array G1 and G2.

The FBP multicast routing of packets take place in the 3D bufferless NoC mesh architecture. The pseudo code of the algorithm for the routing scheme is shown in Table 3. The function judges the coordinate of current node and destination node, then collects multicast destination node IDs into array G1, G2, G3 and G4.

Table 2. The TBP algorithm for bufferless 3D mesh architecture

---

Algorithm: Two block partitioning (TBP)
Input: Multicast destination address dst_add Coordinate of current node (x_d, y_d, z_d)
Multicast current node Coordinate is (x_c, y_c, z_c)
Output: group1 (G1) and group2 (G2)

1: begin
2: for j in 0 to N-1 loop
3:   if $dst\_add[j] = 1$ then
4:     if $z_d > z_c or (z_d = z_c and x_d < x_c)$ then
5:       $G1 \leftarrow dst\_add[i]$
6:     else
7:       $G2 \leftarrow dst\_add[i]$
8:     end if
9:   end if
10: end loop
11: end TBP

5.1 Deadlock and Livelock Avoidance

Deflection routing is deadlock-free, because of the packets never have to wait in a router. However, when a packet does not acquire the optimal port, it will deflect to another port away from destination node. Thus, livelock must be avoided by limiting the number of deflection. In our multicast routing algorithm, the multicast packets are prioritized based on its age that the number of hops already routed in the network. The age-based priority mechanism guarantees the oldest packet will first win the link arbitration and direct to its destination. Once the oldest packet reaches its destination, another packet becomes the oldest. Thus livelock can be avoided.

6 Performance Evaluation

We evaluate the performance of the proposed multicasting mechanism for the 3D mesh interconnection network, a cycle-accurate NoC simulator developed in VHDL. The based multicast routing scheme is use the path-based multicast routing algorithm. There multicast routing algorithms were analyzed for synthetic traffic patterns. Nostrum [19] router is as a baseline router structure. For the 3D mesh architecture, routers have 7 input/output ports. The arbitration scheme for the switch allocator is age-based.

The performance of the network was evaluated using latency curves and the packet injection rate function. The packet latency is the time duration from when the packet is created at the source node to the packet is delivered to the destination node. To perform the simulations, a packet generator is attached to

Table 3. The FBP algorithm for bufferless 3D mesh architecture

Algorithm: Four block partitioning (FBP)
Input: Multicast destination address dst_add Coordinate of current node (x_d, y_d, z_d)
Multicast current node Coordinate is (x_c, y_c, z_c)
Output: group1 (G1), group2 (G2), group3(G3), group4(G4)
1: begin
2: for j in 0 to N-1 loop
3:   if $dst\_add[j] = 1$ then
4:     if $(z_d > z_c and y_d > y_c) or (z_d = z_c and x_d >= x_c and y_d > y_c)$ then
5:       $G1 \leftarrow dst\_add[i]$
6:     elsif $(z_d > z_c and y_d < y_c) or (z_d = z_c and x_d > x_c and y_d <= y_c)$ then
7:       $G2 \leftarrow dst\_add[i]$
8:     elsif $(z_d < z_c and y_d >= y_c) or (z_d = z_c and x_d < x_c and y_d >= y_c)$ then
9:       $G3 \leftarrow dst\_add[i]$
10:     else
11:       $G4 \leftarrow dst\_add[i]$
12:     end if
13:   end if
14: end loop
15: end TBP

each router and uses a FIFO to buffer the packets which cannot be injected into the network immediately due to the fact that there is no free output port to route the packet. It is use A combination of unicast (80 %) and multicast (20 %) traffic. For the unicast portion of the traffic, we use six traffic patterns: uniform random, transpose, bit reverse, bit complement, shuffle, tornado. In uniform random traffic, each resource node sends packet randomly to other nodes with an equal probability. For transpose traffic, resource node coordinate is (x, y, z)(!(x = y = z)) sends package to the destination node coordinate is (z, y, x). If the four-bit source address is s3, s2, s1, s0 the destination address for bit reverse traffic is s0, s1, s2, s3 and for shuffle traffic is s2, s1, s0, s3. For bit complement traffic. The four-bit source node ID $\{si|i \in [0,3]\}$ sends packets to destination $\{\sim si|i \in [0,3]\}$. For tornado traffic, each (radix-k) digit of the destination address Dx is a function of a digit Sx of the source address, which is $D_x = S_x + (k/2-1) \bmod k$. For multicast packet, the destination nodes are uniformly distributed. The simulations are performed on a $4 \times 4 \times 4$ 3D mesh architecture.

In the experiment set, the number of destination nodes has been set to 8. The average packet latency curves for uniform random (i.e. 80 % uniform random unicast 20 % uniform multicast), transpose, bit reverse, bit complement, shuffle, tornado are shown in Fig. 3. It can be observed for all six traffic patterns, that FBP and TBP multicast scheme achieves less average latency than the Path-based multicast scheme. The main reason is that the two proposed multicasting scheme shorten the long path latency.

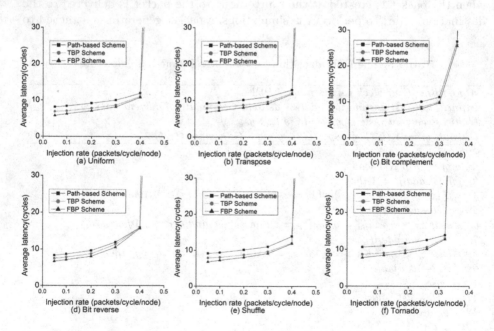

Fig. 3. Latency versus average packet inject rate with 8 multicast nodes

7   Conclusion and Future Work

In this paper, we propose two region patition multicast routing strategy for the 3D NoC mesh architecture, improving the overall NoC performance. The proposed architecture exploits region partition to shorten long path latency to provide high-performance hardware multicast support. Our simulations with different traffic profiles showed that the two multicast routing algorithms can achieve significant performance improvements over the pat-based multicast routing algorithm. In the future, our work will be extended by introducing faulty links for proposed architecture and simulating it using a set of realistic workloads. We will also measure power consumption and area for this architecture.

References

1. Dally, W.J., Towles, B.: Route packets, not wires: on-chip interconnection networks. In: Design Automation Conference (DAC), pp. 684–689 (2001)
2. Carloni, L.P., Pande, P., Xie, Y.: Networks-on-chip in emerging interconnect paradigms: advantages and challenges. In: Proceedings of the 2009 3rd ACM/IEEE International Symposium on Networks-on-Chip, pp. 93–102 (2009)
3. Rahmani, A.-M., Latif, K., Vaddina, K.R., Liljeberg, P., Plosila, J., Tenhunen, H.: Congestion aware, fault tolerant and thermally efficient inter-layer communication scheme for hybrid NoC-bus 3D architectures. In: Proceedings of the 5th ACM/IEEE International Symposium on Networks-on-Chip, pp. 65–2 (2011)
4. Feero, B.S., Pande, P.P.: Networks-on-chip in a three-dimensional environment: a performance evaluation. IEEE Trans. Comput. $58(1)$, 32–45 (2009)
5. Pavlidis, V.F., Friedman, E.G.: 3-D topologies for networks-on-chip. IEEE Trans. Very Large Scale Integr. Syst. $15(10)$, 1081–1090 (2007)
6. Kim, J., Nicopoulos, C., Park, D., Das, R., Xie, Y., Vijaykrishnan, N., Yousif, M., Das, C.: A novel dimensionally-decomposed router for on-chip communication in 3D architectures. In: Proceedings of the International Symposium on Computer Architecture (ISCA 2007), pp. 138–149 (2007)
7. Li, F., Nicopoulos, C., Richardson, T., Xie, Y., Narayanan, V., Kandemir, M.: Design and management of 3D chip multiprocessors using network-in-memory. In: Proceedings of the International Symposium on Computer Architecture, pp. 130–141, June 2006
8. Ramanujam, R.S., Lin, B.: Randomized partially-minimal routing on three-dimensional mesh networks. IEEE Comput. Archit. Lett. $7(2)$, 37–40 (2008)
9. Moosavi, S.R., Rahmani, A.M., Liljeberg, P., et al.: Enhancing performance of 3D interconnection networks using efficient multicast communication protocol. In: 21st Euromicro International Conference on Parallel, Distributed and Network-Based Processing (PDP), pp. 294–301. IEEE (2013)
10. Rahmani, A.-M., Vaddina, K.R., Latif, K., Liljeberg, P., Plosila, J., Tenhunen, H.: Generic monitoring and management infrastructure for 3D NoC-Bus hybrid architectures. In: Proceedings of the 6th ACM/IEEE International Symposium on Networks-on-Chip, pp. 177–184 (2012)
11. McKinley, P.K., Xu, H., Ni, L.M., Esfahanian, A.H.: Unicast-based multicast communication in wormhole-routed networks. IEEE Trans. Parallel Distrib. Syst. $5(12)$, 1252–1265 (1994)

12. Lin, X., Ni, L.M.: Multicast communication in multicomputer networks. IEEE Trans. Parallel Distrib. Syst. **4**, 1105–1117 (1993)
13. Daneshtalab, M., Ebrahimi, M., Mohammadi, S., Afzali-Kusha, A.: Low distance path-based multicast algorithm in NOCs. IET (IEE) -Comput. Digital Tech. Spec. Issue NoC **3**(5), 430–442 (2009)
14. Jerger, N.E., Peh, L.-S., Lipasti, M.: Virtual circuit tree multicasting: a case for on-chip hardware multicast support. In: Proceedings of the 35th Annual International Symposium on Computer Architecture, pp. 229–240 (2008)
15. Hu, W., Lu, Z., Jantsch, A., Liu, H.: Power-efficient tree-based multicast support for networks-on-chip. In: Proceedings of 16th Asia and South Pacific Design Automation Conference, Piscataway, NJ, USA, pp. 363–368 (2011)
16. Wang, L., Kim, H., Kim, E.J.: Recursive partitioning multicast: a bandwidth-efficient routing for networks-on-chip. In: International Symposium on Networks-on-Chip (NOCS), San Diego, CA, May 2009
17. Chaochao, F., Zhonghai, L.U., Jantsch, A., et al.: Support efficient and fault-tolerant multicast in bufferless network-on-chip. IEICE Trans. Inf. Syst. **95**(4), 1052–1061 (2012)
18. Feero, B., Pande, P.P.: Performance evaluation for three-dimensional networks-on-chip. In: Proceedings of IEEE Computer Society Annual Symposium On VLSI (ISVLSI), pp. 305–310, 9th-11th May 2007
19. Millberg, M., Nilsson, E., Thid, R., Kumar, S., Jantsch, A.: The nostrum backbone-a communication protocols stack for networks on chip. In: Proceedings of IEEE Computer Society, International Conference on VLSI Design, pp. 693–696 (2004)

Thermal-Aware Floorplanner for Multi-core 3D ICs with Interlayer Cooling

Wei Guo[✉], Minxuan Zhang, Peng Li, Chaoyun Yao, and Hongwei Zhou

College of Computer, National University of Defense Technology,
Changsha 410073, People's Republic of China
{wineer_guowei,mxzhang,hwzhou}@nudt.edu.cn, {li1986p,ycy021417}@163.com

Abstract. Internal thermal problem has become a critical challenge in multi-core 3D ICs. The interlayer cooling system provided a new solution for this problem, and expanded the design space of multi-core microprocessor floorplan. This work proposes a thermal-aware floorplanner for multi-core 3D ICs with interlayer cooling, with iterative algorithm based on simulated annealing method. The results show that the maximal temperature is reduced by $15°C$, and the temperature gradient is reduced by $28.4°C$ compared to the baseline design with 3 active device layers.

Keywords: 3D ICs · Interlayer cooling · Floorplan · Multi-core · Thermal

1 Introduction

According to the ITRS roadmap [1], the develop of integrated circuit technology continues to proceed, the performance improved exponentially, while the feature sizes became smaller but closer to the physical extreme limit. Three-dimensional integrated circuits (3D ICs) offer an feasible solution to overcome the limit of long wire delay in 2D processor and extend the capabilities of one single processor [2].

The density of power consumption in processor has increased sharply in the past years, which results higher internal temperature. Too high temperature influences the performance and reliability. As the temperature increases, the mobility of carriers decades and the resistance of metal wires increases, which both make the speed of processor descended. Reliability, the other key character of processor, has more direct relationship with temperature. The time to failure of processor's integrated circuits can be predicted as $e^{Ea/kT}$, where T is the absolute temperature, k is the Boltzmann's constant, and Ea is the activation energy of the failure mechanism being accelerated by the increased temperature [3]. Furthermore, electro-migration of the metal wires, which influenced by the temperature gradient, can also reduce the reliability of integrated circuits [4].

W. Guo–The research is supported by National Natural Science Foundation of China with Grant No. 61303066 and 61303069.

W. Xu et al. (Eds.): NCCET 2015, CCIS 592, pp. 23–30, 2016.
DOI: 10.1007/978-3-662-49283-3_3

In 3D ICs, thermal problem gets more concerns, the power density increases significantly compared to 2D ICs due to the reduce distances between units, and the thermal conductivity of bond and insulation layers between the silicon layers is too low compared to silicon and metal, the external heat removal solutions, like heat sink with fans or even fluid cooling, have little influence on the internal temperature gradient [5,6].

Interlayer cooling can remove the internal heat flux of processor effectively, and is the only feasible heat removal solution for multiple active layers in vertically integrated chips so far [2,7]. In this scheme, the coolant pass through the fluid cavities between the active layers, and remove the internal heat flux as Fig. 1 shows.

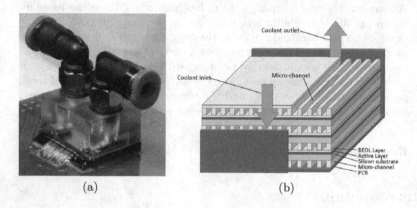

(a)   (b)

Fig. 1. Interlayer cooling system

Floorplaning algorithms are designed for minimizing chip area in original, but the thermal-aware floorplanning algorithms decide the placement of units according their thermal characteristics, to even out the internal temperature of processor through thermal diffusion effect. The units are classified as hot and cool ones, they are considered as thermal sources and sinks separately, and arranged by the multi-objective algorithm combined with liner programming or simulated annealing methods [3]. In the interlayer cooling system, the distribution of heat removal coefficient is also influenced by the relative location of units and fluid cavities.

This work proposes a thermal-aware floorplanner with iterative floorplanning algorithm based on simulated annealing method, to solve the thermal problem in multi-core 3D ICs with interlayer cooling system, considering the balance between the maximal temperature, temperature gradient and total wire length in the design with 3 active device layers.

2   Design Flow

The floorplanner proposed in this work is design to reduce the temperature of the multi-core 3D ICs, especially the internal temperature. To achieve the end with efficiency, the algorithm is divided into two phases. One for initializing, and the other for optimizing. The main process of design flow is shown in Fig. 2.

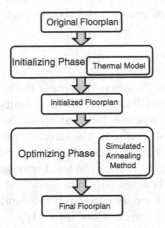

Fig. 2. Design flow of the floorplanner

To obtain the temperature of chip under different floorplan solutions, a simplified thermal model is used in this algorithm, which is derived from Ref. [3]. The chip is divided into cubical thermal cells as Fig. 3 shows.

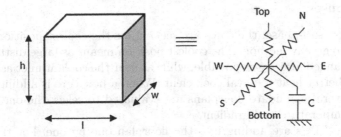

Fig. 3. The equivalent RC circuit of thermal model

The thermal resistance in 6 directions and thermal capacitance of the thermal cell are calculated by the follow expressions:

$$R_{Top} = R_{Bottom} = \frac{h/2}{k_{Si} \times l \times w} \tag{1}$$

$$R_N = R_S = \frac{w/2}{k_{Si} \times l \times h} \tag{2}$$

$$R_E = R_W = \frac{l/2}{k_{Si} \times w \times h} \tag{3}$$

$$C = sc_{Si} \times (l \times w \times h) \tag{4}$$

where k_{Si} is the thermal conductivity of silicon, and sc_{Si} is specific heat capacity per volume of silicon. These cells constitute the thermal RC grid for the chip, the temperature of each cells can be achieved through an iterative method.

3   Initializing Phase

The first phase initializes the floorplan according to the characters of units, such as power density and critical level. For the hot units like cores, the primary target is to find the coolest position far away from the similar hot ones and get better heat removal coefficient refer to the interlayer cooling system.

The rest ones like last level caches (LLCs) and Switch-buses are arranged close to the connected units to reduce the total wire length and act as the heat sink to reduce the internal temperature [8].

The units to be arranged are selected from the candidate units list according the power density. The units are classified into 3 types, such as cores, LLCs and Switch-buses. For fairness, the units of the same type have same power density in this phase, according to the homogeneous baseline design.

Therefore, this phase is divided into 3 sub-phases:

1. **Hot** units seek for coolest positions, like **cores**;
2. **Medium** units seek for the positions most close to the connected units arranged already, like **LLCs**;
3. **Coolest** units seek for the positions with minimum total wire length, like **Switch-buses**.

In the first sub-phase, the cores are seeking for the coolest positions one by one similar to greedy method. The coolest position means as large distance from the cores arranged already as possible, while as near the coolant inlet as possible, where have better heat removal coefficient. When a new core is adding into the floorplan, several candidate floorplans are evaluated to select the one with the minimum temperature and gradient.

Then, the LLCs are adding into the floorplan one by one. For their lower power density refer to cores, they are considered as heat sink. The primary goal in this sub-phase is finding the minimum distance for LLCs to their corresponding cores arranged already in the previous sub-phase, to reduce the total wire length.

Switch-buses are adding into the floorplan at last. They are considered to be heat sink as LLCs, and arranged carefully to reduce the total wire length, for a Switch-bus is connected to a group of LLCs. The processes in the latter two sub-phases are similar to linear programming method.

4   Optimizing Phase

The floorplan achieved by prior phase has some limits due to the sequential operations. The design space has not been explored sufficiently.

Simulated annealing method is a widely used optimization solutions. It can get a good approximation to the global optimum result in large search space. During the searching for the better solutions, a worse one can be accepted by an acceptance probability to explore the solution space.

Table 1. Pseudo-code of optimizing phase

$k \Longleftarrow 0,\ S \Longleftarrow S_0,\ T \Longleftarrow T_0$
$Cost \Longleftarrow Cost\_calc(S)$
$while(k < k_{max}\ and\ T > T_{cold})$
$\quad S_{new} \Longleftarrow Random\_move(S)$
$\quad Cost_{new} \Longleftarrow Cost\_calc(S_{new})$
$\quad if(Cost_{new} < Cost\ or\ Random\_frac() < e^{-(\triangle Cost)/T})$
$\quad\quad S \Longleftarrow S_{new}$
$\quad\quad if\ (Cost_{new} < Cost)$
$\quad\quad\quad S_{best} \Longleftarrow S_{new}$
$\quad T \Longleftarrow T \times Ratio_{cool},\ k{+}{+}$

The pseudo-code of simulated annealing method used in this phase is shown as Table 1, S_{new} is the new solution, which is generated based on the previous accepted solution, through a random move selected in the follow ones:

- **Move** a unit in the **same layer**;
- **Rotate** a unit by 90°;
- **Swap** the positions of two units;
- **Adjust** the shape of unit with same area;
- **Move** a unit to **different layer**.

The cost of a solution is calculated by the equation:

$$Cost = \lambda_{T_{max}} \times T_{max} + \lambda_{T_{grad}} \times T_{grad} + \lambda_W \times W \tag{5}$$

where T_{max} is the maximum temperature of chip, T_{grad} is the maximum temperature gradient of chip, and W is the total wire length of chip. $\lambda_{T_{max}}$, $\lambda_{T_{grad}}$ and λ_W are the corresponding weight coefficients, respectively. After the whole process, S_{best} refers to the best solution with minimum cost.

5   Experimental Results

The floorplan designs in our work are realized in the simulation platform named 3D Interlayer Cooling Emulator (3D-ICE), which simulates the transient thermal behaviour of 3D IC structures with interlayer cooling system, to perform thermal analysis of 3D ICs in the early design stages of processor [7].

The baseline design for the multi-core 3D ICs is shown as Fig. 4. 30 cores are distributed in 3 active layers, 10 ones for each layer using same floorplan as

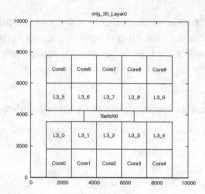

Fig. 4. The floorplan for a layer in baseline design

Fig. 4 shows. The total area of chip is fixed at $10 \times 10 \, mm^2$, as minimizing chip area is not the primary goal in this work.

The 3D stack structure for our work is shown in Fig. 1(b), the chip starts with a $10 \, \mu m$ thick PCB layer at the bottom, followed by the first micro-channel cooling layer, which is $100 \, \mu m$ thick. A $50 \, \mu m$ thick silicon substrate layer is place above the micro-channel, and bellow the bottom active device layer, which is $2 \, \mu m$ thick. There is a $10 \, \mu m$ thick BEOL (Back End Of Line) layer for bonding between the bottom active device layer and the second micro-channel cooling layer. Then, the second and third micro-channel cooling layer, silicon substrate layer, active device layer and BEOL layer are placed above. At the top of chip, there are top micro-channel layer and a silicon layer to finish the stack.

In this work, we use the power information from ESESC, a fast microprocessor architecture simulator [9]. The benchmarks binding to the cores are the same one with similar power to the medium level, for fairness in the comparison with baseline design.

Figure 5 shows the temperature maps for the 3 layers of baseline design, where the green arrows are the directions of coolant flow. The average temperature of layers are $59.20° \, C$, $67.75° \, C$ and $70.15° \, C$ for Layer_0 to Layer_2 separately, and the maximum temperature of whole chip is $122.95° \, C$ in the bottom active layer, the maximum temperature gradient is $71.30° \, C$ in the same layer.

The floorplan designs achieved by our floorplanner are shown in Fig. 6. The 3 figures above are the initialized designs for 3 active device layers respectively, as shown in Fig. 6(a), and the 3 ones bellow refer to the final result of our floorplanner as Fig. 6(b).

The initialized floorplan achieved by the first phase of our floorplanner obtain a cooler design, the average temperature of each layer are $57.18° \, C$, $64.01° \, C$ and $65.05° \, C$, and the maximum temperature gradient is $55.10° \, C$. But the maximum temperature of chip raises to $134.15° \, C$.

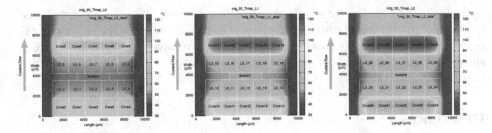

Fig. 5. The temperature maps for layer 0–2 in baseline design

After the optimizing phase with simulated annealing method, the average temperature of each layer are 57.79° C, 64.46° C and 68.47° C, while the maximum temperature of chip is 107.95° C with a reduced maximum temperature gradient of 42.9° C.

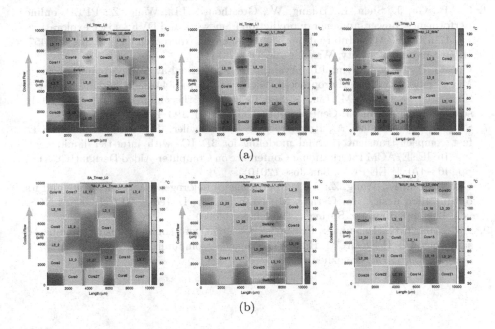

Fig. 6. The temperature maps for layer 0–2 in initialized design(a) and final design(b)

6   Conclusion

This work proposes a thermal-aware floorplanner to solve the thermal problem in multi-core 3D ICs with interlayer cooling. This solution achieves the final design through two phases, the first phase achieves initial floorplan through greedy method and linear programming method, and the second one achieves the optimized result design by simulated annealing method, considering an balance between temperature, thermal gradient and total wire length. The experimental results obtained in a 30 cores design with 3 active layers realized by 3D-ICE show that the maximal temperature is reduced by $15°C$, and the temperature gradient is reduced by $28.4°C$ compared to the baseline design.

References

1. International Technology Roadmap for Semiconductors (ITRS) (2013). http://www. itrs.net/Links/2013ITRS/Home2013.htm
2. Brunschwiler, T., Paredes, S., Drechsler, U., Michel, B., Cesar, W., Leblebici, Y., Wunderle, B., Reichl, H.: Heat-removal performance scaling of interlayer cooled chip stacks. In: 12th IEEE Thermal and Thermomechanical Phenomena in Electronic Systems (ITherm), pp. 1–12. IEEE, Barcelona (2010)
3. Ayala, J.L., Sridhar, A., Cuesta, D.: Thermal modeling and analysis of 3D multi-processor chips. Integr. VLSI J. **43**(4), 327–341 (2010)
4. Su, B., Gu, J., Shen, L., Huang, W., Greathouse, J.L., Wang, Z.: PPEP: online performance, power, and energy prediction framework and DVFS space exploration. In: 47th IEEE/ACM International Symposium on Microarchitecture, pp.445–457. IEEE Computer Society, Washington, DC (2014)
5. Cuesta, D., Risco-Martin, J.L., Ayala, J.L.: 3D thermal-aware floorplanner using a MILP approximation. Microprocess. Microsyst. **36**(5), 344–354 (2012)
6. Shuang-xi, Q., Zhang, M., Liu, G., Liu, T.: Dynamic thermal management by greedy scheduling algorithm. J. Central South Univ. **19**(1), 193–199 (2012)
7. Sridhar, A., Vincenzi, A., Ruggiero, M., Brunschwiler, T., Atienza, D.: 3D-ICE: fast compact transient thermal modeling for 3D ICs with inter-tier liquid cooling. In: IEEE/ACM International Conference on Computer-Aided Design (ICCAD), pp. 463–470. IEEE Press, San Jose (2010)
8. Guo, J., Dai, K., Wang, Z.: A high performance heterogeneous architecture and its optimization design. In: Gerndt, M., Kranzlmüller, D. (eds.) HPCC 2006. LNCS, vol. 4208, pp. 300–309. Springer, Heidelberg (2006)
9. Ardestani, E.K., Renau, J.: ESESC: a fast multicore simulator using time-based sampling. In: IEEE/ACM High Performance Computer Architecture (HPCA), pp. 448–459. IEEE, Shenzhen (2013)

The Improvement of March C+ Algorithm for Embedded Memory Test

Yongwen Wang[✉], Qianbing Zheng, and Yin Yuan

School of Computer, National University of Defense Technology,
Changsha 410073, China
yongwen@nudt.edu.cn

Abstract. March C+ is commonly used as a memory test algorithm. The basic principle is to use finite state machines to read and write all the addresses one by one. This paper analysis the sensitivity conditions of several fault types not covered by the March C+ algorithm, and derived a new $22\,N$ algorithm, March Y, which increase the fault coverage of WDF, CFdsxwx and CFwd. March Y has the same symmetry as the March C+ algorithm, and achieves the coverage of all of the single unit fault types and coupling faults.

Keywords: Single unit faults · Coupling faults · March C+ algorithm · March Y algorithm

1 Introduction

The proportion of embedded memory has gradually increased in SoC [1]. In order to detect the defects and malfunctions effectively in the embedded memory, a high-quality embedded memory test method must be designed, which can improve the overall yield and substantially save the cost of test and manufacturing.

Simple failure is the most common type of fault in the memory. The following single unit fault type and coupling fault type contained in simple faults will be introduced.

The single unit fault type is not subject to the other memory cell and the failure occurs only in a unit, including the following basic types:

- Stuck-at Fault (SAF): the logical value of the storage unit or the connection is always 0 or 1.
- State Fault (SF): the status of the storage unit may automatically jump to state 0 or 1 from 1 or 0.
- Transition Fault (TF): the storage unit can not be changed from 0 to 1 or from 1 to 0.
- Write Disturb Fault (WDF): the write operation which does not change the data of the memory cell changes the data.

Y. Wang—This work is supported in part by National Natural Science Foundation of China under grants 61170045.

© Springer-Verlag Berlin Heidelberg 2016
W. Xu et al. (Eds.): NCCET 2015, CCIS 592, pp. 31–37, 2016.
DOI: 10.1007/978-3-662-49283-3_4

- Read Destructive Fault (RDF): the read operation changes the value of the memory cell, and reads out the value after the change.
- Deceptive Read Destructive Fault (DRDF): the read operation changes the value of the memory cell, and reads out the value before the change [2].
- Incorrect Read Fault (IRF): the read operation does not change the data of storage unit, but reads out the error data.
- Address Decoder Fault (ADF): the error of decoding memory address, and can not access the correct address.

Because prior works have proofed that the address decoding failure fault and stuck-at fault can be covered by other fault types [3], the other six types of fault are studied in this paper.

Coupling failure usually occurs in two or more units, the state of a unit will be subject to the state or operation of other units, including the following type of fault.

- State Coupling Fault (CFst): the state of a unit jump to 0 or 1 caused by its coupling unit.
- Disturb Coupling Fault (CFds): the read/write operations of a unit causing its coupling unit data jump. Such failures include: CFdsrx CFdsxwx and CFdsxw!x. CFdsrx refers to the read operation of a unit, including the "read 0" or "read 1". CFdsxwx means that the write operation does not change the state of a unit, including "0 write 0" or "1 write 1". CFdsxw!x means that the write operations change the state of a unit, including "0 write 1" or "1 write 0".
- Transition Coupling Fault (CFtr): the state of a unit makes the data of its coupling unit jump.
- Write Destructive Coupling Fault (CFwd): the state of a unit makes the WDF of its coupling unit.
- Read Destructive Coupling Fault (CFrd): the state of a unit makes the RDF of its coupling unit.
- Deceptive Read Destructive Coupling Fault (CFdrd): the state of a unit makes the DRDF of its coupling unit.
- Incorrect Reading Coupling Fault (CFir): the state of a unit makes the IRF of its coupling unit.

In this paper, the sensitivity conditions of faults not covered by the March C+ algorithm are analyzed. And March Y, a new 22 N algorithm, is presented to increase the fault coverage of WDF, CFdsxwx and CFwd.

This paper is organized as follows. In Sect. 2, the fault coverage of various March algorithms is analyzed. In Sect. 3 the March Y is described. In Sect. 4, the simulation results of March Y is shown. And this paper is concluded in Sect. 5.

2   Fault Coverage of March Algorithms

March algorithms are the most popular memory test method. These algorithms have a series of operations for each unit of the memory, known as MARCH elements.

Table 1. Description of different March algorithm

Algorithm	Complexity	March elements
MATS+	5 N	$\updownarrow (w0) \Uparrow (r0, w1) \Downarrow (w1, r0)$
March B	17 N	$\updownarrow (w0) \Uparrow (r0, w1, r1, w0, r0, w1) \Uparrow (r1, w0, w1) \Downarrow$ $(r1, w0, w1, w0) \Downarrow (r0, w1, w0)$
March C–	10 N	$\updownarrow (w0) \Uparrow (r0, w1) \Uparrow (r1, w0) \Downarrow (r0, w1) \Downarrow (r1, w0) \updownarrow (r0)$
March C+	14 N	$\updownarrow (w0) \Uparrow (r0, w1, r1) \Uparrow (r1, w0, r0) \Downarrow (r0, w1, r1) \Downarrow$ $(r1, w0, r0) \updownarrow (r0)$

Table 2. Description of different March algorithm

Algorithm	Total fault	Fault coverage
MATS+	27/84	32.14 %
March B	41/84	48.81 %
March C–	56/84	66.67 %
March C+	66/84	78.57 %

A MARCH element can be a simple operation, or a series of read and write sequence. There are four major March algorithms [4] as shown in Tables 1 and 2.

Through the data analysis of the above statistics of two tables, we find that even if the March C+ algorithms have a relative high fault coverage, WDF, CFdsxwx and CFwd are still not covered.

This paper will focus on this situation and make further improvements to March C+ algorithm.

3 March Y Algorithm

March Y algorithm increases the fault coverage of WDF, CFdsxwx and CFwd based on March C+ algorithm. This section will gradually deduce March Y algorithm through the description and fault coverage analysis of the March algorithm, and the analysis of three kinds of fault sensitization conditions.

3.1 The Fault Sensitization Conditions of WDF, CFdsxwx and CFwd

Figure 1 shows that the sensitization conditions of WDF in terms of $0w0$ or $1w1$.

According to the sensitized conditions $0w0$, you must initialize all of the memory cell data to 0, then w0, r0 operation. If the read data is 1, the storage unit is indicated to be failure. Therefore, the sensitivity of the March element is $\updownarrow (w0) \updownarrow (w0, r0)$.

According to the sensitized conditions $1w1$, you must initialize all of the memory cell data to 1, then $w1, r1$ operation. If the read data is 0, the storage

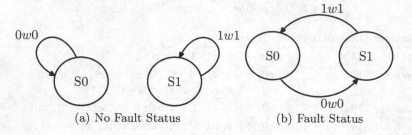

Fig. 1. WDF fault state transition diagram

unit is indicated to be failure. Therefore, the sensitivity of the March element is $\updownarrow (w1) \updownarrow (w1, r1)$.

In summary derivation, we can see the most streamlined March $(6\,N)$ for WDF algorithm:

$$\updownarrow (w0) \updownarrow (w0, r0, w1) \updownarrow (w1, r1) \tag{1}$$

$$\updownarrow (w1) \updownarrow (w1, r1, w0) \updownarrow (w0, r0) \tag{2}$$

Disturb Coupling Fault (CFdsxwx): According to the defines of CFdsxwx, the correct status and fault status as the following state diagram (S01 said that the state of original address is 0, the state of the coupled address is 1, and the address location is $0 <$ coupling address $<$ the original address $< N$):

Figure 2 shows that the sensitization conditions of CFdsxwx in four ways: $(0w0, 0)$, $(1w1, 1)$, $(0w0, 1)$ or $(1w1, 0)$.

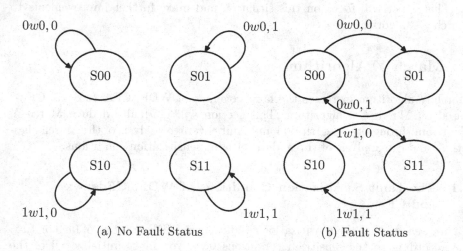

Fig. 2. CFdsxwx fault state transition diagram

According to the sensitized conditions $(0w0, 0)$, First initialize the storage unit to 0, then do $w0$ operation on the memory in descending order, with the $r0$

operation before $w0$ operating to read out unit data to determine whether the failure. Therefore, the March element is $\updownarrow (w0) \Downarrow (r0, w0)$.

According to the sensitized conditions $(1w1, 1)$, First initialize the storage unit to 1, then do $w1$ operation on the memory in descending order, with the $r1$ operation before $w1$ operating to read out unit data to determine whether the failure. Therefore, the March element is: $\updownarrow (w1) \Downarrow (r1, w1)$.

According to the sensitized conditions $(0w0, 1)$, First initialize the storage unit to 1, then do $(r1, w0, w0)$ operation continuous on the memory in descending order, through the twice $(w0)$ operations of the original address to sensitize the condition $(0w0)$, and detect the failure when do r1 operation to the coupled address. Therefore, the March element is $\updownarrow (w1) \Downarrow (r1, w0, w0)$.

According to the sensitized conditions $(1w1, 0)$, First initialize the storage unit to 0, then do $(r0, w1, w1)$ operation continuous on the memory in descending order, through the twice $(w1)$ operations of the original address to sensitize the condition $(1w1)$, and detect the failure when do r0 operation to the coupled address. Therefore, the March element is $\updownarrow (w0) \Downarrow (r0, w1, w1)$.

In summary derivation, we can see the most streamlined March $(9N)$ for CFdsxwx algorithm:

$$\updownarrow (w0) \Downarrow (r0, w0, w1, w1) \Downarrow (r1, w1, w0, w0) \tag{3}$$

$$\updownarrow (w1) \Downarrow (r1, w1, w0, w0) \Downarrow (r0, w0, w1, w1) \tag{4}$$

Write Destructive Coupling Fault (CFwd): According to the defines of CFwd, the correct status and fault status as the following state diagram (S01 said that the state of original address is 0, the state of the coupled address is 1, and the address location is $0 <$ coupling address $<$ the original address $< N$):

Figure 3 shows that the sensitization conditions of CFdsxwx in four ways: $(0, 0w0)$, $(1, 1w1)$, $(0, 1w1)$ or $(1, 0w0)$.

According to the sensitized conditions $(0, 0w0)$, First initialize the storage unit to 0, then do $w0$ operation on the memory in Ascending order to sensitize condition $(0, 0w0)$, and detect the failure with $r0$ operation at last. Therefore, the March element is $\updownarrow (w0) \Uparrow (w0) \updownarrow (r0)$.

According to the sensitized conditions $(1, 1w1)$, First initialize the storage unit to 1, then do $w1$ operation on the memory in Ascending order to sensitize condition $(1, 1w1)$, and detect the failure with r1 operation at last. Therefore, the March element is $\updownarrow (w1) \Uparrow (w1) \updownarrow (r1)$.

According to the sensitized conditions $(0, 1w1)$, First initialize the storage unit to 0, then do $(w1, w1)$ operation on the memory in Ascending order, and detect the failure with $r1$ operation at last. Therefore, the March element is $\updownarrow (w0) \Uparrow (w1, w1) \updownarrow (r1)$.

According to the sensitized conditions $(1, 0w0)$, First initialize the storage unit to 1, then do $(w0, w0)$ operation on the memory in Ascending order, and detect the failure with $(r1)$ operation at last. Therefore, the March element is $\updownarrow (w1) \Uparrow (w0, w0) \updownarrow (r0)$.

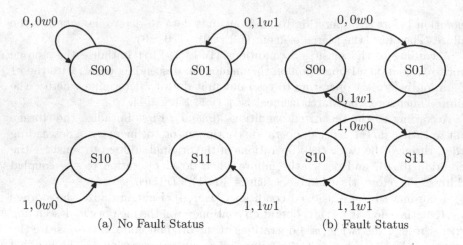

(a) No Fault Status   (b) Fault Status

Fig. 3. CFwd fault state transition diagram

In summary derivation, we can see the most streamlined March (11 N) for CFwd algorithm:

$$\updownarrow (w0) \Uparrow (w1, w1, r1) \Uparrow (w1, r1) \Uparrow (w0, w0, r0) \Uparrow (w0, r0) \tag{5}$$

$$\updownarrow (w1) \Uparrow (w0, w0, r0) \Uparrow (w0, r0) \Uparrow (w1, w1, r1) \Uparrow (w1, r1) \tag{6}$$

$$\updownarrow (w0) \Uparrow (w0, r0) \Uparrow (w1, w1, r1) \Uparrow (w1, r1) \Uparrow (w0, w0, r0) \tag{7}$$

$$\updownarrow (w1) \Uparrow (w1, r1) \Uparrow (w0, w0, r0) \Uparrow (w0, r0) \Uparrow (w1, w1, r1) \tag{8}$$

3.2 Detailed Steps of Algorithm Derivation

March C+ algorithm add the fault coverage of WDF: Compalred with the march elements of WDF we can see that Simply add a ($w0$ operation in M2 and add a ($w1$) operation in M3 of March C+ algorithm to cover the WDF.

$$\updownarrow (w0) \Uparrow (w0, r0, w1, r1) \Uparrow (w1, r1, w0, r0) \Downarrow (r0, w1, r1) \Downarrow (r1, w0, r0) \updownarrow (r0) \tag{9}$$

Formula 9 adds the fault coverage of CFdsxwx. Comaring the March elements of Formulas 3 and 9, we can see that simply add ($w0, w1$) operations in M4 and add ($w1, w0$) operations in M5 of Formula 9 to cover the CFdsxwx, as follows:

$$\updownarrow (w0) \Uparrow (w0, r0, w1, r1) \Uparrow (w1, r1, w0, r0) \Downarrow (r0, w0, w1, w1, r1) \Downarrow (r1, w1, w0, w0, r0) \updownarrow (r0) \tag{10}$$

Formula 10 adds the fault coverage of CFwd. Comparing the March elements of Formulas 7 and 10, we can see that simply add a ($w1$) operation in M2 and add a ($w0$) operation in M3 of Formula 10 to cover the CFwd, as follows:

$$\updownarrow (w0) \Uparrow (w0, r0, w1, w1, r1) \Uparrow (w1, r1, w0, w0, r0) \Downarrow (r0, w0, w1, w1, r1) \Downarrow (r1, w1, w0, w0, r0) \updownarrow (r0) \tag{11}$$

Formula 11 which named March Y has covered WDF, CFdsxwx and CFwd.

4   The Simulation Results of March Y Algorithm

The algorithm as the same as the March C+ algorithm, from the first step of the algorithm $\Updownarrow$ ($w0$) to the last $\Updownarrow$ ($r0$), a complete test needs to undergo six states. We designed and implemented the MBIST controller base on March Y, and simulate the function of MBIST controller. Part of the waveform is shown in Fig. 4.

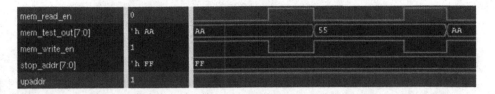

Fig. 4. The second step of March Y algorithm

In Fig. 4, the red line position is the beginning of the second step of March Y algorithm, AA represents data 0, 55 represents data 1, the diagram suggest that do write 0, read 0, write 1, write 1, read 1 operations on the memory in Ascending order.

5   Conclusions

In summary, March Y algorithm inherits the advantages of March C+ algorithms which has six steps of the symmetrical structure, increases the coverage of three kinds of failures which named WDF, CFdsxwx, CFwd with reasonable algorithm complexity.

References

1. Arden, W.M.: The international technology roadmap for semiconductors—perspectives and challenges for the next 15 years. Curr. Opin. Solid State Mater. Sci. **6**, 371–377 (2002)
2. Adams, R., Cooley, E.: Analysis of a deceptive destructive read memory fault model and recommended testing. In: Proceedings of IEEE North Atlantic Test Workshop, pp. 27–32 (1996)
3. Dekker, R., Beenker, F., Thijssen, L.: A realistic fault model and test algorithms for static random access memories. IEEE Trans. Comput.-Aided Des. Integr. Circ. Syst. **9**, 567–572 (1990)
4. Marinissen, E.J., Prince, B., Keltel-Schulz, D., Zorian, Y.: Challenges in embedded memory design and test. In: Proceedings of Design, Automation and Test in Europe, pp. 722–727. IEEE (2005)

Mitigating Soft Error Rate Through Selective Replication in Hybrid Architecture

Chao Song[1(✉)] and Minxuan Zhang[1,2]

[1] College of Computer, National University of Defense Technology,
Changsha 410073, China
xiatiandf0109@163.com
[2] National Laboratory for Parallel and Distributed Processing,
National University of Defense Technology, Changsha 410073, China

Abstract. With the rapid development of integrated circuit technology, soft error has increasingly become the major factor for the reliability of microprocessors. The researchers employ a variety of methods to reduce the influence of soft errors. Besides the lower delay and increasing bandwidth, 3D integration technology also has the ability of heterogeneous integration. STT-RAM is a new storage technology with broad prospects. The characteristic that STT-RAM is immune to soft errors makes it ideal candidate for improving reliability and STT-RAM can be integrated into the 3D chip through heterogeneous integration. In this paper, we proposed a selective replication mechanism for soft error rate reduction in hybrid reorder buffer architecture based on the 3D integration technology and STT-RAM. Instructions will be replicated or migrated to STT-RAM for reliability improvement in certain situations. The experimental results show that the soft error rate of the proposed hybrid structure is reduced by 15 % on average and the AVF decreased 54.3 % further on average through the in-buffer selective replication mechanism while the performance penalty is 2.8 %.

Keywords: Soft error rate · Selective replication · Hybrid architecture

1 Introduction

With the development of the manufacturing process, the feature size of integrated circuits, operating voltage and the parasitic capacitance are reducing, which makes the reliability of integrated circuits become more prominent [1]. Studies have shown that soft error problem has become a major aspect of the IC reliability [2, 3] and has caused great damage [4–6]. Typically, soft error is induced by the striking of the high energy particles. Different from the traditional hard errors, soft errors are not permanent, which means that the state of the circuit is temporary changed, and will back to normal in a short time. The high energy particles are mainly from the atmosphere, and the chip packaging materials [7].

The 3D integration technology [8] brings about new structure of the chip. The 3D chip is made by stacking some traditional 2D circuits in the vertical direction using 3D integration technology, and connecting the adjacent circuit layer using interlayer

© Springer-Verlag Berlin Heidelberg 2016
W. Xu et al. (Eds.): NCCET 2015, CCIS 592, pp. 38–47, 2016.
DOI: 10.1007/978-3-662-49283-3_5

interconnection technology, such as TSVs (Through Silicon Vias). The new integrated technology can reduce the overall length of the chip wiring and improve the latency and power consumption. And more, it is capable of heterogeneous integration [9], i.e., different circuit layers may take different manufacturing processes.

Therefore, new opportunities are provided by the 3D integration technology, which is employing STT-RAM (Spin-transfer Torque Random Access Memory) technology to reduce the possibility of the occurrence of soft errors. STT-RAM is a novel storage technology. High-energy particles can cause soft error in conventional memory cell, such as SRAM, but the STT-RAM is not affected. The STT-RAM holds information by Magnetic Tunnel Junctions (MTJs), instead of storing electric charges in SRAM. The STT-RAM has the same read performance as SRAM, but the write latency is relatively long.

In this paper, based on the heterogeneous integration provided by 3D integration technology and the feature of STT-RAM that is immune to soft error, we construct a hybrid reorder buffer structure. In the new structure, the long STT-RAM write latency is handled properly by the long latency of instructions. We also observed that only a part of entries in reorder buffer are occupied at most of cycles. We proposed an in-buffer replication mechanism for AVF reduction in hybrid architecture. The experimental results show that the soft error rate of the proposed hybrid structure is reduced by 15 % on average and the AVF reduction decreased 54.3 % on average through the in-buffer replication mechanism while the performance penalty is 2.8 %.

The remainder of this paper is organized as follows. Section 2 briefly reviews the background of soft errors, 3D integration technology and STT-RAM. Section 3 presents the proposed hybrid architecture. Section 4 describes our experimental methodology. Section 5 presents simulation results, and discussion. Related work is discussed in Sect. 6. Finally, conclusions are drawn in Sect. 7.

2 Background

Soft errors are caused by high energy particles. When high energy particles strike and go through the silicon material, producing large amounts of electric charge, causing a voltage pulse. If the data stored in the storage elements are changed by the pulse, a soft error occurs.

A soft error in circuit does not mean the corruption of the final result, because the soft error may be masked. For example, if it is a new write operation but not a read operation that is executed in memory cell after a soft error happened in the cell, the soft error is masked. Architectural Vulnerability Factors (AVF) is proposed to quantify the effect of masking [13], which is the probability that a soft error in circuit leads to a visible error in the final output. The final SER is the product of raw SER of the circuit (SER_{RAW}) and the AVF, which is expressed by the following equation:

$$SER = SER_{RAW} * AVF \tag{1}$$

The AVF can be calculated through ACE analysis [13]. ACE analyze find the instructions which are essential for the architectural correct execution. Errors in un-ACE instructions would not affect the final reliability.

Figure 1 is a schematic view of 3D integration technology, showing a 3D chip stacking two layers, which can be carried out through two bonding techniques, Face-to-Face (F2F), i.e. two metal layer are adjacent, or Face-to-Back (F2B), i.e., the metal layer and the substrate are adjacent.

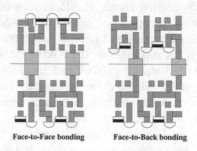

Face-to-Face bonding   Face-to-Back bonding

Fig. 1. Schematic view of 3D integration technology

In the 3D chip, circuit layers are produced in accordance with conventional techniques, and then stacked in the vertical direction. Between the adjacent circuit layers, vertical wire connections are built for signal and data transmission. Each circuit layer of a 3D circuit can be manufactured separately using different process technology, and 3D chip is capable of integrating heterogeneous technology, such as STT-RAM.

STT-RAM is a new storage technology with several attractive features. In addition to the non-volatility, high storage density and low leakage current, STT-RAM is immune to soft errors. Figure 2 presents a schematic structural view of STT-RAM memory cell. Traditional SRAM and DRAM technology uses electric charges to store information, while STT-RAM using MTJ (Magnetic Tunnel Junctions). A MTJ consists of two ferromagnetic layers and a oxide barrier layer. If the two ferromagnetic layers are in the same direction, the resistance of MTJ is low, indicating a logic state 0, otherwise represents 1. The direction of the ferromagnetic layer can be changed by applying a driving current. The memory unit may be designed as a transistor (NMOS) connecting a MTJ in series [10]. NMOS gate connected to a word line (WL). If need to access the MTJ during read or write operation, the NMOS is opened.

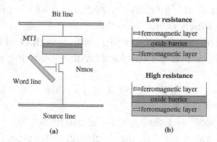

Fig. 2. Schematic view of STT-RAM cell (a) and MTJ (b)

3   Architectural Modification

In this section, we analyze the distribution of different instruction type and AVF of the ROB at fine-grained level. Based on the analysis and combined with 3D integration technology, hybrid architecture and selective replication are proposed to reduce the soft error rate.

3.1   Instruction and AVF Analysis

The uncommitted instructions are stored in ROB and each instruction occupies a ROB entry. Instructions are classified into the following categories: ACE instructions, trivial instructions and unknown instructions. All bits in ACE instruction are critical for AVF, while only a part of bits in trivial instructions are critical for ACE analysis. The unknown instructions cannot be determined in the instruction analysis window. In order to understand the influence of each instruction type on the overall AVF, we carry out a fine-grained analysis with a out-of-order issue and execution microprocessor simulator. We assume that the ROB consists of 80 entries (specific settings are in Table 1).

Figure 3 shows the distribution of different type instructions and AVF originated from each type. The prefetch, NOP and FDDTDD instructions are trivial instructions [11]. The unknown, ACE and trivial instructions account for 0.6 %, 44.3 % and 55.1 % respectively, but the AVFs account for 4.2 %, 84.4 % and 11.4 % respectively. ACE instructions cover large percent AVF in spite of less than half the proportion of instructions. Then the ACE instructions are the key to reduce AVF. Sophisticated analysis is essential for the identification of all instruction type and finding out all ACE instructions is hard when the soft error rate reduction mechanism is working.

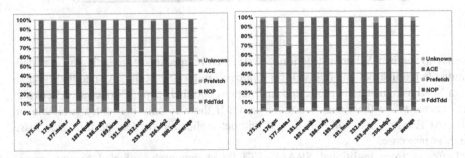

Fig. 3.   (a). The distribution of instructions (b). The distribution of AVFs (Color figure online)

3.2   Architectural Optimization

Some ACE instructions cannot be determined until the analysis after their commitment, but other ACE instructions such as unconditional branch, jump, PALcode instruction

Table 1. The flow of replication and migration

Each new instruction
1:**if** (available entry in SRAM) **then**
2:　　**if** (instruction is ACE instruction) **then**
3:　　　　**if** (available entry for replication) **then**
4:　　　　　　instruction is replicated;
5:　　　　**else**
6:　　　　　　instruction replication is abandoned;
7:　　　　**end if**
8:　　**else**
9:　　　　instruction replication is abandoned;
10:　　**end if**
11:**else**
12:　　wait for available entry;
13:**end if**

Each new cycle
1:**for** (all occupied entry in SRAM) **do**
2:　　check the resident time of instruction;
3:　　**if** (the instruction stayed too long for migration) **then**
4:　　　　**if** (the instruction has been replicated) **then**
5:　　　　　　instruction is migrated to STT-RAM;
6:　　　　　　two entries in SRAM is available after migration;
7:　　　　**else**
8:　　　　　　instruction is migrated to STT-RAM;
9:　　　　　　one entry in SRAM is available after migration;
10:　　　　**end if**
11:　　**else**
12:　　　　instruction migration is abandoned;
13:　　**end if**
14:**end for**

are easy to confirm. When instructions are decoded in previous stage, a flag bit is added to indicate the instructions that will be replicated in reorder buffer. A specified field is put in ROB to indicate the replicated instructions and their copy. Correctness checking will execute when these instructions commit. If there is only one entry available in ROB, ACE instruction will still be put without replication for less performance loss, which is rare case.

Different from traditional SRAM, STT-RAM cannot be affected by soft error. Hybrid structure is feasible for reliability improvement, although STT-RAM write speed is slower than mature technology. Placing more instructions to the STT-RAM is better for reducing soft error rate, but the performance will be more affected. For performance considerations, the number of instructions in STT-RAM needs to be handled reasonably. Figure 4 shows the distribution of cycles that instructions stay in the ROB. And it can be seen that only a small part of instructions have long resident time. The instructions that resident time is less than 30 cycles account for 96 %.

Therefore, migrating instructions with long resident time to the STT-RAM will achieve better trade-off between the reliability and performance. Figure 5 is the percentage of the migrated instructions when the maximum cycle number that instructions stay in SRAM based entry changed. We can see that if the instructions stay in traditional entry for less than 15 cycles, a plenty of instructions will be migrated. For the benefit of reducing overhead, it is suitable that instructions stay in traditional entry for 25 cycles. In our design, instructions that resident time is more than 25 cycles will be migrated to STT-RAM based entries.

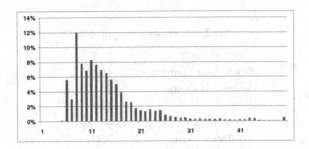

Fig. 4. The distribution of cycles instructions stayed in ROB

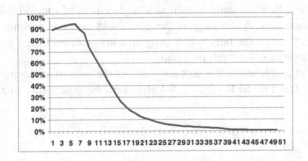

Fig. 5. The distribution of cycles instructions stayed in ROB

Table 1 shows the flow of replication and migration. New instruction in ROB would be replicated if it is ACE instruction and an entry is available. Each instruction is checked at each cycle for the migration to STT-RAM regardless of whether it is ACE instruction or not. If migration is done, there will be new available entries available for new instruction in SRAM. When the instruction is migrating, the data in SRAM entry is valid. New entry is not available until the completion of write operation in STT-RAM entry and instruction will not stalled for the benefit of performance.

4 Experimental Methodology

To evaluate the soft error rate reduction performance of the above presented hybrid architecture, we carry out the Sim-SODA, an architectural reliability simulations tool [11]. We assume that the entire design is implemented at the 65-nm technology node and the processor works at 2.0-GHz frequency. Table 2 lists the simulator configuration parameters. The number of ROB entries is 120, including 80 traditional entries and 40 STT-RAM based entries and for STT-RAM the write operation latency is set to 20 cycles [10].

Table 2. Processor Configuration

Pipeline stages	7
Fetch, issue, commit width	4/4/4
Instruction Queue	20
ROB	120
Register File	80
Load/store Queue	32/32
Instruction/Data TLB	128/128

The integer and floating point benchmark applications of the SPEC2000 suite are used for the simulation. According to the Sim-Point analysis technology [12], the representative sections of the benchmark programs are selected to run and one million instructions are executed for each program.

For the hybrid architecture, the soft error rate is the sum of traditional part and the STT-RAM part. The raw SER of STT-RAM is zero because of its immunity to soft error.

5 Results

In this section, we list the results obtained by simulation.

Figure 6 shows the distribution of instructions migrated to STT-RAM and the normalized AVF reduction. Figure 6 shows that, for a majority of benchmark, only a small part of instructions migrated to STT-RAM. Except *lucas* and *eon*, in which 9.5 % and 15.5 % instructions have migrated respectively, 3.3 % instructions should be migrated to STT-RAM on average. Figure 6 shows that, the AVF reduction is 14.6 % on average, and *mesa* has the highest AVF reduction of 53 %, although only 3.2 % instructions are migrated. In this case, a small part of instructions stay in the structure for a long time, taking a large proportion of AVF.

Figure 7 shows distribution of replicated instructions and the normalized AVF reduction. As can be seen, the percentage of replicated instructions has the same trend with the results of AVF reduction basically. For all applications, there are 29.5 % instructions replicated in buffer on average, resulting in the AVF reduction by 54.4 % on average.

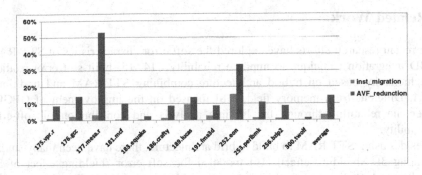

Fig. 6. The distribution of instructions migrated to STT-RAM and AVF reduction (Color figure online)

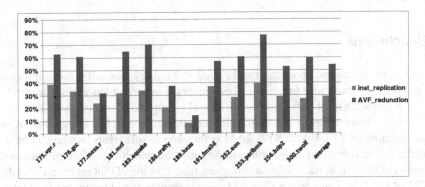

Fig. 7. The distribution of replicated instructions and AVF reduction (Color figure online)

In buffer replication will lead to performance degradation. Figure 8 shows the normalized IPC degradation. For most of applications, the performance penalty is acceptable, which is 2.8 % on average. The performance loss is 15.2 % for *mesa*, which is significant higher than the other applications. We can see from Fig. 6 that a small part of instructions in *mesa* stay in the structure for a long time, which means that instructions are difficult to commit. If instructions are not replicated, there would be more entries for instructions.

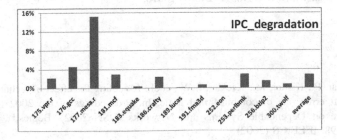

Fig. 8. The IPC degradation (Color figure online)

6   Related Work

Many recent research efforts have explored the soft error characteristics of STT-RAM and 3D integration technique to improve reliability. [14, 15] built soft error-resilient cache hierarchy based on hybrid architecture combining STT-RAM and traditional SRAM. Different from memory field, [18] focused on the improvement of GPGPU register file reliability through the lifetime analysis and contribution of soft-error vulnerability.

Besides using STT-RAM to build hybrid architecture, there have been many studies integrating 3D shielding effect. [16] modeled the soft error shielding effect of 3D vertically stacked dies and further proposed architectural optimization for processor core. [17] targeted for cache hierarchy using shielding effect provided by 3D integrated technology, reducing SER by migrating data blocks among soft error invulnerable die and protected die.

7   Conclusions

With the rapid development of integrated circuit technology, the soft error problem also has become more and more important. Researchers have presented various methods to reduce the probability of soft error occurring. 3D integrated technology is capable of heterogeneous integration in the chip, which enables the on chip integration of new storage technology STT-RAM. STT-RAM is immune to soft errors, which can be used to reduce the influence of soft errors, improving the reliability of chip. This paper presented the hybrid reorder buffer architecture based on the 3D integration technology and STT-RAM. The latency of STT-RAM write operation is hidden by the long latency of instructions and the overall soft errors rate is reduced. The experimental results show that the soft error rate of the proposed hybrid structure is reduced by 15 % on average. We observed that only a part of entries in reorder buffer are occupied at most of cycles. In this paper, we proposed a selective replication mechanism for soft error rate reduction in hybrid architecture. The experimental results show that the AVF decreased 54.3 % further on average through the in-buffer replication mechanism while the performance penalty is 2.8 %.

Acknowledgments. The research is supported by National Natural Science Foundation of China with Grant No. 61076025, and by Specialized Research Fund for the Doctor Program of Higher Education of China with Grant No. 20124307110016.

References

1. Shivakumar, P., Kistler, M., Keckler, S.W., et al.: Modeling the effect of technology trends on the soft error rate of combinational logic. In: Proceedings of the 2002 International Conference on Dependable Systems and Networks (DSN 2002), Bethesda, MD, USA, pp. 389–398. IEEE CS (2002)

2. Mitra, S., Seifert, N., Zhang, M., Shi, Q., Kim, K.S.: Robust system design with built-in soft-error resilience. IEEE Trans. Comput. **38**(2), 43–52 (2005)
3. Baumann, R.C.: Radiation-Induced soft errors in advanced semiconductor technologies. IEEE Trans. Device Mater. Reliab. **5**(3), 305–316 (2005)
4. Baumann, R.C: Soft errors in commercial semiconductor technology: overview and scaling trends. In: IEEE Reliability Physics Tutorial Notes, Reliability Fundamentals 7 April 2002
5. Zielger, J.F., Puchner, H.: SER—History, Trends and Challenges. Cypress Semiconductor Corporation, San Jose (2004)
6. Michalak, S.E., Harris, K.W., Hengartner, N.W., Takala, B.E., Wender, S.A.: Predicting the number of fatal soft errors in Los Alamos National Laboratory's ASC Q supercomputer. Trans. Device Mater. Reliab. **5**(3), 329–335 (2005)
7. Baumann, R.C.: Soft errors in advanced semiconductor Devices Part I: the three radiation sources. IEEE Trans. Device Mater. Reliab. **1**, 17–22 (2001)
8. Banerjee, K., Souri, S.J., Kapur, P., Saraswat, K.C.: 3-D ICs: a novel chip design for improving deep-submicrometer interconnect performance and systems-on-chip integration. Proc. IEEE **89**(5), 602–633 (2001)
9. Xie, Y.: Processor architecture design using 3D integration technology. In: VLSID 2010, pp. 446–451 (2010)
10. Hosomi, M., Yamagishi, H.Y., Yamamoto, T., Bessho, K., Higo, Y., Yamane, K., Yamada, H., Shoji, M., Hachino, H., Fukumoto, C., Nagao, H., Kano, H.: A novel nonvolatile memory with spin torque transfer magnetization switching: Spin-RAM. In: IEDM 2005
11. Fu, X., Li, T., Fortes, J.: Sim-SODA: A unified framework for architectural level software reliability analysis. In: Proceedings of Workshop on Modeling, Benchmarking and Simulation (2006)
12. Sherwood, T., Perelman, E., Hamerly, G., Calder, B.: Automatically characterizing large scale program behavior. In: ASPLOS 2002
13. Mukherjee, S.S., Weaver, C.T., Emer, J., Reinhardt, S.K., Austin, T.: A systematic methodology to compute the architectural vulnerability factors for a high-performance microprocessor. In: MICRO 2003
14. Sun, H., Liu, C., Xu, W., Zhao, J., Zheng, N., Zhang, T.: Using magnetic RAM to build low-power and soft error-resilient L1 cache. IEEE Trans. VLSI **20**(1), 19–28 (2010)
15. Sun, G., Kursun, E., Rivers, J., Xie, Y.: Exploring the vulnerability of CMPs to soft errors with 3D stacked non-volatile memory. In: Proceedings of the 29th International Conference on Computer Design (ICCD) October 2011, pp. 366–372 (2011)
16. Zhang, W., Li, T.: Microarchitecture soft error vulnerability characterization and mitigation under 3D integration technology. In: Proceedings of the 41st Annual International Symposium on Micro-architecture (MICRO) December 2008, pp. 453–446 (2008)
17. Sun, H., Ren, P., Zheng, N., Zhang, T., Li, T.: Architecting high-performance energy-efficient soft error resilient cache under 3D integration technology. Microprocess. Microsyst. **35**(4), 371–381 (2011)
18. Tan, J., Li, Z., Fu, X.: Soft-error reliability and power co-optimization for GPGPUS register file using resistive memory. In: Proceedings of the Design, Automation & Test in Europe Conference & Exhibition (DATE) March 2015, pp. 369–374 (2015)

Application Specific Processors

A New Memory Address Transformation for Continuous-Flow FFT Processors with SIMD Extension

Chao Yang[✉], Haiyan Chen, Sheng Liu, and Sheng Ma

The School of Computer, National University of Defense Technology,
Changsha 410073, Hunan Provience, China
yc.nudt@gmail.com,
{hychen,liusheng83,masheng}@nudt.edu.cn

Abstract. The property of addresses accessed by one butterfly in FFT processors arises the difficulty for parallel accessing during computation. And the address reversal at input or output stage increases the difficulty for parallel I/O. In this paper, a new and simple generalized memory address transformation method supporting parallel accessing for computation is proposed to accelerate 2^n-point Mixed-Radix FFT for memory-based FFT processors with SIMD extension. To make I/O clock cycles match up with computation cycles, a new I/O addresses parallel generation method is also proposed. The advantages of the method proposed in this paper lie in the fact that they support the maximum throughput SIMD memory with multi-bank structures and in-place policy for both I/O and computation with continuous data flow. And most importantly, the address transformation circuit for FFT computations is low-complexity with only XOR gates; the I/O addresses parallel generation circuit is also simple with just counters.

Keywords: FFT · SIMD · Mixed-Radix · Memory-based · Parallel access · Continuous-flow

1 Introduction

With the performance needs increasing for FFT computation in many digital signal processing applications, such as communication signal processing, image analysis, energy detection [12], electrochemistry [13], many solutions were proposed for accelerating the computation.

Nowadays, the architecture of numerous FFT processors can be classified into two popular types: the pipelined architecture and the memory-based architecture. The FFT processors based on pipelined architecture such as in [3, 4, 14] are high-throughput but cost more power and area. And the FFT processors based on memory-based architecture such as in [1, 5, 6, 11] are effective for area reduction and memory size minimum. In recent years, memory-based architecture in FFT processors has gained more and more attention for its high hardware efficiency.

SIMD (single instruction multiple data) extension in both pipelined and memory-based architectures is effective to satisfy real-time processing. For example,

© Springer-Verlag Berlin Heidelberg 2016
W. Xu et al. (Eds.): NCCET 2015, CCIS 592, pp. 51–60, 2016.
DOI: 10.1007/978-3-662-49283-3_6

[7] used k radix-b BF(butterfly) processing units and k*b memory modules to acquire the speedup of the FFT algorithms by a factor of k.

For memory system, one of the techniques to improve the bandwidth is low-order address interleaved scheme with more memory modules. However, the actual bandwidth of low-order address interleaved memory system in FFT processors is dissatisfied because of the property of addresses needed for one BF operation. To solve this problem, for radix-2 FFT processors based on pipelined architecture, Ma in [2] come up with a method supporting memory access simultaneously. In memory-based FFT processors the parallel access schemes proposed in [1] for fixed radix-b with single BF and in [7] for fixed radix-b with multiple BFs are effective. Parallel access schemes in [8, 9] are effective for constant geometry FFT algorithms.

This paper presents a new memory address transformation method and I/O address schedule, which allow conflict-free parallel memory access in hardware implementation of memory-based FFT processors and increase the speed of the Mixed-Radix-2^r FFT algorithm by a factor equal to the number of BFs. This paper is organized as followings. Section 2 explains the FFT algorithms. Section 3 proposes address transformation to support conflict-free parallel access and address generation methods for I/O. Section 4 compare some methods supporting parallel access to show that our method is effective.

2 Mixed-Radix-2^r FFT Algorithms

The DFT (discrete fast Fourier) transformation of the N-point is defined by:

$$X(k) = \sum_{n=0}^{N-1} x(n) * W_N^{nk} \tag{1}$$

In (1), $W_N^k = e^{-j*2k\pi/N}$, and k is integer ranging from 0 to N-1. When $N = 2^n$, the DFT series can be divided into small series processed with radix-2/4/8 and other radix-2^r algorithms. For examples, radix-8 algorithms will be used for calculating 64-point FFT in two stages(radix-8, and radix-8). Radix-8 and radix-4 algorithms can be used to compute 32-point FFT in two stages (radix-8, and radix-4). And radix-4, radix-2 algorithms could be used to calculate 32-point FFT in three stages(radix-4, radix-4, and radix-2), which are called Mixed-Radix-2^r algorithm. Figure 1 shows the signal flow graph of radix-2/4/8.

3 Memory Address Generation

3.1 Address Transformation for Fixed-Radix-2^r Using Single BF

Fixed-Radix-2^r (r is integer) FFT processors with single BF unit is a special case of Mixed-Radix-2^r SIMD FFT processors. Assuming address a represented as $a_{n-1}a_{n-2}...a_0$ (or a[n-1:0], in this paper, a_i is the same as a[i]), in the familiar low-order address interleaved scheme, a[r-1:0] represents the memory modules index and a[n-1:r]

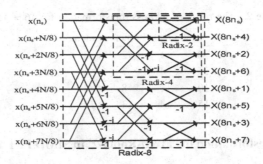

Fig. 1. Signal flow graph of the radix-2/4/8 algorithm

represents the row address in one module. For radix-2^r FFT, the number of operators for one BF is 2^r. In every stage of FFTs, there are r bits different for the 2^r operator addresses accessed for one BF. For example, in Table 1, for FFT size $16 = 4*4$, in the first stage for each BF operation the bits of a[3:2] are different and in the second stage for each BF operation the bits of a[1:0] are also different.

Table 1. Binary codes of 0 to 15.

0	1	2	3
0000	0001	0010	0011
4	5	6	7
0100	0101	0110	0111
8	9	10	11
1000	1001	1010	1011
12	13	14	15
1100	1101	1110	1111

So according to this property of addresses needed for one BF operation, we could arrange addresses accessed by one BF operation in different memory modules. To achieve that, we divide address a by r-bits, starting from the least significant bit of a, and acquire vectors $F_0, F_1, \ldots, F_{[n/r-1]}$, viz., $F_0 = a[r-1:0]$, $F_1 = a[2r-1:r]$, $\ldots$, here $F_{[n/r-1]}$ may be only n mod r bits when n is not multiples of r. Then m[r-1:0] is the result of performing bit-wise XOR operation between all F_i. Because r and only r bits are different from the addresses accessed by one BF operation in every stage, m[r-1:0] ranges from 0 to 2^r-1. If a[r-1:0] is replaced by m[r-1:0], these addresses accessed by one BF could be distributed into 2^r memory modules, which indicates that data consumed by one BF can be accessed simultaneously.

In Table 2 we find that the four addresses needed by one BF in every stage can be accessed in one cycle. And the address transformation is below:

m[1:0] = F_1^F_0 = {a[3]^a[1], a[2]^a[0]};

aa[3:0] = {a[3:2],m[1:0]};

Here, F_0 is a[1:0], F_1 is a[3:2], aa[3:0] is address after be transformed.

Table 2. The result of address transformation for 16 = 4*4.

mem0	mem1	mem2	mem3
0	1	2	3
5	4	7	6
10	11	8	9
15	14	13	12

3.2   Address Transformation for Fixed-Radix-2^r in SIMD FFT Processors

In SIMD FFT processors, there are more than two BF units. Assuming the number of BF units is 2^p, so 2^{r+p} memory modules are needed. Here address a is divided into three parts: a[n-1:p + r] represented as the row address of memory modules, a[p-1:0] represented as 2^p memory blocks, each of which is composed of 2^r memory modules. And a[p + r-1:p] index the module in the block, which is shown in Fig. 2.

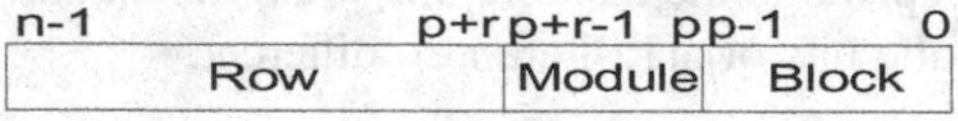

Fig. 2. The division of address a[n-1:0].

In each stage there are r bits different for the operator addresses accessed by one BF operation. These different bits can be represented as a[d + r-1:d], here d is not fixed. To arrange all addresses accessed by BFs in one cycle into different memory modules, we segment address a[n-1:p] by r-bits, starting from the least significant bit of a[n-1:p], and acquire vectors, F_0, F_1, ..., $F_{[(n-p)/r-1]}$, viz., $F_0 = a[p + r-1:p]$, $F_1 = a[p + 2r-1:p + r]$, ..., here $F_{[(n-p)/r-1]}$ may be only (n-p) mod r bits when (n-p) is not multiples of r. Then m [r-1:0] is the result of performing bit-wise XOR operation between F_i. And new address aa[n-1:0] is same as a[n-1:0] except a[p + r-1:p] replaced by m[r-1:0].

There always exist r bits different in aa[p + r-1:0] for the transformed addresses accessed by one BF in a cycle. Because in each stage, when d ranges from n-r to p, each aa[p + r-1:p] is different from the transformed addresses corresponding to initial addresses; when d ranges from p-r to 0, there exists r bits different in aa[p-1:0] and when d ranges from p-1 to p-r + 1 there exists r-p + d bits different in aa[p + r-1:p] and p-d bits different in aa[p-1:0].

In aa[p + r-1:0], these different bits are defined as aa[dd + r-1:dd], here dd is not fixed. Then for all BFs in the same stage, dd is the same, and other p bits in aa [p + r-1:0] can represent 2^p BFs. In a nutshell, our address transformation can support parallel access for all 2^p BFs in SIMD architecture.

Table 3 displays that our address transformation supports eight addresses accessed by two radix-4 BFs in a cycle. The address transformation for Table 3 is below:

m[1:0] = F_2^F_1^F_0 = {a[2]^a[4], a[1]^a[3]^a[5]};

aa[5:0] = {a[5:3],m[1:0],a[0]};

Here, F_0 is a[2:1], F_1 is a[4:3], F_2 is a[5].

Table 3. The result of address transformation for 64 = 8*8.

block0				block1			
mem0	mem2	mem4	mem6	mem1	mem3	mem5	mem7
0	2	4	6	1	3	5	7
10	8	14	12	11	9	15	13
20	22	16	18	21	23	17	19
30	28	26	24	31	29	27	25
34	32	38	36	35	33	39	37
40	42	44	46	41	43	45	47
54	52	50	48	55	53	51	49
60	62	56	58	61	63	57	59

3.3 Address Transformation for Mixed-Radix-2^r in SIMD FFT Processors

Assuming FFT points $N = 2^n$ is processed with radix-2^{r1} and radix-2^{r2}(r1, r2 are integers) algorithms. Here r1 is bigger than r2 and radix-2^{r2} computations are done at the final FFT stage. In this subsection, we will prove that the memory system supporting conflict-free parallel access for radix-2^{r1} algorithm also supports conflict-free parallel access for radix-2^{r2} algorithm.

In the stage of radix-2^{r2} FFT computations, there exist r2 bits different from the addresses accessed by one radix-2^{r2} BF. These different bits are taken as a[d + r2-1:d] in which d is not fixed. When d ranges from n-r2 to p, there exist r2 bits different in aa [p + r1-1:p], and when d ranges from p-r2 to 0, there exists r2 bits different in aa[p-1:0] and when d ranges from p-1 to p-r2 + 1 there exists r2-p + d bits different in aa [p + r1-1:p] and p-d bits different in aa[p-1:0]. So for one radix-2^{r2} BF in a stage, there always exist r2 bits different in aa[p + r1-1:0]. So as like in Sect. 3.2, the data needed by number of $2^{p+r1-r2}$ radix-2^{r2} BF units in one stage can be accessed in one cycle. Table 4 shows that our address transformation can support parallel access for 32-points processed by radix-8, radix-4 algorithms. The addresses accessed by two radix-4 BFs in one cycle are blacked in Table 4. The address transformation for Table 4 is below:

m[2:0] = F_1^F_0 = {a[2], a[4]^a[1], a[3]^a[0]};

aa[4:0] = {a[4:3], m[2:0]};

Here, F_0 is a[2:0], F_1 is a[4:3].

Table 4. The result of address transformation for FFT sizes 32 = 8*4.

block0							
mem0	mem1	mem2	mem3	mem4	mem5	mem6	mem7
0	1	2	3	4	5	6	7
9	8	11	10	13	12	15	14
18	19	16	17	22	23	20	21
27	26	25	24	31	30	29	28

In summary, for Mixed-Radix-2^r FFT processors with SIMD extension, if 2^{r1} is the biggest radix and 2^p is the number of radix-2^{r1} BFs, the procedures proposed in this paper are below:

1: Divide address a[n-1:0] into three parts: a[n-1:p + r1], a[p + r1-1:p], a[p-1:0], then divide a[n-1:p] by r1-bits, starting from the least significant bit of a[n-1:p], F_0, F_1, ..., $F_{[(n-p)/r1-1]}$, viz., $F_0 = a[p + r1-1:p]$, $F_1 = a[p + 2r1-1:p + r1]$, ..., here $F_{[(n-p)/r-1]}$ may be only (n-p) mod r1 bits;

2: Get m[r-1:0] from performing bit-wise XOR operation between F_i, m $[r-1:0] = F_{[(n-p)/r-1]}{}^{\wedge}...^{\wedge}F_1{}^{\wedge}F_0$;

3: Get new address aa[n-1:0] from a[n-1:0] after replacing a[p + r-1:p] with m [r-1:0]. So the new address aa[n-1:0] is what we want.

Next, we will explain this new address transformation is one-to-one mapping.

In address a[n-1:0], a[p-1:0] is different from each block, and a[p + r-1:p] is different from each module in the same block. In the new transformation, F_0 is a [p + r-1:p]. Assume x[r-1:0] is the result of performing bit-wise XOR between F_1, F_2, ..., $F_{[(n-p)/r1-1]}$. So at the same row of each bank in the same block, x[r-1:0] is the same and F_0 is different corresponding to each module in a same block. If perform bit-wise XOR between x[r-1:0] and F_0, the result corresponding to each module in a same block ranges from 0 to 2^r-1. So this new transformation is one-to-one mapping. For example, the transformation from binary codes {00, 01, 10, 11} to {01, 00, 11, 10} by performing bit-wise XOR with 2`b01 is one-to-one mapping.

3.4 Address Transformation for I/O

In FFT, bit reversal must take place either at the input or at the output for correct operation. Our architecture does bit reversal at the output. For a FFT series processed with the order of radix-2^{r1}, 2^{r2} and 2^{r3}(r1, r2, r3 are integers), the address a of the computation result and the reversed address ra is shown in Fig. 3.

Fig. 3. Address reversal for output

For FFT processors based on memory-based architecture, only work existed in [1] can finish all the mentioned tasks within 2N clock cycles for the N-point FFT, and the clock cycles needed for I/O is 2N. To decrease the clock cycles needed, because the computation rate and the I/O rate should be matching and computation cycles could be decreased through high-radix algorithm or SIMD architecture, cycles needed for I/O should be decreased to match up with the computation cycles. But the reversed address arise the difficulties for parallel I/O.

To speed up the I/O rate by a factor of 2^s, addresses for I/O issued each cycle should obey the following principles, here I/O is assumed as MM(Main Memory) owing 2^s memory modules with low-order address interleaved scheme:

1: load 2^s data each cycle in order; and store 2^s data each cycle in the following principles;

2: each ra[s-1:0] in reversed addresses ra[n-1:0] based on each addresses a[n-1:0] issued each cycle should be different;

3: each aa[s-1:0] in transformed addresses aa[n-1:0] corresponding to each address a[n-1:0] issued each cycle should be different;

The three principles are easy to achieve. And it is easy to load data parallel, now we discuss principle 2 and 3 for storing data. For example, for a FFT processor composed with eight memory modules, the FFT size is 2^6 processed by radix-8 algorithm. The available minimum computation cycle is 32 clock cycles. To match I/O clock cycles up with computation cycles, 4 addresses should be issued for I/O each cycle. On the principle 2, ra[1:0] should be different from 4 reversed addresses corresponding to addresses a[5:0] issued each cycle. So a[4:3] are different from 4 addresses issued. After address transformed in this paper, aa[1:0] are also different. So the four addresses issued each cycle should be below, here ga[3:0] is a counter and Ai is a[5:0](a_5a_4... a_1a_0):

A_0 = {ga[3], 0, 0, ga[2:0]}; A_1 = {ga[3], 0, 1, ga[2:0]};
A_2 = {ga[3], 1, 0, ga[2:0]}; A_3 = {ga[3], 1, 1, ga[2:0]}.

In Fig. 4, at the start of output ga[3:0] is 2'b0000, and ga[3:0] adds 1 each cycle until ga[3:0] is again 2'b0000. The data for output can be read from RAM via addresses aa[5:0], and data should be written to I/O via addresses ra[5:0]. Because 4 addresses issued each cycle, the I/O cycle is also 32 clock cycles. In fact, according to the principles, I/O cycle can be decreased to 2 N/(2 ^{s})(s ranges from 0 to r1 + p, and 2^{r1} is the biggest radix used) cycles.

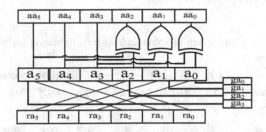

Fig. 4. Address generation for output

4 Implementation and Comparison

The architecture of the continuous-flow memory-based FFT processor is shown in Fig. 5. Here CU is Control Unit, AGU is Address Generation Unit for computation and I/O, BF is butterfly unit and TF is Twiddle Factor, AT is Address Transformation unit,

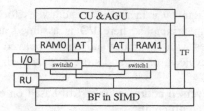

Fig. 5. Architecture of memory-based FFT processors

and RU is address Reversed Unit. It owns RAM0 and RAM1 to support I/O and computation via switch0 and switch 1.

The comparison of some address transformation methods is shown in Table 5. Dual port memory modules which is expensive to realize because of area cost, is used in [10]. Constant geometry in [8–10] is less flexibility. Mixed-Radix is not supported in [2, 7, 10]. And the circuit of address transformation proposed in this paper is simple with only some XOR gates. XOR gates are also used in [8, 9], but a rotation unit is also used in [8] and the number of XOR gates used in [9] is bigger than the number of XOR gates used in this paper. For example, in a processor owning two radix-4 BFs and eight memory modules in one RAM, the XOR gates needed in our proposed approach is 16 and the XOR gates needed in [9] is 24. At last, we synthesis the address transformation units. By comparing the area, when the degree of parallelism is 1 or 2, the area of the methods proposed in this paper and in [6, 8, 9] is almost the same, and area of methods in other papers are almost $0.1 \sim 0.2$ bigger than area of methods in [6, 8, 9] and this paper. When the degree of parallelism is bigger than 2, the area of methods proposed in other papers is $0.1 \sim 0.5$ bigger than the area of method proposed in this paper. This indicates that when the degree of parallelism is 1 or 2, methods proposed in [6, 8, 9] and this paper are better, and when the degree of parallelism is bigger than 2, only the method proposed in this paper is optimal.

Table 5. Comparison of some address transformation methods.

	[10]	[6][1][11]	[2]	[7]	[8][9]	proposed
radix	r	MR-2/4 or R	2	2^r	MR-2^r	MR-2^r
(BF)SIMD	r^p	1	1	2^p	2^p	2^p
port	dual	single	single	single	single	single
constant geometry	yes	no	no	no	yes	no
FFT sizes	r^n	16-4096/2^n	2^n	2^n	2^n	2^n
cost	registers	adder/module	counters/s hifters	look-up tables	XOR/ rotation	XOR

Table 6 (in Table 6 some data is from [1]) shows the available minimum FFT computation cycles corresponding to methods proposed in [1, 6, 10] and this paper. Note that the computation cycle needed in our work is within N clock cycles. And the I/O clock cycle in our work could be also within N clock cycles, which has been illustrated in Sect. 3.4. This indicates that only our work could finish tasks of processing FFT sizes less than N clock cycles.

Table 6. Computation cycles of some different methods.

	[10]		[6]		[1]		proposed (SIMD) 2 radix-8 BFs	
	cycle	radix	cycle	radix	cycle	radix	cycle	radix
1024	2560	4	2560	4	1024	2,8	512	2,8
2048	22528	2	6144	2,4	2048	4,8	1024	4,8
4096	4096	8	12288	4	4096	8	2048	8
8192	106496	2	28672	2,4	10240	2,8	5120	2,8

References

1. Hsiao, C.F., Chen, Y., Lee, C.Y.: A generalized mixed-radix algorithm for memory-based FFT processors. IEEE Trans. Circuits Syst. II Exp. Briefs **57**(1), 26–30 (2010)
2. Ma, Y.: An effective memory addressing scheme for FFT processors. IEEE Trans. Signal Process. **47**(3), 907–911 (1999)
3. Lin, Y.T., Tsai, P.Y., Chiueh, T.D.: Low-power variable-length fast Fourier transform processor. IEEE Proc. Comput. Digit. Technol. **152**(4), 499–506 (2005)
4. Lin, Y.W., Lee, C.Y.: Design of an FFT/IFFT processor for MIMO-OFDM systems. IEEE Trans. Circuits Syst. I, Regul. Pap. **54**(4), 807–815 (2007)
5. Lin, Y.W., Liu, H.Y., Lee, C.Y.: A dynamic scaling FFT processor for DVB-T applications. IEEE J. Solid State Circuits **39**(11), 2005–2013 (2004)
6. Jo, B.G., Sunwoo, M.H.: New continuous- flow mixed-radix(CFMR) FFT processor using novel in-place strategy. IEEE Trans. Circuits Syst. I, Regul. Pap. **52**(5), 911–919 (2005)
7. Reisis, D., Vlassopoulos, N.: Conflict-free parallel memory accessing techniques for FFT architectures. IEEE Trans. Circuits Syst. I, Regul. Pap. **55**(11), 3438–3447 (2008)
8. Takala, J.H., Jarvinen, T., Sorokin, H.: Conflict-free parallel memory access scheme for FFT processors. In: Proceedings of International Symposium on Circuits and Syst. (ISCAS 2003), vol. 4, 524–527. IEEE (2003)
9. Sorokin, H., Takala, J.: Conflict-free parallel access scheme for mixed-radix FFT supporting I/O permutations. In: Proceedings of IEEE International Conference on Acoustics, Speech, Signal Processing, pp. 1709–1712 (2011)
10. Hidalgo, J.A., Lopez, J., Arguello, F., Zapata, E.L.: Area-efficient architecture for fast Fourier transform. IEEE Trans. Circuits Syst. II, Analog Digit. Signal Process. **46**(2), 187–193 (1999)
11. Jacobson, A.T., Truong, D.N., Baas, B.M.: The design of a reconfigurable continuous-flow mixed-radix FFT processor. In: Proceedings of IEEE International Symposium on Circuits and Systems, pp. 1133–1136 (2009)

12. Takai, R., Uchida, S., Sato, A., Sanada, Y.: Experimental investigation of signal sensing with overlapped FFT based energy detection. Wireless Pers. Commun. **77**(1), 553–569 (2014)
13. Norouzi, P., Alahdadi, I., Shahtaheri, S.J.: Determination of ochratoxin at nanocomposite modified glassy carbon electrode combine with FFT coulometric admittance voltammetry and flow injection analysis. Int. J. Electrochem. Sci. **10**, 3400–3413 (2015)
14. Wang, Z., Liu, X., He, B., Yu, F.: A combined SDC-SDF architecture for normal I/O pipelined radix-2 FFT. IEEE Trans. VLSI Syst. **23**, 973–977 (2015)

Designing Parallel Sparse Matrix Transposition Algorithm Using ELLPACK-R for GPUs

Song Guo[1]([✉]), Yong Dou[1], Yuanwu Lei[1], Qiang Wang[1], Fei Xia[2], and Jianning Chen[3]

[1] National Laboratory for Parallel and Distribution Processing,
National University of Defense Technology, Deya Road 109#,
Changsha 410073, People's Republic of China
{songguo,yongdou,yuanwulei,qiangwang}@nudt.edu.cn
[2] Electronic Engineering College, Naval University of Engineering,
Wuhan 430033, China
xcyphoenix@hotmail.com
[3] Guangzhou Military Tactical Luzhai Base, Guangzhou 510000, China
jianningchen@hotmail.com

Abstract. In this paper, we proposed a parallel algorithm to implement the sparse matrix transposition using ELLPACK-R format on the graphic processing units. By utilizing the tremendous memory bandwidth and the texture memory, the performance of this algorithm can be efficiently improved. Experimental results show that the performance of the proposed algorithm can be improved up to 8x times on Nvidia Tesla C2070, compared with the implementation on the Intel Xeon E5-2650 CPU. It also can be concluded that it is not wise to accelerate the transposition algorithm for the matrices in the ELLPACK-R format with violent divergence in the number of nonzero elements among the rows.

Keywords: Parse matrix transposition · ELLPACK-R · Graphic processing units

1 Introduction

Matrix transposition is a basic operation in linear algebra, which exchanges the rows and columns of the matrix without altering the values of the elements. It is an essential kernel in many scientific computations such as iterative linear solvers, which can be found in many commonly used software packages including MATLAB and LIN-PACK. For the dense matrix, the transposition is trivial and can be implemented by addressing an element with the stride of the number of the row in the matrix. However, due to different sparsity patterns of different sparse matrices, this method does not work on sparse matrices, and this will also result in irregular memory accesses to the nonzero elements to incur the ineffective use of the memory bandwidth. This is the main reason for the low performance of sparse matrix computation on modern central processing units (CPUs) platforms.

© Springer-Verlag Berlin Heidelberg 2016
W. Xu et al. (Eds.): NCCET 2015, CCIS 592, pp. 61–68, 2016.
DOI: 10.1007/978-3-662-49283-3_7

Since the emergence of the graphics processing units (GPUs) in the high performance computing domain, there has been a substantial body of works to be transplanted onto the throughput-oriented platform. The reason for the wide use of GPU is that it features with many concurrency threads and high peak performance and memory bandwidth. These characteristics make GPUs good candidates for executing the sparse matrix transposition efficiently. However, the irregular access patterns in the sparse matrix transposition are still a challenge for the performance improvement. It needs more effort to design the parallel sparse matrix transposition algorithm for GPUs. In this paper, we choose the ELLPACK-R format to store the sparse matrix, and propose a parallel sparse matrix transposition algorithm for GPUs. Through the utilization of the abundant concurrency threads, texture memory and high memory bandwidth of the Nvidia GPUs, the performance is improved up to 8 x, compared with the implementation on the Intel Xeon E5-2650 CPU platform. It also can be concluded that it is not wise to accelerate the transposition algorithm for the matrices in the ELLPACK-R format with violent divergence in the number of nonzero elements among the rows.

The remainder of the paper is organized as follows. The ELLPACK-R format and the related works are briefly reviewed in Sect. 2. In Sect. 3, the parallel algorithm of sparse matrix transposition using ELLPACK-R format is addressed in detail. The performance evaluation and comparison are given in Sect. 4. Finally, this paper ends with the main conclusion in Sect. 5.

2 Background and Related Work

2.1 ELLPACK-R Format

The ELLPACK-R format is one variant of ELLPACK format [1]. As illustrated in Fig. 1, the ELLPACK-R format consists of three arrays, *val*, *col* and *rowLen*. The former two arrays, *val* and *col*, are of dimension N_MEPR, and the left array *rowLen* is an integer array with dimension N, where N represents the dimension of the sparse matrix, and *MEPR* is the maximum number of nonzero elements of each row. The rows, the number of the nonzero elements of which is less than *MEPR*, should be padded to meet the alignment requirement (as the asterisk in the *val* and *col*). The arrays, *val* and *col*, are used to store the values and column indices of the nonzero elements in one-to-one manner, respectively. The array *rowLen* is introduced to store the actual length of each row, regardless of the number of the elements padded.

$$A = \begin{pmatrix} a & 0 & b & 0 \\ c & d & 0 & e \\ 0 & 0 & f & 0 \\ 0 & g & 0 & 0 \end{pmatrix} \quad val = \begin{pmatrix} a & b & * \\ c & d & e \\ f & * & * \\ g & * & * \end{pmatrix} \quad col = \begin{pmatrix} 0 & 2 & * \\ 0 & 1 & 3 \\ 2 & * & * \\ 1 & * & * \end{pmatrix} \quad rowLen = \begin{pmatrix} 2 \\ 3 \\ 1 \\ 1 \end{pmatrix}$$

(a) sparse matrix   (b)   ELLPACK-R Format

Fig. 1. The structure of ELLPACK-R format

2.2 Related Work

As the general use in the linear algebra computation, there has been a substantial body of work to implement and optimize the matrix transposition. Krishnamoorthy *et al.* proposed an efficient parallel algorithm for the transposition of the out-of-core matrix [2]. Mateescu *et al.* developed a matrix transpose implementation running on POWER7 machine by utilizing its cache model and prefetching techniques [3]. However, these two works were only suitable to the dense matrices. Gustavson proposed two fast serial algorithms for sparse matrix multiplication and permuted transposition using compressed sparse row format [4]. However, they were serial codes. Pyrrhos Stathis, *et al.* implemented one novel Sparse Matrix Transposition Mechanism using the Hierarchical Sparse Matrix (HiSM) storage format [5]. It was nontrivial to transform the sparse matrix into the HiSM format. Tien-Hsiung Weng et al. proposed two parallel algorithms for sparse matrix transposition and vector multiplication using CSR format: with and without actual transposition. Both algorithms are parallelized using OpenMP [6]. Based on the tremendous computational power and memory bandwidth of the GPU offered by parallel platform in CUDA, Tien-Hsiung Weng *et al.* proposed a parallel algorithm for sparse matrix transposition using CSR format to run on many-core GPUs [7].

3 Parallel Transposition Algorithm on GPUs

In this section, we give an in-depth insight into the overall structure of the fully-pipelined dual-mode double precision reduction circuit. As shown in Fig. 1, the reduction circuit is mainly divided into two modules, accumulator and summator. The elements in the vector are streamed into the accumulator module and accumulated into L partial sums in the striding mode, where L is the pipeline stage of the adder. When the last item in the vector is accepted, the partial sums are fed into the summator module to gain the final result, and meanwhile the accumulator module can receive the elements from the new vectors.

In this section, we give an in-depth insight into the parallel transposition algorithm on GPUs. As other sparse matrix computation kernels, the sparse matrix transposition is of memory-bandwidth-bound. The main idea of the proposed parallel transposition algorithm is to reduce the number and latency of the memory accesses with the coalesced global memory access and the use of texture memory of GPUs.

As illustrated in Fig. 2, the parallel transposition algorithm is divided into two parts, host code and kernel code. The host code runs on the CPU. Firstly, the sparse matrix A is loaded into the CPU Memory in the ELLPACK-R format to initialize the arrays, $A.val$, $A.idx$ and $A.rowLen$. And then the offset of each nonzero element (*off*) and the number of nonzero elements in each row of the transposed matrix $A.rowLen$ are calculated. Meanwhile, the maximum numbers of the nonzero elements of the rows in the transposed matrix can be gained by one maximum reduction operation as the statement in line 3 in the Host Code on CPU section. After the preprocessing phase finishes, the variables, including *matSize*, $A.val$, $A.idx$, $A.rowLen$ and *off*, are copied from the CPU Memory to the GPU Memory, and the transposition kernel is launched and executed on the GPU device. Finally, the transposed matrix is transferred from the GPU Memory to

---

Input: Sparse Matrix A in the ELLPACK-R Format
Ouput: Sparse Matrix A^T in the ELLPACK-R Format
Parameter:
    matSize: the dimension of the sparse matrix A
    A.val: store the values of the nonzero elements in A
    A.idx: store the column indices of the nonzero elements in A
    A.rowLen: the actual number of nonzero elements in each row
    off: the offsets of each nonzero element in the row of the A^T
    A^T.idx: store the column indices of the nonzero elements in A^T
    A^T.val: store the values of the nonzero elements in A^T
    A^T.rowLen: the number of each nonzero elements in each row of A^T

Host Code on CPU:
    1.Load A into the array A.val, A.idx and A.rowLen
    2.Calculate the number of nonzeros in each row and the offset of
      each nonzero elements:
      For i=1 to matSize do
        For k=0 to A.rowLen[i]
          off[k*matSize+i]=A^T.rowLen[$A.idx$[k*matSize+i]]++;
        EndFor
      EndFor
    3.Calculate the maximum number of nonzeros in one row
      maxNonEntriesPerRow=max(A^T.rowLen)
    4.Copy Memory from CPU to GPU devices
    5.Launch the kernel to transpose the sparse matrix A
    6.Copy data from the device memory to the host memory

Kernel Code on GPU:
    1. For thread *tid*=0 to matSize parallel do
    2. For *j*=0 to A.rowLen[*tid*]
    3.   colIndex = tex1Dfetch(A.idx, *j**matSize+*tid*);
    4.   value = tex1Dfetch(A.val, *j**matSize+*tid*);
    5.   offIndex = tex1Dfetch(off, *j**matSize+*tid*);
    6.   idx = offIndex*matSize+colIndex;
    7. A^T.val[idx] = value;
    8. A^T.idx[idx] = tid;
    9. EndFor
   10. EndFor

Fig. 2. Parallel transposition algorithm using ELLPACK-R format

the CPU Memory in the ELLPACK-R format. In the transposition kernel, each thread is assigned to process one row of the sparse matrix. In order to reduce the redundant computations, the actual number of the iteration for each thread is determined by the number of the nonzero elements in the responding row with no regard to the zero paddings. Firstly, the column index, value and offset of each nonzero element are read from the corresponding texture memory, and secondly, the corresponding index (*idx*) in the transposed matrix is calculated. Finally, the value and column index of each nonzero element are stored back into the transposed matrix in the ELLPACK-R format. Due to the column-major-order storage scheme in the ELLPACK-R format, multiple consecutive rows of the sparse matrix can be accessed in a coalesced way. The memory access pattern for the array val is illustrated in Fig. 3. The array val is stored in a contiguous area in the column-major order, and accessed by the threads in an cyclic fashion. The four threads, labeled as *T0* to *T3*, can access four elements through one read operation instead of four operations, which is named as coalesced access and often used to greatly reduce the number of the memory access to the global memory.

$$tid = (t0 \quad t1 \quad t2 \quad t3 \mid t0 \quad t1 \quad t2 \quad t3 \mid t0 \quad t1 \quad t2 \quad t3)$$
$$val = (a \quad c \quad f \quad g \mid b \quad d \quad * \quad * \mid * \quad e \quad * \quad *)$$

Fig. 3. Fine-grain thread mapping of the parallel transposition kernel

4 Performance Evaluation and Comparison

In this section, we address the platforms used to evaluate and compare the performance. The sparse matrix benchmark and the performance results are listed and analyzed in detail as follows.

4.1 Implementation

For the performance evaluation and comparison, the proposed parallel transposition algorithm is implemented on an Intel Xeon E5-2650 CPU platform, equipped with 128 GB DDR3 DRAM and an Nvidia Tesla C2070 GPU, which has 448 cores with processor clock frequency at 1150 MHz and maximum memory bandwidth of 144 GB/s. The operation system running on this platform is 64-bit Red Hat Enterprise Linux 5.5. The implementation is compiled with GNU nvcc compiler version 4.1 with flag-O3,-use-fast-math and Carch *sm* 20 to use the fast math library and enable double-precision texture memory.

The experiment is conducted on different sparse matrices chosen from the University of Florida Sparse Matrix Collection [8] with different sparsity patterns. As listed in Table 1, many characteristics related to the performance are presented, where AverageRow means the average number of nonzeros in each row, ModeRow and MaxRow presents the mode and maximum of the array AverageRow, and PRatio (PaddingRatio) is calculated as (*maxRow * Dimension - NonzeroNumber*) = (*maxRow * Dimension*) * 100 %, indicating the degree of the difference of the number of the nonzero elements among the rows.

Table 1. Characteristics of the sparse matrix benchmark

No.	Matrix	Dimension	NonzeroNumber	AverageRow	MaxRow	PRatio
1	2cubes_ sphere	101492	1647264	17	31	47.64
2	cant	62451	4007383	65	78	17.73
3	consph	83334	6010480	73	81	10.96
4	cop20k_A	121192	2624331	22	81	73.27
5	crystk03	24696	1751178	71	81	12.46
6	dw2048	2048	10114	5	8	38.27
7	dw8192	8192	41746	6	8	36.3
8	e40r0100	17281	553562	33	62	48.33
9	F2	71505	5294285	75	345	78.54
10	garon2	13535	373235	28	45	38.72
11	lhr10	10672	228395	22	63	66.03
12	mc2depi	525825	2100225	4	4	0.15
13	mhd3200a	3200	68026	22	33	35.58
14	ncvxbqp1	5000	349968	7	9	22.23
15	nd3 k	9000	3279690	365	515	29.24
16	pct20stif	52329	2698463	52	207	75.09
17	pdb1HYS	36417	4344765	120	204	41.52
18	ship_001	34920	3896496	112	362	69.18
19	shipsec1	140874	3568176	26	68	62.75
20	sme3Dc	42930	3148656	74	405	81.89
21	tandem_vtx	18454	253350	14	35	60.78
22	thread	29736	4444880	150	306	51.15
23	bcsstm36	23052	320606	14	103	86.5
24	fp	7548	834222	111	900	87.72
25	gyro_k	17361	1021159	59	360	83.66
26	msc10848	10848	1229778	114	723	84.32
27	net25	9520	401200	43	139	69.68
28	nmos3	18588	237130	13	23	44.53
29	psmigr_1	3140	543160	173	2294	92.46
30	sme3 Da	12504	874887	70	345	79.72

4.2 Performance Comparison and Analysis

The performance comparison results are summarized in Table 2. The execution time of the proposed implementation includes the time spending on the data transfer between the CPU Memory and the GPU Memory. Through Table 2, it can be seen that the tested matrices are divided into two groups, Group A and Group B, according to the performance improvement of the proposed parallel algorithm, compared with the implementation on CPU.

Table 2. Performance comparison of CPU and GPU

No.	CPU (ms)	GPU (ms)	Speedup	No.	CPU (ms)	GPU (ms)	Speedup
Group A							
1	19.487	10.841	1.797	12	7.772	6.012	1.292
2	81.733	16.497	4.954	13	0.669	0.43	1.554
3	191.374	23.296	8.214	14	3.103	1.477	2.099
4	55.411	29.534	1.876	15	41.617	18.523	2.246
5	16.098	6.601	2.438	16	43.546	32.666	1.333
6	0.064	0.054	1.168	17	72.432	27.963	2.59
7	0.626	0.187	3.347	18	65.619	40.286	1.628
8	7.39	3.89	1.899	19	122.423	30.678	3.991
9	144.688	73.104	1.979	20	60.988	50.263	1.213
10	2.945	1.766	1.667	21	2.045	2.015	1.014
11	1.637	1.401	1.168	22	65.487	31.941	2.051
Group B							
23	5.303	6.576	0.806	27	3.34	3.913	0.853
24	9.491	15.088	0.629	28	1.623	1.782	0.91
25	13.72	17.939	0.764	29	12.545	22.661	0.553
26	12.827	22.459	0.571	30	10.789	12.834	0.841

For the Group A, the performance can be improved with the speedup ranging from 1.014 x to 8.214 x. The performance improvement can be derived from the following aspects, the parallel exchanging of multiple nonzero elements using the concurrency threads, the coalesced accesses resulting from the column-major-order storage in the ELLPACK-R format, and the reduced access latency with the use of the texture memory.

For the Group B, the performance is degraded to be lower than the implementation on CPU. There are two main reasons for performance loss. The first is that the overhead of data transfer increases drastically, resulting from the excessive zero paddings in the ELLPACK-R format, due to the vastly different number of nonzero elements for each row, as shown in the PRatio column. The second is the AverageRow is less than the number of threads in one warp, resulting in the waste of the computation power for the matrix *net25* and *nmos3*.

5   Conclusion and Future Work

In order to evaluate the performance of the reduction circuit, we implement the proposed design on a Xilinx Virtex II Pro. FPGA. The hardware design is described in RTL using Verilog HDL, and synthesized using Xilinx ISE v10.1. In this paper, the parameter L is set to 8, and the synthesis result reported by the Xilinx ISE is given in Table 1. Through the table, it can be seen that there is only about 6 % more hardware and 9 % increment in delay in the fully-pipelined dual-mode double precision reduction circuit, compared with the double-precision floating-point one of the same architecture.

In this paper, a parallel algorithm to implement the sparse matrix transposition on GPU using ELLPACK-R format is proposed. By utilizing the concurrency threads, texture memory and high memory bandwidth, the performance of the proposed algorithm can be efficiently improved. Experimental results show that the performance of the proposed algorithm can be improved up to 8 times on Nvidia Tesla C2070, compared with the implementation on the Intel Xeon E5-2650. For some matrices with violent difference in the number of the nonzero elements of the rows in the sparse matrix, the data transferring overhead resulting from the zero paddings, will make the performance be lower than the implementation on CPU.

There are many avenues for future work. Firstly, it is essential to design a heuristic method to decide the use of GPU and CPU to implement the transposition. Moreover, it is much more useful to integrate the kernel into the iterative solvers to accelerate the solution of practical applications.

Acknowledgments. This work was supported by the National Science Foundation of China under Grants 61402499 and 61202127, and the National High Technology Research and Development Program of China under Grants 2012AA012706.

References

1. Vazquez, F., Fernandez, J.J., Garzon, E.M.: A new approach for sparse matrix vector product on NVIDIA GPUs. Concurrency Comput.: Pract. Experimence. **23**, 815–826 (2011)
2. Krishnamoorthy, S., Baumgartner, G., Cociorva, D., Lam, C.C., Sadayappan, P.: Efficient parallel out-of-core matrix transposition. Int. J. High Perform. Comput. Netw. **2**, 110–119 (2004)
3. Mateescu, G., Bauer, G.H., Fiedler, R.A.: Optimizing matrix transposes using a POWER7 cache model and explicit prefetching. In: Proceedings of the Second International Workshop on Performance Modeling, Benchmarking and Simulation of High Performance Computing Systems, Seattle, 12-18, pp. 5–6 (2011)
4. Gustavson, F.G.: Two fast algorithms for sparse matrices: multiplication and permuted transposition. ACM. Trans. Math. Software. **4**(3), 250–269 (1978)
5. Stathis, P., Cheresiz, D., Vassiliadis, S., Juurlink, B.: Sparse matrix transpose unit. In: Proceedings of the 18th International Parallel and Distribute Processing Symposium (IPDPS04) (2004)
6. Weng, T.H., Batjargal, D., Pham, H., Hsieh, M.Y., Li, K.C.: Parallel matrix transposition and vector multiplication using OpenMP. In: Juang, J., Huang, Y.C. (eds.) Intelligent Technologies and Engineering Systems. Lecture Notes in Electrical Engineering, vol. 234, pp. 243–249 (2013)
7. Weng, T.H., Pham, H., Jiang, H., Li, K.C.: Designing parallel sparse matrix transposition algorithm using CSR for GPUs. In: Juang, J., Huang, Y.C. (eds.) Intelligent Technologies and Engineering Systems. Lecture Notes in Electrical Engineering, vol. 234, pp. 251–257 (2013)
8. Davis, T.: The University of Florida Sparse Matrix Collection. Technical report, University of Florida (2011)

Channel Estimation in Massive MIMO: Algorithm and Hardware

Chuan Tang[✉], Cang Liu, Luechao Yuan, and Zuocheng Xing

Parallel and Distributed Processing Laboratory,
National University of Defense Technology, Changsha, China
{tc8831,liucang,yuan.luechao,zcxing}@nudt.edu.cn

Abstract. Currently 5G is research hotspot in communication field, and one of the most promising wireless transmission technologies for 5G is massive multiple input multiple output (MIMO) which provides high data rate and energy efficiency. The main challenge of massive MIMO is the channel estimation due to the complexity and pilot contamination. Some improvement of traditional channel estimation methods to solve the problem in massive MIMO have been introduced in this paper. Besides, the hardware acceleration is useful for massive MIMO channel estimation algorithm. We discuss the relate work about hardware accelerator of matrix inversion and singular value decomposition which are the main complex operations of channel estimation. We find that the memory system, network of processing elements and the precision will be the main research directions for the hardware design of large-scale data size.

Keywords: Massive MIMO · Channel estimation · Hardware accelerator · FPGA

1 Introduction

Nowadays 4G has been commercialized, popularizing around the world. The increased data rate makes people shift more activities, like surfing, online video, online games and so on, to mobile terminals, which further promotes the expansion of the scale of wireless communication networks. Due to the explosive growth of wireless communication requirement, the research for the next generation mobile communication system (5G) has begun long before [1].

Broadly speaking, the objective of 5G can be described in four words: *Fast, Green, Ubiquitous, Intelligent. Fast* means very high data rate to satisfy the explosive requirement. Environmental pollution is another problem of current wireless communication industry. Currently, 70 % of the electricity is consumed by base stations (BSs) for cellular operators [2], and mobile terminals ask for low power chip for signal processing due to limited battery. Therefore, *Green* communication calling for low energy consumption and high energy efficiency is necessary. The objective of *Ubiquitous* is to furnish wireless communication

© Springer-Verlag Berlin Heidelberg 2016
W. Xu et al. (Eds.): NCCET 2015, CCIS 592, pp. 69–84, 2016.
DOI: 10.1007/978-3-662-49283-3_8

service in whatever place and diversified scenario, e.g. high-speed rail, indoor, device-to-device (D2D), wireless sensor network. However, to support the ubiquitous and heterogeneous networks, 5G must be *Intelligent* to switch seamlessly among heterogeneous networks and manage or reconfigure the networks adaptively. For achieving the goals above, there are two major research directions: wireless transmission technology and wireless network. Massive MIMO [3,4] is one of the promising wireless transmission technology for 5G, which claims to provide high data rates and high energy efficiency.

Massive MIMO was first proposed by Marzetta in 2010 [3]. Compared to traditional MIMO (4×4, 8×8), massive MIMO has hundreds of antennas in BSs and serves a few tens of users. More antennas can acquire multiplexing gain and diversity gain, which will improve data rate and reliability respectively. Moreover, massive MIMO has improved energy efficiency and is not sensitive to noise which makes approximate optimal performance be achieved by linear method of signal processing (e.g. precoding, detection) with perfect channel state information (CSI) [4]. However,there also exist some challenges, a major one of which is channel estimation. Channel estimation is a technique to obtain the estimation of CSI. In modern wireless communication system, the performance of many wireless communication technology like precoding, beamforming, detection and physical layer security, depends on the quality of CSI, hence the channel estimation is important [5]. However due to limited independent pilots resource, there is a problem of pilot contamination which is harmful to the quality of CSI. Furthermore, the augment of antennas obviously increase the dimensions of matrix handled by signal processing, hence asking for more powerful hardware chips in the physical layer, especially the ability of dealing with a large scale matrix operation.

According to whether assisted by data, the channel estimation can be classified into three kind: pilot-based methods, blind methods and semi-blind methods. Pilot-based methods insert pilot signal known by receiver into the sequence of data, and the receiver works out the CSI, i.e. channel matrix, on the basis of pilot signal and corresponding received signals. Matrix inversion is the main complex calculation in Pilot-based methods. Because some data are replaced by pilot signals, pilot-based methods reduce the data rate. With no need for pilot signals, blind methods estimate the CSI using the statistics features of received signals. Although blind methods do not lose the data rate, it induced higher computation complexity, slower convergence and also a problem of ambiguity [6,7] compared to pilot-based methods. Semi-blind methods is a compromising proposal. It uses few pilot signals to get a initiatory CSI, which can speed up the convergence of blind methods and solve the problem of ambiguity, or be used to obtain precise CSI by iteration.

As concerning the challenge in massive MIMO channel estimation, there are improvements and upgrades in the traditional algorithms and hardware design, or combination with other advanced techniques, which will be discussed in latter sections. In the rest of paper, we present the background about massive MIMO channel estimation in Sect. 2, show the channel estimation algorithm in Sect. 3, describe the hardware accelerators about the main complex operations of massive MIMO channel estimation in Sect. 4, and conclude the paper in Sect. 5.

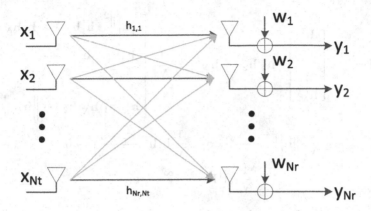

Fig. 1. Massive MIMO system model.

Notation: Column vectors and matrices are represented by lower case and upper case boldface respectively, $\mathbf{x}$ and $\mathbf{X}$. $(\cdot)^T, (\cdot)^\dagger, (\cdot)^{-1}, (\cdot)^+$ donate transpose, conjugate transpose, inverse and pseudo-inverse. $\| \cdot \|$ donates the Euclidean norm. $det(\cdot)$ donates the determinant, and $adj(\cdot)$ donates the adjoint matrix of $(\cdot)$.

2 Background

In this section, we will introduce the characteristic of channel matrix in massive MIMO, and reveal the challenge of massive MIMO channel estimation using mathematical model.

2.1 Massive MIMO System Model

In this paper, we consider there are N_r receive antennas and N_t transmitter antennas. Vector $\mathbf{x} = (x_1, x_2, \cdots, x_{N_t})^T \in \mathbb{C}^{N_t \times 1}$ and $\mathbf{y} = (y_1, y_2, \cdots, y_{N_r})^T \in \mathbb{C}^{N_r \times 1}$ represents the complex transmitted signal and received signal, the channel matrix $\mathbf{H} \in \mathbb{C}^{N_r \times N_t}$ can be represented as $(\mathbf{h}_1, \mathbf{h}_2, \cdots, \mathbf{h}_{N_t})$, where the $\mathbf{h}_i = (h_{1,i}, h_{2,i}, \ldots, h_{N_r,i})^T \in \mathbb{C}^{N_r \times 1}$, and $h_{m,n}$ means the complex channel gains from transmit antennas n to receive antennas m. The system illustrated in Fig. 1 can be modeled as

$$\mathbf{y} = \mathbf{Hx} + \mathbf{w}, \tag{1}$$

where the $\mathbf{w} = (w_1, w_2, \cdots, w_{N_r})^T \in \mathbb{C}^{N_r \times 1}$ is the complex additive white Gaussian noise (AWGN) vector whose element is mutually independent. The elements of $\mathbf{H}, \mathbf{x}, \mathbf{w}$ are all zero mean random variable, and i.i.d with each other.

2.2 Channel Matrix Characteristics in Massive MIMO

Taking the uplink transmission of realistic time-division duplex (TDD) massive MIMO system for example, considering the case of extreme that N_r (base station) is infinite and N_t (user) is constant, then

$$\frac{1}{N_r}\mathbf{H}^\dagger\mathbf{H} = \frac{1}{N_r}\begin{bmatrix} \mathbf{h}_1^\dagger \\ \mathbf{h}_2^\dagger \\ \vdots \\ \mathbf{h}_{N_t}^\dagger \end{bmatrix}\begin{bmatrix} \mathbf{h}_1 & \mathbf{h}_2 & \cdots & \mathbf{h}_{N_t} \end{bmatrix} = \frac{1}{N_r}\begin{bmatrix} \left\|\mathbf{h}_1^\dagger\right\|^2 & \mathbf{h}_1^\dagger\mathbf{h}_2 & \cdots & \mathbf{h}_1^\dagger\mathbf{h}_{N_t} \\ \mathbf{h}_2^\dagger\mathbf{h}_1 & \left\|\mathbf{h}_2^\dagger\right\|^2 & \cdots & \vdots \\ \vdots & \vdots & \ddots & \vdots \\ \mathbf{h}_{N_t}^\dagger\mathbf{h}_1 & \mathbf{h}_{N_t}^\dagger\mathbf{h}_2 & \cdots & \left\|\mathbf{h}_{N_t}^\dagger\right\|^2 \end{bmatrix} \tag{2}$$

$$\frac{1}{N_r}\left\|\mathbf{h}_i^\dagger\right\|^2 \xrightarrow{N_r\to\infty} \sigma_h^2, \frac{1}{N_r}\mathbf{h}_i^\dagger\mathbf{h}_j \xrightarrow{N_r\to\infty, i\neq j} 0 \tag{3}$$

$$\frac{1}{N_r}\mathbf{H}^\dagger\mathbf{H} \xrightarrow{N_r\to\infty} \sigma_h^2\mathbf{I}. \tag{4}$$

The $\left\|\mathbf{h}_i^\dagger\right\|^2$ is the N_r times variance of channel gain, which is a constant. Because the different $\mathbf{h}_i$ is independent, $\mathbf{h}_i^\dagger\mathbf{h}_j$ dividing by N_r approaches zero when i is not equal to j. So in massive MIMO system, we can get the transmitted signal by matched filtering (5). In (5), the $\mathbf{w}$ is also independent with $\mathbf{H}$, hence the second item approaches zero like (3).

$$\frac{1}{\sigma_h^2 N_r}\mathbf{H}^\dagger\mathbf{y} = \frac{1}{\sigma_h^2 N_r}\mathbf{H}^\dagger\mathbf{H}\mathbf{x} + \frac{1}{\sigma_h^2 N_r}\mathbf{H}^\dagger\mathbf{w} \xrightarrow{N_r\to\infty} \mathbf{x} \tag{5}$$

2.3 Pilot Contamination

The pilot-based method is still the most popular channel estimation technique. The pilot signals of different users must be orthogonal to each other. However, the number of orthogonal pilot signals is limited by the coherence time. Therefore, in massive MIMO system, there are not enough orthogonal pilot signals, and the pilot signals must be reused among multiple cells. Due to the broadcast nature of wireless communications, if two identical pilot signal transmit from two users in different cell concurrently, the estimated channel gain will be the superposition of the two channels. This is the pilot contamination, which will induce the interference among cells. A simple model considering two cells is shown in Fig. 2. Assuming that the cell a and cell b have the same number of users N_t with single antenna, and use the same pilot signal vector $\mathbf{p} \in \mathbb{C}^{N_t\times 1}$ with zero mean and unit variance. All the BSs has the same number of N_r antennas. The channel matrix between users in cell a and base station in cell a is $\mathbf{H}_{aa} \in \mathbb{C}^{N_r\times N_t}$, and the channel matrix between users in cell b and base station in cell a is $\mathbf{H}_{ab} \in \mathbb{C}^{N_r\times N_t}$.

Considering the worst case that all the users in both the cell a and cell b transmit the pilot signal at the same time, the received signal in cell a base station $\mathbf{y}$ can be represented as

$$\mathbf{y} = \mathbf{H}_{aa}\mathbf{p} + \mathbf{H}_{ab}\mathbf{p} + \mathbf{w}. \tag{6}$$

Base station in cell a estimates the channel matrix using the known pilot signal $\mathbf{p}$. For brief description, we ignore the noise in (6), the estimated channel matrix $\hat{\mathbf{H}}_{aa} \in \mathbb{C}^{N_r\times N_t}$ is

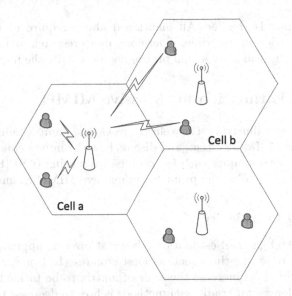

Fig. 2. The system model of pilot reuse.

$$\hat{\mathbf{H}}_{aa} = \mathbf{y}\mathbf{p}^+ = \mathbf{H}_{aa} + \mathbf{H}_{ab}. \tag{7}$$

With the estimated channel matrix $\hat{\mathbf{H}}_{aa}$, when adopting the matched filtering to get the transmitted signals $\mathbf{x}_a \in \mathbb{C}^{N_t \times 1}$ from users in cell a, we must consider the transmitted signals $\mathbf{x}_b \in \mathbb{C}^{N_t \times 1}$ from users in cell b. The mathematical description is

$$\frac{1}{\sigma_h^2 N_r}\hat{\mathbf{H}}_{aa}^\dagger \mathbf{y} = \frac{1}{\sigma_h^2 N_r}(\mathbf{H}_{aa} + \mathbf{H}_{ab})^\dagger(\mathbf{H}_{aa}\mathbf{x}_a + \mathbf{H}_{ab}\mathbf{x}_b + \mathbf{w}) \xrightarrow{N_r \to \infty} \mathbf{x}_a + \mathbf{x}_b. \tag{8}$$

Because the $\hat{\mathbf{H}}_{aa}$, $\hat{\mathbf{H}}_{ab}$, $\mathbf{w}$ are independent, the (8) approaches $\mathbf{x}_a + \mathbf{x}_b$ in the same reason for (5). To sum up, the pilot contamination can induce serious interference among cells reusing the same pilot sequence.

2.4   Computation Complexity

For various channel estimation methods, there are many complex operations about matrix such as inversion and singular value decomposition (SVD). Taking the matrix inversion for example, we adopt the TDD system model in (1) using the pilot-based minimum mean square error (MMSE) channel estimation method. The covariance matrix $\mathbf{R} \in \mathbb{C}^{N_t N_r \times N_t N_r}$ of channel matrix needs to take inversion operation, which is of $O((N_t N_r)^3)$ computation complexity [8] and a tough thing in channel estimation. Besides, the hardware design of matrix inversion is complex, some research employs software to implement the channel estimation [9]. Moreover, the mobility of user is higher, the speed of user is faster and the wireless communication environment is more complex, hence the coherence time is smaller. All mentioned above require us fulfilling more complex computation in less time. Therefore, more research focus on hardware acceleration for physical layer signal processing, especially the matrix operation.

3   Channel Estimation for Massive MIMO

In this section, we illustrate the related research about channel estimation method in massive MIMO system, and discuss how the improvement or the combination with new techniques such as compressive sensing (CS) [10] and spatial modulation (SM) [11] solve the problems in massive MIMO channel estimation.

3.1   Reducing Complexity

For massive MIMO channel estimation, the most obvious approach is adopting traditional pilot-based method such as least squares (LS) or MMSE. However the large-scale antennas increase the scale of matrix to be tackled notably. One of the main challenges for traditional methods is how to decrease the complexity of the algorithm. Polynomial expansion (PE) is a solution for reducing the complexity of matrix inversion, which bases on the Taylor expansion. PE transforms the matrix inversion to L-order matrix polynomial (9), and is widely used in other wireless communication techniques [12–14].

$$\mathbf{X}^{-1} = \alpha(\mathbf{I} - (\mathbf{I} - \alpha\mathbf{X}))^{-1} \approx \alpha \sum_{l=0}^{L} (\mathbf{I} - \alpha\mathbf{X})^l \qquad (9)$$

Nafiseh Shariati [8] and Z. Chen [15] have proposed to use PE in MMSE channel estimation, replacing the matrix inversion. Z.Chen is mainly focusing on the orthogonal frequency division multiplexing (OFDM) system with large-scale subcarrier. Nafiseh Shariati researches the massive MIMO system with single carrier. In [8] the inversion of channel covariance matrix is replaced by L-order PE operation. Assuming the number of pilot signals is P, the complexity drops from $O(P^3 N_r^3)$ to $O(LP^2 N_r^2)$. As the augment of L, it gradually converges the performance to that of the MMSE estimator. If the α in (9) is not the same, we can config the optimal coefficient α^l for different orders of the polynomial item. In this way, we can get the near optimal mean square error (MSE) with a small L. What is more, with the identical performance requirement, L is not scaled with the matrix dimensions. Although PE has been used in other field of wireless communication as mentioned above, the optimal coefficient α^l is not in common use due to different performance objective. Therefore the computation of optimal coefficient is the critical process of PE.

3.2   Pilot Decontamination

Except for the complexity of signal processing, the pilot-based method in massive MIMO system also has the problem of pilot contamination. Concerning this problem, Hanfan Yin proposes a coordinated channel estimation method to eliminate the contamination [16]. Reference [16] exploits the second-order statistical information about the channels to improve the precision of the channel estimation (compared to LS). With the communication and coordination of BSs in each cells, the slow changing statistical information is shared. Due to the nature of slow changing, it is cheap to construct the shared backhaul link. According to the information shared among the cells, the pilot signals can be assigned in a proper way, in which the performance of channel estimation can approach the case without contamination.

Another solution is adopting CS technique to reduce the requirement of pilots signals. CS technique can use less samples to recovery more information, which means that to estimate the same channel matrix we can use less pilot signals by CS-based methods. Reference [17] has considered the case that it only has limited scatterers in the realistic propagation environment for massive MIMO system. Therefore, the channel matrix is not only sparse, but also has relevant sparsity due to common shared scatterers. With the nature of sparsity, we can use less samples (i.e. pilot signals) getting more information to recovery the channel matrix, which is also good for frequency-division duplex (FDD) system because of reducing the feedback cost of CSI. Therefore, reference [17] proposes a distributed channel estimation using CS for FDD massive MIMO. In this article, the channel matrix is transformed to angular domain, where the element (m,n) being non-zero means that there is a path from the m-th transmit direction to the n-th receive direction [18]. Due to limited scatterers, there are few propagation paths inducing that few elements of angular domain channel matrix are non-zero. In FDD system, the base station transmits only a few pilot signals, and the users feed back the compressed measurements (i.e. transformed received pilot signals) to base station to do CS-based channel estimation. This method reduces the cost of feedback, and exploits the implicit jointed sparsity resulting from the common scatterers to improve performance of CS recovery algorithm. Reference [19] adopts the CS-based channel estimation for TDD massive MIMO system. The main idea is based on the fact that the degree of freedom of channel matrix is less than its free parameters. Therefore, the problem can be converted to CS-based low-rank matrix approximation, which could be solved by quadratic semi-define programming. Considering the limited scatterers The method is better than traditional LS method, and does not need the statistical information about channel.

To avoid the pilot contamination, Some researches employ blind or semi-blind method. Reference [20] adopts a blind method based on subspace projection. Assuming the coherence time contains C symbol intervals, the receive signal block $\mathbf{Y} \in \mathbb{C}^{N_r \times C}$ among the internals of coherence time is conducted with SVD, attaining the signal space basis $\mathbf{S} \in \mathbb{C}^{N_r \times N_t}$. Then the received signal block is project onto the signal subspace getting $\widetilde{\mathbf{Y}} = \mathbf{S}^{\dagger}\mathbf{Y} \in \mathbb{C}^{N_t \times C}$. Instead of estimating the channel matrix $\mathbf{H}$, it is just needed to estimate the subspace channel matrix $\widetilde{\mathbf{H}} \in \mathbb{C}^{N_t \times N_t}$ with traditional SVD-based blind method. Besides, concerning the inter-cell interference, which singular values corresponds

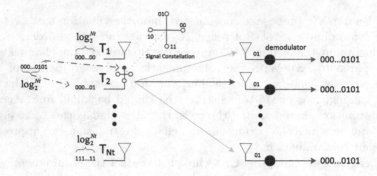

Fig. 3. An example of spatial modulation.

to the channel vectors from objective cell instead of other cells needs to be distinguished. For massive MIMO system, the small-scale fading vanishes, so the norm of the channel vectors only determines by the large-scale fading which mainly depends on the distance. Obviously the users in objective cell is closer than those in other cells, and even concerning the user in the border land the interference can be avoid by employing proper frequency re-use patterns. The main complexity of [20] is induced by the matrix operation of SVD, which is hard to tackle even in traditional MIMO system. What is more, there also exists the problem of ambiguity. Reference [21] combinds the subspace-based blind method and the pilot-based method. It conducts the SVD on received signals using the subspace-based blind method attaining a preliminary channel matrix of ambiguity. Then the preliminary channel matrix can be refined and eliminate the ambiguity by few pilot signals. However this method has limitations due to the assume of ideal propagation condition.

3.3 Channel Estimation for SM Massive MIMO

SM technique is based on MIMO system. The information is not only presented by signals constellation mapping, but also contained in the antenna index. when transmitting data, only one or a few antennas are activated, which reduces the cost of hardware (number of RF chains) and the complexity of signal processing. Therefore, the combination of SM and massive MIMO is a promising technique in 5G [1]. An example is shown in Fig. 3. When a series of binary to be transmitted, the first $\log_2^{Nt}$ bits selects the antenna T_2, the next two bits 01 is mapped to the signal constellation and then be transmitted via the antenna T_2. The receiver gets the signal 01, and then the demodulator identifies the index of transmit antenna with the difference of channel gains among different channels, and in the end recovers the whole data.

Currently, there is not any public literature about the channel estimation in SM massive MIMO system, however we could learn the advantage and challenge of it by researching the relate works in SM MIMO system. Reference [22] proposed that due to one or a few activated antennas the channel estimation can only be taken on these active channels. In another word, the estimation period is in direct proportion to the number of transmit antennas. Considering the correlation among channels, the author exploits the slow varying feature of the deviation among different channel gains to get the estimation of all antennas. When estimating the activated antennas, the other unactivated antennas get their estimation by adding the recorded deviations to the estimated value of activated antennas, and the deviations is always updating for each estimation. In this way, the estimation period is equal to that of traditional MIMO system with equal pilot rate of traditional SM MIMO system.

Because the SM only activate one or a few antennas, it is free from the effect of inter-channel interference (ICI). So the SM MIMO system does not require complex data detector, and usually adopts iteration-based joint channel estimation and data detection. Adopting decision-directed channel estimator combining with data detector [23,24] needs to exchange information between estimator and detector by iterations. Concerning the inherent iteration nature of turbo detector, Reference [25] insert the channel estimator into the outer loop of turbo detector, which do not induce any extra iteration. Simulation results show that this method can attain approximately optimal channel capacity in the condition of near identical complexity compared to only turbo detector.

In conclusion, the main challenge for SM MIMO channel estimation is long estimation period, which is more serious in SM massive MIMO system, and the advantage is making use of the low complexity of data detection to implement high performance semi-blind channel estimation.

4 Hardware Acceleration

Concerning the popular channel estimation algorithm, the most complex operations are the large-scale matrix inversion and SVD, which are not only used in channel estimation but also the detection and precoding. Software-based implementation is inefficient, especially for massive MIMO system. To meet the requirement of real-time signal processing, the hardware implementation based on FPGA or multicore is necessary. In this section, we mainly introduce the research about hardware acceleration on matrix inversion and SVD.

4.1 Matrix Inversion

The main methods of matrix inversion are analytic method, decomposition method, Gaussian elimination method and Newton iteration method.

- Analytic method is based on the formula

$$\mathbf{A}^{-1} = \frac{1}{\det(\mathbf{A})} \times adj(\mathbf{A}). \tag{10}$$

For the matrix whose dimensions is more than 4×4, the hardware design is very complicated, asking for lots of resource and iterations which is not suitable for large-scale matrix inversion.

- Decomposition method is mainly based on matrix decomposition, such as LU, QR and Cholesky decomposition. For decomposition method, the objective matrix is decomposed into triangular matrix or unitary matrix which are easy for matrix inversion. Then the product of the inversion of decomposing matrices (triangular or unitary) is the inversion of objective matrix. Decomposition method is common in current research.
- Gaussian elimination method carries out finite times elementary matrix transformation on the objective matrix to attain the unit matrix, then the product of the elementary transformation matrix sequence is the inversion of the objective matrix.
- Newton iteration method first takes a rough estimation getting a original inversion matrix $\mathbf{X}_0$, then the iteration estimation is taken as

$$\mathbf{X}_{n+1} = \mathbf{X}_n(2\mathbf{I} - \mathbf{A}\mathbf{X}_n), \tag{11}$$

until the precision satisfies, where $\mathbf{A}$ donates the objective matrix and $\mathbf{X}_i$ is the i-th estimated inversion of $\mathbf{A}$. However, to be converged, the original inversion matrix $\mathbf{X}_0$ must meet the convergence condition

$$\|\mathbf{I} - \mathbf{A}\mathbf{X}_0\| < 1, \tag{12}$$

which needs extra computation for $\mathbf{X}_0$ amd limits the practical applicability of this method.

Reference [26] adopts LU decomposition implementing the 2×2 matrix inversion hardware design. The QR decomposition matrix inversion has many related research, which can be implemented by various algorithms, such as Givens rotation [27], Gram-Schmidt orthogonalization [28] method and so on.

For matrix bigger than 4×4, it is the block-wise matrix inversion [29,30] that is often adopted. In this way, the objective matrix is divided into small matrices (4×4 or 2×2), then computation the inversion matrix of each small matrix in traditional methods. Reference [31] designs a processor for coping with matrix inversion based on the architecture of Very Long Instruction Word (VLIW). Concerning that the traditional MIMO is usually 4×4, the author adopts the block-wise method dividing the objective matrix into 2×2 submatrix, then uses the analytic method implement the inversion of submatrix.

Reference [32,33] adopt the Gaussian elimination method implementing the hardware design of matrix inversion, which can avoid the complex computation such as matrix multiplication and square root. Reference [32] makes the matrix dimensions configurable, and [33] implements the inversion of 4×4, 8×8, 16×16 respectively. Given the design of [32], the reference [34] discusses the influence of error propagation for different data representation precision. From matrix dimensions $n = 5$ to $n = 120$, the author carries out experiments on Matlab for single, double and custom floating-point precision, finding that the error varies observably as the matrix dimensions increases, and different precisions have some difference on the error changing laws. Therefore the author design a matrix dimensions and precision configurable matrix inversion accelerator based on FPGA. This design ensures the low computation error for different precisions, and optimizes the hardware cost.

Reference [35] design a accelerator for large-scale matrix inversion. The accelerator adopts twelve scalable linear array processing elements (PEs) with QR decomposition algorithm, implementing seconds level (1.758 s for 1024×1024) FPGA-based matrix inversion accelerator for large matrix. However the computations speed can not meet the require of massive MIMO system. Reference [36] claims that it first implements the FPGA-based matrix inversion for the data detector of massive MIMO. In this article, the matrix inversion adopts PE algorithm, supporting the antennas configure of 128(BS) $\times$ 16(user). However, for uplink detection algorithm, it just need to do a 16×16 matrix inversion. Reference [37] researches the relationship between the approximation error of PE algorithm designed in [36] and the number of antennas. Compared with a precise implementation FPGA accelerator based on Cholesky decomposition algorithm, the author finds that the PE algorithm is suitable for large BS-antenna-to-user ratio, and the precise implementation is suitable for small one.

Currently, large-scale matrix inversion hardware accelerator for channel estimation is still worth to research. Due to the nature for channel matrix show in (4), the Newton iteration [38] method maybe a good choice for low cost implementation for large-scale matrix inversion. Because the diagonal elements of objective matrix are dominant, the original inversion matrix $\mathbf{X}_0$ can just be a diagonal matrix whose elements are the reciprocal of the corresponding diagonal elements of the objective matrix. Therefore, the complex computation for $\mathbf{X}_0$ to meet convergence condition is avoid.

4.2 Singular Value Decomposition

QR decomposition and Jacobi algorithm are the main SVD solutions.

- For QR-based method [39], the objective matrix carries out Householder transformation attaining a bidiagonal matrix. The bidiagonal matrix further carries out an iteration of QR decompositions making it to converge at a diagonal matrix. QR-based method has lower precision and is harder for parallelization compared to Jacobi algorithm, so most hardware designs adopt Jacobi algorithm.
- Jacobi algorithm is a block-wise-based method, which includes two-sided Jacobi and one-sided Jacobi. For the two-sided method, the objective matrix $\mathbf{A}$ is divided into multiple 2×2 submatrix, and then each of them carries out the Jacobi rotation for both columns and rows of the submatrix to implement diagonalization as shown in (13)

$$\mathbf{J}_i^{l^T} \mathbf{A}_i \mathbf{J}_i^r = \begin{pmatrix} \cos(\theta^l) & \sin(\theta^l) \\ -\sin(\theta^l) & \cos(\theta^l) \end{pmatrix}^T \begin{pmatrix} a_i^{11} & a_i^{12} \\ a_i^{21} & a_i^{22} \end{pmatrix} \begin{pmatrix} \cos(\theta^r) & \sin(\theta^r) \\ -\sin(\theta^r) & \cos(\theta^r) \end{pmatrix} = \begin{pmatrix} \sigma_1 & 0 \\ 0 & \sigma_2 \end{pmatrix},$$
(13)

where the A_i donate the i-th submatrix, and $\mathbf{J}_i^l$, $\mathbf{J}_i^r$ donate the Jacobi matrices rotate for the angle of θ^l, θ^r. After a serious of Jacobi transformations which compose of the two unitary matrices of SVD, the objective matrix is developed into a diagonal matrix, which is the singular value matrix of it. For one-sided Jacobi method, the objective matrix $\mathbf{A}$ just carries out Jacobi rotation for columns to get a orthogonal matrix $\mathbf{V}$ that $\mathbf{AV} = \mathbf{W}$, where each column of $\mathbf{W}$ is orthogonal. Then normalizing the matrix $\mathbf{W}$, we can get $\mathbf{W} = \mathbf{U\Sigma}$, where $\mathbf{U}$ is unitary matrix, and $\mathbf{\Sigma}$ is a diagonal matrix. Then the objective matrix can be represented as $\mathbf{A} = \mathbf{U\Sigma V}^T$. One-sided Jacobi method is mainly based on the orthogonalization of the columns pairs, which induces no conflicts for data sharing, so it is more suitable for parallelization design of hardware [40].

Brent, Luk and Van Loan proposed a FPGA-based SVD named BLV [41]. The BLV adopts expandable systolic array consisting of 2×2 PEs which most of relate researches are based on. For efficient implementation of Jacobi rotation, Reference [42] combines the design in [41] with the CORDIC-based SVD architecture [43]. Reference [44] implements the one-sided Jacobi method in a PC FPGA joint system. In this system, FPGA board communicates with the PC via the Peripheral Component interface (PCI), and can be reconfigured dynamically. Reference [45] designs a system consisting of multiple identical PEs, and adopts enhanced CORDIC module to solve the SVD of large-scale asymmetry matrices. The author conducts experiments on matrix dimensions of 2×2, 8×7, 16×32, and 32×127, and has verified the precision. Focusing on the small-scale matrix SVD for real-time system, [46] designs a 4×4 SVD processor using a vector product module and 8 special CORDIC units which can more efficiently implement the orthogonalization of complex vectors. Reference [40] proposed an extensible parallel SVD processor architecture, which can cope with large-scale asymmetry matrices. In this design, two PEs can be used for the objective of minimum hardware cost, or $n/2$ (n is the number of matrix columns) PEs can be used for the objective of maximum performance. It also introduce a decision device based on threshold to optimize the convergence threshold. Reference [47] adopts a structure similar with [40], and analyses the performance restraining factor in large-scale data size. The result shows that as the increase of data size, the performance of data transforming will gradually predominate the system performance, so how to design the network and memory system of PEs will be a important research field for hardware accelerator design.

4.3   Design Principles

Concerning the design mentioned above, the data accessing and transforming gradually become the bottleneck as the matrix dimensions increasing. The design key point of the architecture for large-scale data size is no longer only the powerful PE, but also the memory system and network of PEs, which is similar for multi-core processor system as the number of cores increases. What is more, due to the increase of data, the hardware cost of high precision data representation is enormous, how to trade-off between the precision and the cost is also worth to research.

5   Conclusion

Massive MIMO is a promising wireless transmission technology for 5G communication, and the channel estimation is the key challenge of massive MIMO due to the complexity and pilot contamination. In this paper, we illustrate the problem of complexity and pilot contamination and introduce some channel estimation methods of massive MIMO to solve these problems. What is more, given the algorithm complexity and requirement of real-time processing, the hardware acceleration for channel estimation is necessary. We discuss the relate research about hardware design of matrix inversion and SVD which are the main complex operation of channel estimation, finding that precision, memory system and network of PEs are the key of hardware design for large-scale matrix computation.

Acknowledgments. This work was supported in part by the NSF of China (Grant No. 61170083, 61373032) and Specialized Research Fund for the Doctoral Program of Higher Education (Grant No. 201143071110001).

References

1. Wang, C.X., Haider, F., Gao, X., You, X.H., Yang, Y., Yuan, D., Aggoune, H., Haas, H., Fletcher, S., Hepsaydir, E.: Cellular architecture and key technologies for 5G wireless communication networks. IEEE Commun. Mag. **52**(2), 122–130 (2014)
2. Han, C., Harrold, T., Armour, S., Krikidis, I., Videv, S., Grant, P.M., Haas, H., Thompson, J.S., Ku, I., Wang, C.X.: Green radio: radio techniques to enable energy-efficient wireless networks. IEEE Commun. Mag. **49**(6), 46–54 (2011)
3. Marzetta, T.L.: Noncooperative cellular wireless with unlimited numbers of base station antennas. IEEE Trans. Wireless Commun. **9**(11), 3590–3600 (2010)
4. Rusek, F., Persson, D., Lau, B.K., Larsson, E.G., Marzetta, T.L., Edfors, O., Tufvesson, F., Print, P., Rusek, F., Persson, D.: Scaling up MIMO: opportunities and challenges with very large arrays. IEEE Sig. Process. Mag. **30**(1), 40–60 (2013)
5. Marzetta, T.L., Caire, G., Debbah, M., Chih-Lin, I., Mohammed, S.K.: Special issue on massive MIMO. J. Commun. Netw. **15**(4), 333–337 (2013)
6. Shin, C., Heath Jr., R.W., Powers, E.J.: Blind channel estimation for MIMO-OFDM systems. IEEE Trans. Veh. Technol. **2**, 670–685 (2007)
7. Tu, C.C., Champagne, B.: Subspace blind MIMO-OFDM channel estimation with short averaging periods: performance analysis. In: Wireless Communications and Networking Conference, WCNC 2008, pp. 24–29. IEEE (2008)
8. Shariati, N., Bjornson, E., Bengtsson, M., Debbah, M.: Low-complexity channel estimation in large-scale MIMO using polynomial expansion, ePrint arXiv, pp. 1157–1162 (2013)
9. Shepard, C., Yu, H., Zhong, L.: Argosv2: a flexible many-antenna research platform, pp. 163–166. (2013). http://nms.csail.mit.edu
10. Cands, E.J.: Compressive sampling. Marta Sanz Sol **25**(2), 1433–1452 (2007)
11. Renzo, M.D., Haas, H., Ghrayeb, A., Member, S., Sugiura, S., Member, S., Hanzo, L.: Spatial modulation for generalized MIMO: challenges, opportunities and implementation. Proc. IEEE **102**(1), 56–103 (2013)

12. Lei, Z.D., Lim, T.J.: Simplified polynomial-expansion linear detectors for DS-CDMA systems. Electron. Lett. **34**(16), 1561–1563 (1998)
13. Hoydis, J., Debbah, M., Kobayashi, M.: Asymptotic moments for interference mitigation in correlated fading channels. In: 2011 IEEE International Symposium on Information Theory Proceedings (ISIT), pp. 2796–2800 (2011)
14. Kammoun, A., Muller, A., Bjornson, E., Debbah, M.: Linear precoding based on polynomial expansion: large-scale multi-cell MIMO systems. IEEE J. Sel. Top. Sig. Process. **8**(5), 861–875 (2014)
15. Chen, Z., Hou, X., Han, S., Yang, C., Wang, G., Lei, M.: Low complexity channel estimation in TDD coordinated multi-point transmission systems. In: 2013 IEEE Wireless Communications and Networking Conference (WCNC), pp. 3128–3133 (2013)
16. Yin, H., Fellow, D.G., Liu, Y.: A coordinated approach to channel estimation in large-scale multiple-antenna systems. IEEE J. Sel. Areas Commun. **31**(2), 264–273 (2012)
17. Rao, X., Lau, V.K.N.: Distributed compressive csit estimation and feedback for fdd multi-user massive MIMO systems. IEEE Trans. Sig. Process. **62**(12), 3261–3271 (2014)
18. Tse, D., Viswanath, P.: Fundamentals of wireless communication. Eth Zrich Lect. Script **3**(5), B6–1–B6–5 (2005)
19. Nguyen, S.L.H., Ghrayeb, A.: Compressive sensing-based channel estimation for massive multiuser MIMO systems. In: 2013 IEEE Wireless Communications and Networking Conference (WCNC), pp. 2890–2895 (2013)
20. Mller, R., Cottatellucci, L., Vehkapera, M.: Blind pilot decontamination. IEEE J. Sel. Top. Sig. Process. **8**(5), 1016–1020 (2013)
21. Ngo, B.Q., Larsson, E.G.: EVD-based channel estimation in multicell multiuser MIMO systems with very large antenna arrays. In: International Conference on Acoustics, Speech, and Signal Processing (ICASSP), pp. 3249–3252 (2012)
22. Wu, X., Renzo, M.D., Haas, H., Wu, X.: Channel estimation for spatial modulation. IEEE Trans. Commun. **62**(12), 4362–4372 (2013)
23. Chen, S., Sugiura, S., Hanzo, L.: Semi-blind joint channel estimation and data detection for space-time shift keying systems. IEEE Sig. Process. Lett. **17**(12), 993–996 (2010)
24. Zhang, P., Dey, I., Sugiura, S., Chen, S.: Semi-blind adaptive space-time shift keying systems based on iterative channel estimation and data detection. IEEE Veh. Technol. Conf. **120**(2226), 1–5 (2011)
25. Zhang, P., Chen, S., Hanzo, L.: Reduced-complexity near-capacity joint channel estimation and three-stage turbo detection for coherent space-time shift keying. IEEE Trans. Commun. **61**(5), 1902–1913 (2013)
26. Yokoyama, S., Matsumoto, K. Sedukhin, S.G.: Matrix inversion on thecell/b.e. processor. In: 11th IEEE International Conference on High Performance Computing and Communications, HPCC 2009, pp. 148–153 (2009)
27. Huang, Z.Y., Tsai, P.Y.: Efficient implementation of qr decomposition for gigabit MIMO-OFDM systems. IEEE Trans. Circ. Syst. I Regul. Pap. **58**(10), 2531–2542 (2011)
28. Singh, C.K., Prasad, S.H., Balsara, P.T.: VLSI architecture for matrix inversion using modified Gram-Schmidt based QR decomposition. In: Proceedings of the IEEE International Conference on VLSI Design, pp. 836–841 (2007)
29. Eilert, J., Wu, D., Liu, D.: Efficient complex matrix inversion for MIMO software defined radio. In: IEEE International Symposium on Circuits and Systems, ISCAS 2007, pp. 2610–2613 (2007)

30. Ma, L., Dickson, K., Mcallister, J., Mccanny, J.: QR decomposition based matrix inversion for high performance embedded MIMO receivers. IEEE Trans. Sig. Process. **59**(4), 1858–1867 (2011)
31. Zhang, L., Li, F., Shi, G.: Efficient matrix inversion based on VLIW architecture. J. Syst. Eng. Electron. **25**(3), 393–398 (2014)
32. Arias-Garcia, J., Jacobi, R.P., Llanos, C.H., Ayala-Rincon, M.: A suitable FPGA implementation of floating-point matrix inversion based on Gauss-Jordan elimination. In: 2011 VII Southern Conference on Programmable Logic (SPL), pp. 263–268 (2011)
33. Moussa, S., Razik, A.M.A., Dahmane, A.O., Hamam, H.: FPGA implementation of floating-point complex matrix inversion based on Gauss-Jordan elimination. In: Canadian Conference on Electrical & Computer Engineering, pp. 1–4 (2013)
34. Arias-Garcia, J., Llanos, C.H., Ayala-Rincon, M., Jacobi, R.P. : FPGA implementation of large-scale matrix inversion using single, double and custom floating-point precision. In: 2012 VIII Southern Conference on Programmable Logic (SPL), pp. 1–6 (2012)
35. Zhou, J., Dou, Y., Zhao, J., Xia, F., Lei, Y., Tang, Y.: A fine-grained pipelined implementation for large-scale matrix inversion on FPGA. In: Dou, Y., Gruber, R., Joller, J.M. (eds.) APPT 2009. LNCS, vol. 5737, pp. 110–122. Springer, Heidelberg (2009)
36. Wu, M., Yin, B., Vosoughi, A., Studer, C., Cavallaro, J.R., Dick, C.: Approximate matrix inversion for high-throughput data detection in the large-scale MIMO uplink. In: 2013 IEEE International Symposium on Circuits and Systems (ISCAS), pp. 2155–2158 (2013)
37. Yin, B., Wu, M., Studer, C., Cavallaro, J.R., Dick, C.: Implementation trade-offs for linear detection in large-scale MIMO systems. In: 1988 International Conference on Acoustics, Speech, and Signal Processing, ICASSP 1988, vol. 32, no. 3, pp. 2679–2683 (2013)
38. Ylinen, M., Burian, A., Takala, J.: Direct versus iterative methods for fixed-point implementation of matrix inversion. In: Proceedings of the 2004 International Symposium on Circuits and Systems, ISCAS 2004, vol. 3, pp. III–225–8 (2004)
39. Kaji, T., Yoshizawa, S., Miyanaga, Y.: Development of an ASIP-based singular value decomposition processor in SVD-MIMO systems. In: 2011 International Symposium on Intelligent Signal Processing and Communications Systems (ISPACS), pp. 1–5 (2011)
40. Bildosola, I., Martinez-Corral, U., Basterretxea, K.: Adaptive scalable SVD unit for fast processing of large LSE problems. In: 2014 IEEE 25th International Conference on Application-specific Systems, Architectures and Processors (ASAP), pp. 17–24 (2014)
41. Brent, R.P., Luk, F.T., Van Loan, C.: Computation of the singular value decomposition using mesh-connected processors. J. VLSI Comput. Syst. **1**(3), 242–270 (1983)
42. Cavallaro, J.R., Luk, F.T.: Architectures for a CORDIC SVD processor. In: 30th Annual Technical Symposium, pp. 45–53 (1986)
43. Sibul, L.H., Fogelsanger, A.L.: Application of coordinate rotation algorithm to singular value decomposition. In: IEEE International Symposium on Circuits and Systems, pp. 821–824 (1984)
44. Bobda, C., Danne, K., Linarth, A.: Efficient implementation of the singular value decomposition on a reconfigurable system. In: Cheung, P.Y.K., Constantinides, G.A. (eds.) FPL 2003. LNCS, vol. 2778. Springer, Heidelberg (2003)

45. Ledesma-Carrillo, L.M., Cabal-Yepez, E., Romero-Troncoso, R.D.J., Garcia-Perez, A., Osornio-Rios, R.A. Carozzi, T.D.: Reconfigurable FPGA-based unit for singular value decomposition of large m × n matrices. In: International Conference on Reconfigurable Computing and FPGAs, pp. 345–350 (2011)
46. Milford, D., Sandell, M.: Singular value decomposition using an array of CORDIC processors. Sig. Process. **102**(9), 163–170 (2014)
47. Martinez-Corral, U., Basterretxea, K., Finker, R.: Scalable parallel architecture for singular value decomposition of large matrices. In: 2014 24th International Conference on Field Programmable Logic and Applications (FPL), pp. 1–4 (2014)

A ML-Based High-Accuracy Estimation of Sampling and Carrier Frequency Offsets for OFDM Systems

Cang Liu[1]($\boxtimes$), Luechao Yuan[1], Zuocheng Xing[1],
Xiantuo Tang[2], and Guitao Fu[3]

[1] National Laboratory for Parallel and Distributed Processing,
National University of Defense Technology, Changsha, China
{liucang,yuan.luechao,zcxing}@nudt.edu.cn
[2] National Digital Switching System Engineering and Technological R&D Center,
Zhengzhou, China
tangxiantuo@nudt.edu.cn
[3] Beijing Satellite Navigation Center (BSNC), Beijing, China
fgtnudt@nudt.edu.cn

Abstract. This paper addresses the problem of acquiring the sampling frequency offset (SFO) and carrier frequency offset (CFO), which severely degrade the performance of orthogonal frequency division multiplexing (OFDM) system. Using two identical frequency domain (FD) long training symbols in preamble, we propose a novel maximum-likelihood (ML) estimation method to simultaneously acquire the values of SFO and CFO, which extend the Kim's and Wang's estimation methods. The main contribution of this paper is that the first-order Legendre series expansion is used to obtain the SFO and CFO values in closed-form. For obtaining the performance of the proposed estimation scheme, we built the OFDM system model according to IEEE 802.11a. The results show that the proposed scheme achieves the best performance to the existing schemes.

Keywords: Sampling frequency offset · Carrier frequency offset · Orthogonal frequency division multiplexing · Legendre series expansion

1 Introduction

Orthogonal frequency division multiplexing (OFDM) has received increasing attention in broadband wireless transmission systems due to its robustness against frequency-selective fading channels and high spectral efficiency. OFDM technique has been adopted in various broadband communication systems, such as IEEE 802.11a [1], IEEE 802.16a [2], digital video broadcasting (DVB-T) [3] and digital radio mondiale (DRM) [4]. However, a well-known drawback is its susceptibility to synchronization errors such as sampling frequency offset (SFO)

© Springer-Verlag Berlin Heidelberg 2016
W. Xu et al. (Eds.): NCCET 2015, CCIS 592, pp. 85–93, 2016.
DOI: 10.1007/978-3-662-49283-3_9

and carrier frequency offset (CFO) [5,6], which may destroy the orthogonality, cause inter-carrier-interference (ICI) and degrade the performance at the receiver.

SFO and CFO are caused by the mismatch sampling clocks and Doppler shift, respectively. Precise synchronization is vital for realizing the potential performance. So far, lots of methods have been proposed to estimate the SFO and CFO, respectively [7–11]. The schemes of joint SFO and CFO estimation have also been proposed in some literatures. A method of tracking the residual SFO and CFO by pilot signals in OFDM symbols was presented in [12]. In [13], an estimation scheme based on maximum-likelihood (ML) was proposed, which needs the perfect channel state information (CSI). A joint estimation scheme was proposed for the fractional SFO and CFO infrequency domain (FD) by Speth et al. [14], using the correlation operations between two identical long training symbols. In [15], the received signals of time domain (TD) version were used to estimate SFO and CFO values.

The scheme of using TD signals to estimate the SFO and CFO parameters needs an IFFT block [15]. And it may result in significant instability in SFO and CFO estimation. In order to avoid the IFFT block and the instability in SFO and CFO estimation, Nguyen-Le et al. [16] proposed a ML estimator for the coarse estimation of SFO and CFO values, using two identical long training symbols in the preamble. Y.-H. Kim et al. [17] proposed a joint SFO and CFO ML estimation scheme, which extend the Nguyen-Le's ML estimator. Its performance is superior to previous schemes. However, all these ML algorithms require a two-dimensional exhaustive search in [16–18], resulting in the undesired computational complexity. For solving the problem of computational complexity, X. Wang et al. [19] proposed a low-complexity ML estimator for SFO and CFO, in which the CFO was solved in closed-form, and the SFO was obtained by one-dimensional exhaustive search. In order to obtain the SFO value in closed-form, Wang et al. [19] proposed an approximate ML scheme, which takes a second-order Taylor series expansion. The Wang's ML scheme and approximate ML scheme reduce the computational complexity significantly, and achieve almost the same performance as [17]. Further improving the estimation performance is vital for future wireless communication systems, especially in low SNR(Signal Noise Ratio).

In this paper, we propose a ML estimator for acquiring the SFO and CFO in closed-form. In order to obtain the SFO in closed-form, the approach of first-order Legendre series expansion is taken. Then, the value of SFO is used to calculate the CFO value in closed-form. We also built the IEEE 802.11a system model to verify various estimation schemes. The numerical results demonstrate that the proposed ML estimation scheme is superior to the scheme proposed by [16,17,19]. In particular, the proposed estimation scheme does not need exhaustive search. Hence, the computational complexity of the proposed algorithm is significantly reduced than the schemes in [16,17].

The remainder of this paper is organized as follows: In Sect. 2, the to-be-considered OFDM system is described. Section 3 proposes the ML-based estimation of SFO and CFO values in closed-form. The simulation result is presented in Sect. 4. Section 5 provides some conclusions.

2 System Model

The considered OFDM system model is showed in Fig. 1. The M-ary modulation signal set is fed to the IFFT unit, and it is converted to the signal in TD. After the cyclic prefix (CP) insertion, the TD signal is transmitted over the multipath channel. The TD signal is sampled with period T at receiver. Then, discard the CP part of the received TD signal, FFT unit is used to convert the TD signal back to the FD signal.

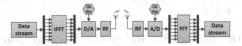

Fig. 1. System model

Let N be the total number of subcarriers, N_g the length of the cyclic prefix, K the number of used subcarriers, and N_m the sum $N + N_g$. We assume that the SFO, CFO and f are ΔT, Δf and the radio carrier frequency, respectively. The normalized SFO and CFO are denoted by $\eta = \Delta T/T$ and $\varepsilon = \Delta f NT$, respectively. The FD received signal can be expressed as follows [16]:

$$R_m(k) = \Phi_{kl}(m) X_m(k) H(k) + ICI_m(k) + W_m(k) \tag{1}$$

where

$$ICI_m(k) = \sum_{l=-K/2, l\neq 0, k}^{K/2} \Phi_{kl}(m) X_m(i) H(i) \tag{2}$$

$$\Phi_{kl}(m) = \delta_{kl} e^{j\frac{2\pi}{N}(N_g + m(N+N_g))(l\eta + \varepsilon(1+\eta))} \tag{3}$$

$$\delta_{kl} = \frac{1}{N} \sum_{n=0}^{N-1} e^{j\frac{2\pi n}{N}(l\eta + \varepsilon(1+\eta) + l - k)}$$

$$\approx e^{j\frac{\pi(N-1)}{N}(l\eta + \varepsilon(1+\eta) + l - k)} \tag{4}$$

$$\times \frac{\sin(\pi(l\eta + \varepsilon(1+\eta) + l - k))}{N \sin(\pi(l\eta + \varepsilon(1+\eta) + l - k)/N)} .$$

and $H(k)$ stands for the channel frequency response, $\Phi_{kl}(m)$ represents attenuation factor, $ICI_m(k)$ is ICI, $W_m(k)$ is the additive white Gaussian noise (AWGN). As shown above, CFO would introduce a phase rotation in the TD, and SFO would introduce the additional phase rotation, which linearly grows with the subcarrier index k. Thus, estimation the SFO and CFO is vital in OFDM system, that would be used to compensate the synchronization errors caused by SFO and CFO for improving the receiver performance.

3   ML-based Joint SFO and CFO Estimation

3.1   Conventional ML Estimation Method

Nguyen-Le et al. [16] first proposed the ML-based estimator for SFO and CFO in FD, using two identical long training symbols in the preamble. Kim et al. [17] extended the Nguyen-Le's estimation scheme and proposed a joint SFO and CFO estimation algorithm, exhibiting superior performance than the Nguyen-Le's ML scheme. The cost function proposed by Kim is presented as follows [17]:

$$\widehat{\varepsilon}, \widehat{\eta} = \arg\min_{\varepsilon, \eta} \Gamma\left(\varepsilon, \eta\right)$$
$$\Gamma\left(\varepsilon, \eta\right) = \sum_{k=-K/2, k\neq 0}^{K/2} \left| R_1\left(k\right) - e^{j\frac{2\pi N_m}{N}\left[k\eta + \varepsilon(1+\eta)\right]} R_0\left(k\right) \right|^2 \tag{5}$$

where $R_0(k)$ and $R_1(k)$ are the first and second FD long training symbols in the preamble, respectively.

After some straightforward manipulations, X. Wang et al. [19] obtained the value of SFO by one dimensional exhaustive search, and the value of CFO was calculated by SFO in closed-form. The two dimensional exhaustive search is equivalently converted to one dimensional exhaustive search, that can significantly reduce the computational complexity. Equation 7 expresses the ML estimation of CFO in closed-form, and Eq. 6 expresses the cost function of SFO [19].

$$\widehat{\eta} = \arg\max_{\eta} \left| g\left(\eta\right) \right|^2 \tag{6}$$

$$\widehat{\varepsilon} = -\frac{N\angle g\left(\widehat{\eta}\right)}{2\pi N_m \left(1 + \widehat{\eta}\right)} \tag{7}$$

where

$$g\left(\eta\right) = \sum_{k=-K/2, k\neq 0}^{K/2} R_1^*\left(k\right) R_0\left(k\right) e^{j\frac{2\pi N_m}{N} k\eta} \tag{8}$$

The conventional ML estimators require a one or two dimensional exhaustive search. The exhaustive search results in the undesired computational complexity, and the limitation of step size in exhaustive search results in the error floor in high SNR. For reducing the computational complexity, X. Wang et al. [19] proposed an approximate ML scheme, which needs a second-order Taylor series expansion. The estimation performance of the existing approaches need to further improved to meet the demand of future wireless communication systems.

3.2   The Proposed ML Estimation Method

In this subsection, we will show the proposed estimation method for acquiring the SFO and CFO values. We take the first-order Legendre series expansion for acquiring the SFO estimation value in closed-form. And substitute the SFO value into Eq. 7 to obtain the CFO value.

Consider cost function Eq. 6, we take the further proceeding as follows:

$$\widehat{\eta} = \arg \max_{\eta} |g(\eta)|^2$$
$$= \arg \max_{\eta} \sum_{p \neq q} R(p)R(q)^* \varphi_{p,q}(\eta) + C_1 \tag{9}$$

where C_1 denotes the term which is independent of SFO η, $R(x)$ and $\varphi_{a,b}(x)$ are given as follows:

$$R(x) = R_1^*(x) R_0(x) \tag{10}$$

$$\varphi_{a,b}(x) = e^{j \frac{2\pi N m}{N}(a-b)x} \tag{11}$$

We take the first-order derivative to find η, which can satisfy Eq. 9, we get the following equation:

$$\frac{d|g(x)|^2}{d\eta} = 0 \tag{12}$$

We then rewrite Eq. 12 and take some straightforward manipulations as follows:

$$\sum_{p \neq q} (p-q) R(p)R(q)^* \varphi_{p,q}(\eta)$$
$$= \sum_{p > q} (p-q) \operatorname{Im} \left[R(p) R(q)^* \varphi_{p,q}(\eta) \right] \tag{13}$$
$$= 0$$

The SFO η is difficult to calculate by Eq. 13 directly, because the term $\varphi_{p,q}(\eta)$ is not tractable. We can take the first-order Legendre series expansion to approximate $\varphi_{p,q}(\eta)$ in $\eta \subset [-20\,\text{ppm}, 20\,\text{ppm}]$. The boundary of η is enough to contain all the possible SFO values, because the typical tolerance of SFO is $\pm$ 20 ppm (parts per million), mandated by the IEEE 802.11a standard [1].

Because the domain of Legendre polynomial is $[-1, 1]$, we set $t = 50000\eta$. Rewrite $\varphi_{p,q}(\eta)$ as the following form.

$$\varphi_{p,q}(\eta) = e^{j \frac{2\pi N m}{N}(p-q)\eta}$$
$$= e^{j \frac{2\pi N m}{N}(p-q) \times 0.2 \times 10^{-4} t} \tag{14}$$

In order to take the approximation by first-order Legendre polynomial, set $p_0(t) = 1$ and $p_1(t) = t$. We can obtain the approximation of $\varphi_{p,q}(\eta)$ by first-order Legendre series expansion as follows:

$$e^{j \frac{2\pi N m}{N}(p-q) \times 0.2 \times 10^{-4} t} = \alpha + \beta t$$
$$\alpha = \frac{(y, p_0)}{(p_0, p_0)} \tag{15}$$
$$\beta = \frac{(y, p_1)}{(p_1, p_1)}$$

where

$$(p_0, p_0) = \int_{-1}^{1} 1 dt = 2$$
$$(p_1, p_1) = \int_{-1}^{1} t^2 dt = \frac{2}{3}$$
$$(y, p_0) = \int_{-1}^{1} e^{jat} dt = 2 \frac{\sin a}{a} \tag{16}$$
$$(y, p_1) = \int_{-1}^{1} t e^{jat} dt = -2j \frac{a \cos a - \sin a}{a^2}$$

with

$$a = \frac{2\pi N_m}{N} (p - q) \times 0.2 \times 10^{-4} \tag{17}$$

Substitute Eq. 16 into Eq. 15, after some straightforward manipulations, we get the estimation value of SFO $\hat{\eta}$ as follows:

$$\hat{\eta} = \frac{-\sum\limits_{p>q} (p - q) \operatorname{Im} \left\{ R(p) R(q)^* \frac{\sin a}{a} \right\}}{\sum\limits_{p>q} (p - q) \operatorname{Im} \left\{ 3j R(p) R(q)^* \frac{\sin a - a \cos a}{a^2} \right\}} \times 0.2 \times 10^{-4} \tag{18}$$

Equation 18 gives the estimated value of SFO $\hat{\eta}$, according to Eq. 7, we can obtain the estimated value of CFO easily. From aforementioned steps, we know that the value of SFO $\hat{\eta}$ belong to [-20 ppm, 20 ppm] in our scheme. Hence, when the result of Eq. 18 is bigger than 20 ppm, we would set the value of η to be 20 ppm, in contrast, when the result of Eq. 18 is smaller than -20 ppm, we set the value of η to be -20 ppm. Compared with [16, 17, 19], the estimation accuracy of the proposed scheme is better, especially in low SNR. Because the exhaustive search does not needed in the proposed scheme, the computational complexity significantly reduce than the existing ML-based approaches [15–17].

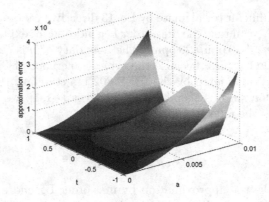

Fig. 2. The change of approximation error with a and t.

The quality of the first-order Legendre series expansion determines the estimation accuracy. We would analysis the approximation error in the following:

$$\Delta = \left| e^{jat} - \alpha - \beta t \right| \\
= \left| e^{jat} - \frac{\sin a}{a} + 3j \frac{a \cos a - \sin a}{a^2} t \right|, \qquad -1 \le t \le 1 \tag{19}$$

where a is presented in Eq. 17, we consider the system parameters according to the IEEE 802.11a standard [1], where N_m and N are 80 and 64 respectively, and $1 \le p-q \le 63, p-q \in N$. We present the change of approximation error with the change of a and t in Fig. 2. We can know that the approximation error is smaller than 4×10^{-5} from Fig. 2, that is better than the approximate ML scheme in [19] and can satisfies the requirement of wireless communication systems.

4   Simulation Results

In this section, computer simulation is conducted to evaluate the proposed joint estimator performance. As an example, we consider the system parameters according to the IEEE 802.11a standard [1], where the total number of subcarrier N, the used number of subcarrier K and the length of CP N_g are 64, 52, and 16, respectively. We consider a Rayleigh fading channel with exponential power delay profile with $E\{|h_l|^2\} = \sigma_0^2 e^{-l/5}, l = 0, ..., 4$. σ_0^2 is a constant for normalizing the channel power to unity. The values of SFO and CFO are set to $\eta = 13\,$ppm and $\varepsilon = 0.012$, respectively.

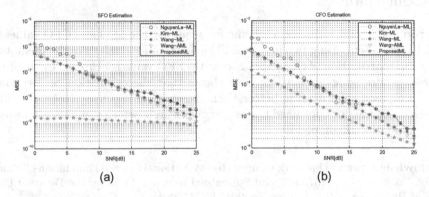

Fig. 3. Normalized MSEs of SFO and CFO estimation vs. SNR in Rayleigh fading channel (CFO = 0.012, SFO = 13 ppm), with 16-QAM constellations: (a) SFO estimation; (b) CFO estimation.

Figure 3(a) and (b) present the mean squared error (MSE) performance of the proposed joint estimator versus SNR. The exhaustive searches of [16, 17, 19] are performed by setting $\eta = 0.00003t$, $\varepsilon = 0.01t$, respectively, where $t \subseteq \{-50, -49, ..., 49, 50\}$. Figure 3(a) shows the estimation performance of SFO, and the estimation performance of CFO is ploted in Fig. 3(b). As expected, the performance of the proposed joint estimation scheme is superior to the existing ML estimation schemes in [16, 17, 19].

Figure 4 illustrates the MSE results of different SFO values between the proposed and the Wang's ML scheme [19]. We obtain the SFO estimation performance in the range of [0 ppm, 20 ppm] with SNR=5 dB. The results show that the proposed scheme exhibits superior estimation accuracy to the Wang's ML scheme [19].

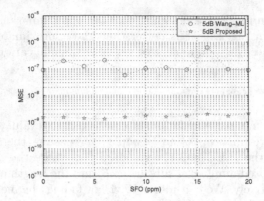

Fig. 4. The SFO values of proposed and Wang's ML scheme, (CFO = 0.012).

5 Conclusion

We proposed a joint estimation scheme for acquiring the SFO and CFO values in the OFDM system, using two identical FD long training symbols in the preamble. The main contribution of this paper is that the SFO value is acquired by the first-order Legendre series expansion. It is shown that the estimation performance of the proposed algorithm is better than the existing schemes [16,18,19]. The proposed scheme does not need the exhaustive search, which significantly reduce the computational complexity.

Acknowledgments. This work is supported by National Science Foundation of China (Grant No. 61170083, 61373032) and Specialized Research Fund for the Doctoral Program of Higher Education (Grant No. 20114307110001).

References

1. IEEE: Supplement to IEEE standard for information technology - telecommunications and information exchange between systems - local and metropolitan area networks - specific requirements. part 11: Wireless lan medium access control (MAC) and physical layer (PHY) specifications: High-speed physical layer in the 5 GHz band. IEEE Std 802.11a (1999)
2. IEEE: IEEE standard for local and metropolitan area networks part 16: Air interface for fixed broadband wireless access systems draft amendment: Management information base extensions. IEEE Unapproved Draft Std P802.16i/D5 (2007)
3. IEEE: Etsi, digital video broadcasting (DVD): frame structure, channel coding and modulation for digital terrestrial television (DVD-T). ETSI EN 300 744 (2004)
4. IEEE: Digital radio mondiale (DRM): System specification. ETSI ES 201 980 v3.1.1 (2009)
5. Wu, H.-C.: Analysis and characterization of intercarrier and interblock interferences for wireless mobile OFDM systems. IEEE Trans. Broadcast. **52**(2), 203–210 (2006)

6. Ai, B., Yang, Z.-X., Pan, C.-Y., Ge, J.H., Wang, Y., Lu, Z.: On the synchronization techniques for wireless OFDM systems. IEEE Trans. Broadcast. **52**(2), 236–244 (2006)
7. Wang, Y.-Y.: A subspace-based CFO estimation algorithm for general ICI self-cancellation precoded OFDM systems. IEEE Trans. Wirel. Commun. **12**(8), 4110–4117 (2013)
8. Zhang, W., Yin, Q.: Blind maximum likelihood carrier frequency offset estimation for OFDM with multi-antenna receiver. IEEE Trans. Sig. Proces. **61**(9), 2295–2307 (2013)
9. Gul, M.M.U., Lee, S., Ma, X.: Carrier frequency offset estimation for OFDMA uplink using null sub-carriers. Digit. Sig. Proces. **29**, 127–137 (2014)
10. Gault, S., Hachem, W., Ciblat, P.: Joint sampling clock offset and channel estimation for OFDM signals: Crame acute;r-Rao bound and algorithms. IEEE Trans. Sig. Proces. **54**(5), 1875–1885 (2006)
11. You, Y.-H., Kim, S.-T., Lee, K.-T., Song, H.-K.: An improved sampling frequency offset estimator for OFDM-based digital radio mondiale systems. IEEE Trans. Broadcast. **54**(2), 283–286 (2008)
12. Morelli, M., Imbarlina, G., Moretti, M.: Estimation of residual carrier and sampling frequency offsets in OFDM-SDMA uplink transmissions. IEEE Trans. Wirel. Commun. **9**(2), 734–744 (2010)
13. Oberli, C.: ML-based tracking algorithms for MIMO-OFDM. IEEE Trans. Wirel. Commun. **6**(7), 2630–2639 (2007)
14. Speth, M., Fechtel, S., Fock, G., Meyr, H.: Optimum receiver design for OFDM-based broadband transmission.ii. a case study. IEEE Trans. Commun. **49**(4), 571–578 (2001)
15. Freda, M.M., Weng, J., Le-Ngoc, T.: Joint channel estimation and synchronization for OFDM systems. In: 2004 IEEE 60th Vehicular Technology Conference, VTC2004-Fall, vol. 3, pp. 1673–1677 (2004)
16. Nguyen-Le, H., Le-Ngoc, T., Ko, C.-C.: RLS-based joint estimation and tracking of channel response, sampling, and carrier frequency offsets for OFDM. IEEE Trans. Broadcast. **55**(1), 84–94 (2009)
17. Kim, Y.-H., Lee, J.-H.: Joint maximum likelihood estimation of carrier and sampling frequency offsets for OFDM systems. IEEE Trans. Broadcast. **57**(2), 277–283 (2011)
18. Nguyen-Le, H., Le-Ngoc, T., Ko, C.-C.: Joint channel estimation and synchronization for MIMO OFDM in the presence of carrier and sampling frequency offsets. IEEE Trans. Veh. Technol. **58**(6), 3075–3081 (2009)
19. Wang, X., Hu, B.: A low-complexity ML estimator for carrier and sampling frequency offsets in OFDM systems. IEEE Commun. Lett. **18**(3), 503–506 (2014)

A High-PSRR CMOS Bandgap Reference Circuit

Chang Liping[1(✉)], An Kang[1], Liu Yao[2], Liang Bin[2], and Li Jinwen[1]

[1] Department of Computer, College of Computer, National University of Defense Technology,
643 Room, Changsha, China
cqupt-changliping@163.com
[2] Institute of Microelectronics and Microprocessor, College of Computer,
National University of Defense Technology, 643 Room, Changsha, China

Abstract. The paper presents a high power supply rejection ratio (PSRR) CMOS bandgap reference (BGR). The circuit adopts a pre-regulator. To facilitate comparison, BGRs with- and without- pre-regulator are, respectively, designed and simulated in the 0.13 μm standard CMOS process technology. Simulation results show that the PSRR of the designed BGR with pre-regulator achieves, respectively, −107.3 dB, −106.6 dB and−75 dB at 100 Hz, 1 kHz and 100 kHz, while PSRR of BGR without pre-regulator has only, respectively, −70.6 dB, −70.5 dB and −65 dB at 100 Hz, 1 kHz and 100 kHz. The BGR with pre-regulator achieves a bandgap voltage reference of 0.76 V, a temperature coefficient of 0.55 ppm/°C in the temperature range from −25 °C to 125 °C, and a deviation of output voltage of 0.08 mV when the power supply voltage changed from 2.6 V to 6.2 V.

Keywords: Bandgap reference · Power supply rejection ratio · Pre-regulator

1   Introduction

Voltage reference is an important circuit block in many analog and mixed-signal system-on-chip (SoC) applications, such as data converters, DC-DC converters, DRAMs, flash memory controlling blocks, and other integrated circuits [1–6]. Voltage reference should be free from the fluctuations of process, power supply voltage, and temperature. In fact, one of the most popular voltage reference is bandgap reference (BGR), whose output is usually a weighted sum of the base-emitter voltage (V_{BE}) of a diode-connected bipolar transistor and the thermal voltage (V_T). As for the bandgap reference used in modern SoC design, it is very important to achieve high power supply rejection ratio (PSRR) over a broad frequency range in order to reject noise from the high speed digital circuits on the chip.

In the recent past, many techniques have been applied to improve the PSRR of BGR [2, 7–10]. For example, the Cascode technique was used to improve the PSRR in N. Qiao's paper [3], but it did not achieve well performance at high frequency. However, to achieve better performances of BGR, the high PSRR BGR needs further research.

In this paper, a BGR, which adopts a pre-regulator, is presented. It has a simple architecture and achieves well performance. In Sect. 2, the analysis of BGR without a pre-regulator will be discussed. The analysis and design of BGR with a pre-regulator will be given in Sect. 3. Section 4 will present the simulation results. Finally, the conclusions are drawn in Sect. 5.

© Springer-Verlag Berlin Heidelberg 2016
W. Xu et al. (Eds.): NCCET 2015, CCIS 592, pp. 94–102, 2016.
DOI: 10.1007/978-3-662-49283-3_10

2   Analysis of Bandgap Reference Without Pre-regulator

As is shown in Fig. 1, the presented bandgap reference consists of pre-regulator, the core circuit of BGR and a start-up circuit. All MOS transistors adopt the long channel transistors so that the channel-length modulation effect is negligibly small. The core circuit of BGR is similar to that reported in Tham's article [7], However, the difference was that its operating supply voltage is the internal regulated supply voltage V_{REG} instead of the power supply voltage V_{dd}. There are two possible equilibrium points in the circuit of BGR, so a start-up circuit is necessary. As shown in Fig. 1(a), the startup circuit is made up of transistor M19, M20, M21. The core circuit of BGR generates a bandgap reference voltage V_{ref}, and have a good temperature characteristic, and will be analyzed in Sects. 2.1 and 2.2. The pre-regulator will provide an internal supply voltage V_{REG}, which is the operating supply voltage of the core circuit of BGR, and will be discussed in Sect. 3.

2.1   A Core Circuit of Bandgap Reference

As is shown in Fig. 1(c), the core circuit of BGR consists of M_1–M_{18}, R_1–R_7, and vertical pnp transistors Q_1–Q_3. Resistor R_1 and R_2 are the entirely same, so it is concluded that ($R_1 = R_2$). Q_1 have an emitter area that is n times that of Q_2's. Transistors M_{13}–M_{16} and resistors R_5–R_6 form the error amplifier, keeping the voltages V_A and V_B be equal, i.e. $V_A = V_B$. Here, V_A and V_B are, respectively, the voltage of node A and node B. In Fig. 1(c), M_1–M_4 are entirely same, so they have the same drain current, i.e. V_{ref}, can be expressed as

$$V_{ref} = \frac{R_0}{R_2}(V_{eb2} + \frac{R_2}{R_1}V_T \ln n)$$
(1)

where, V_{eb2} is the emitter-base voltage of Q_2, V_T is the thermal potential and can be expressed as

$$V_T = \frac{kT}{q}$$
(2)

where, k is Boltzmann's constant, q is electronic charge, T is absolute temperature.

In Eq. (1), V_{eb2} have a temperature coefficient of -2.2 mV/°C at 25 °C, while V_T have a temperature coefficient of $+0.085$ mV/°C. $\frac{\partial V_{ref}}{\partial T}T = 25$ °C $= 0$ can be achieved by proper choice of $\frac{R_2}{R_1}$ and n at 25 °C.

2.2   A Bandgap Reference with Second-Order Curvature Compensation

However, it only analyzed the temperature dependences of the output voltage at the first order. In fact, the V_{BE} voltage of a BJT does not change linearly with the temperature but, according to the relationship proposed in [2], it is given by

$$V_{BE} = V_{G0} - (V_{G0} - V_{BE0})\frac{T}{T_0} - (\eta - \alpha)V_T \ln(\frac{T}{T_0}) \tag{3}$$

Where η depends on the bipolar structure and is around 4, while α is equals 1 if the current in the BJT is PTAT and goes to 0 when the current is temperature independent.

Various approaches to compensate for the nonlinear term have been proposed [11–14]. The solution proposed in [11] can be simply implemented in our circuit. The basic idea is to correct the nonlinear term by a proper combination of the V_{BE} across a junction with a temperature-independent current ($\alpha = 0$) and the V_{BE} across a junction with a PTAT current ($\alpha = 1$). The current in the bipolar transistors (Q1 and Q2) are PTAT ($\alpha = 1$), while the current in the p-channel MOS transistors are at first-order temperature independent. Therefore, if we mirror the current flowing in p-channel MOS transistors (with M17) and we inject it to a diode connected bipolar transistor (Q3), as is shown Fig. 1(c), across Q3 we produce a V_{BE} with a $\alpha \approx 0$. Using Eq. (3), the V_{BE} of bipolar transistors Q3 and Q1,2 can be expressed as

$$V_{BE,Q3} = V_{G0} - (V_{G0} - V_{BE0})\frac{T}{T_0} - \eta V_T \ln\left(\frac{T}{T_0}\right) \tag{4}$$

$$V_{BE,Q1,2} = V_{G0} - (V_{G0} - V_{BE0})\frac{T}{T_0} - (\eta - 1)V_T \ln\left(\frac{T}{T_0}\right) \tag{5}$$

The difference between $V_{BE,Q3}(T)$ and $V_{BE,Q1,2}(T)$ leads to a voltage proportional to the nonlinear term of Eq. (3), given by

$$\Delta V = V_{BE,Q3}(T) - V_{BE,Q1,2}(T) = V_T \ln\left(\frac{T}{T_0}\right) \tag{6}$$

Curvature compensation can now be achieved by subtracting from both $I_{C,Q1}$ and $I_{C,Q2}$ a current proportional to ΔV. Complete bandgap circuit is shown in Fig. 1(c), this is obtained by introducing resistors R_3 and R_4(nominally equal), which drains from M_1 and M_2 the required current (ΔI), thus leading to

$$V_{ref} = R_7 \left\{ \frac{\left[V_{G0} - (V_{G0} - V_{BE0})\left(\frac{T}{T_0}\right) - (\eta - 1)V_T \ln\left(\frac{T}{T_0}\right) \right]}{R_1} + \frac{V_T \ln N}{R_0} + \frac{V_T \ln\left(\frac{T}{T_0}\right)}{R_3} \right\} \tag{7}$$

According to Eq. (7),

$$R_1 = qR_0 \frac{(V_{G0} - V_{BE0})}{KT_0 \ln N} \tag{8}$$

$$R_3 = \frac{R_1}{\eta - 1} \tag{9}$$

$$V_{ref} = IR_7 = V_{G0} \frac{R_7}{R_1} \qquad (10)$$

The proposed implementation of the curvature compensation principle requires an additional current mirror and two resistors only. However, it is more effective than the solution presented in Rincon-Mora's paper [13] and much less complex than other architectures [14–17], which uses operational amplifiers or switched capacitor structures.

However, the BGR can not be applied effectively to SoC designs, because that it can not achieve high PSRR over a broad frequency range. So, a BGR, which adopts pre-regulator to improve its PSRR, would be designed in the next section.

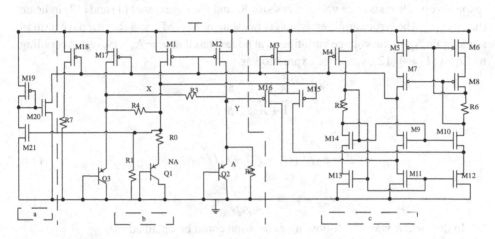

Fig. 1. BGR without pre-regulator (a) start-up circuit; (b) core circuit; (c) error amplifier

3 Analysis and Design of BGR with Pre-regulator

As is shown in Fig. 2, the designed BGR with pre-regulator consists of a pre-regulator, the core circuit of BGR and a start-up circuit. The core circuit of BGR with pre-regulator is similar to that the circuit which was shown in Fig. 1, but its operating supply voltage is the internal regulated supply voltage V_{REG} instead of the power supply voltage V_{dd}. The core circuit of BGR with pre-regulator generates a bandgap reference voltage V_{ref}, and has a good temperature characteristic, whose analysis is similar to that in Sect. 2. To simplify the analysis, this section will not discuss the core circuit of BGR with pre-regulator in detail. The PSRR of V_{ref} will be improved and will be quantitatively analyzed as following.

As is shown in Fig. 2(b), the pre-regulator, which was made up of M_{19}–M_{26}, is adopted to achieve a high PSRR over a wide frequency range. And all MOS transistors are in strong inversion. For convenience, it is assumed that the small-signal current and transconductance of transistor M_i. M_{1-3}, and M_{17-19} which expresses as i_i and g_{mi}, are entirely same. In other words, $g_{m1} = g_{m2} = g_{m3} = g_{m17} = g_{m18} = g_{m19}$. M_{20}–M_{24},

M_{22}–M_{23} have the same aspect ratio respectively, so it conclude that $g_{m20} = g_{m24}$ and $g_{m22} = g_{m23}$. R_2 and R_3 are entirely same, and Q_1 have an emitter area that is n times that of Q_2. Assume that there is an incremental voltage variation v_{reg} at node VREG, so there are incremental voltage variation v_a, v_b and v_c at node A, node B and node C respectively. And, v_a and v_b can be expressed as

$$v_a \approx g_{m1}\left(v_{reg} - v_c\right)\left(r_2//r_{e2}\right) \tag{11}$$

$$v_b \approx g_{m1}\left(v_{reg} - v_c\right)\left[r_2//\left(r_{e1} + r_1\right)\right] \tag{12}$$

where, r_{e1} and r_{e2} are, respectively, the emitter resistor of Q_1 and Q_2, r_1 and r_2 are, respectively, the resistance value of resistor R_1 and R_2. Equations (11) and (12) indicate that $v_a < v_b$. The error amplifier, which is made up of M_4–M_{18} and R_5–R_6, have a small signal gain A_d, so the voltage variation v_c at node C has that $v_c = A_d \times (v_b$-$v_a)$. According to Eqs. (11) and (12), v_c can be expression as

$$v_c = \frac{A_d g_{m1} v_{reg} \beta}{1 + A_d g_{m1} \beta} \tag{13}$$

where,

$$\beta = R_2//\left(r_{e1} + r_1\right) - r_2//r_{e2} \tag{14}$$

$$v_{reg} - v_c = \frac{v_{reg}}{1 + A_d g_{m1} \beta} \tag{15}$$

In the similar way, the following expression could be obtained as

$$\begin{cases} i_{mj} \approx g_{mj}\left(v_{reg} - v_c\right) \\ j = 4, 5, 15, 16 \, and \, 19 \end{cases} \tag{16}$$

$$i_{23} = i_{21} \approx g_{m21}[1 - \frac{g_{m1}\left(r_2//r_{e2}\right)}{1 + A_d g_{m1} \beta}]v_{reg}$$

$$\approx g_{m21} \frac{A_d g_{m1} \beta}{1 + A_d g_{m1} \beta} v_{reg} \tag{17}$$

According to the Kirchhoff current law (KCL) at node V_{REG}, the following equation could be obtained as

$$\frac{v_{dd} - v_{reg}}{r_{o25}} + i_{19} \frac{g_{m24}}{g_{m20}} \frac{g_{m25}}{g_{m26}}$$

$$= i_1 + i_2 + i_3 + i_4 + i_5 + i_{15} + i_{16} + i_{19} + i_{21} + i_{23} \tag{18}$$

where, v_{dd} is the incremental voltage variation of power supply voltage V_{dd}, r_{o25} is the source-drain resistance of the transistor M_{25}. According to Eqs. (11)~(20), the following expression could be obtained as

$$\frac{v_{reg}}{v_{dd}} =$$

$$\frac{1}{1 + \dfrac{4g_{m1} + 2g_{m5} + g_{m15} + g_{m16} - g_{m1}\frac{g_{m25}}{g_{m26}} + 2g_{m21}A_d g_{m1}\beta}{1 + A_d g_{m1}\beta} r_{o25}} \tag{19}$$

In the similar way, the output voltage variation v_{ref} of BGR with pre-regulator could also be written as

$$\frac{v_{ref}}{v_{reg}} \approx \frac{g_{m1}R_4}{1 + A_d g_{m1}\beta} \tag{20}$$

So, the PSRR of BGR with pre-regulator could be expressed as

$$PSRR_{dB} = 20\lg\left|\frac{v_{ref}}{v_{dd}}\right|$$

$$= 20\lg\left|\frac{v_{ref}}{v_{reg}} \times \frac{v_{reg}}{v_{dd}}\right| = 20\lg\left|\frac{v_{ref}}{v_{reg}}\right| + 20\lg\left|\frac{v_{ref}}{v_{dd}}\right| \tag{21}$$

This equation indicated that the designed BGR with pre-regulator achieved an improved PSRR.

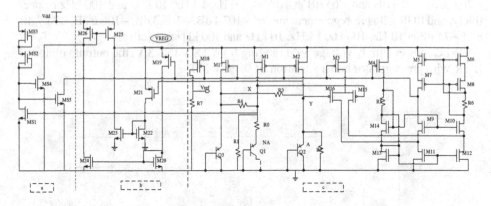

Fig. 2. BGR with pre-regulator (a) start-up circuit; (b) pre-regulator; (c) core circuit of BGR

4   Simulation Results

To verify the functionality of the BGR (bandgap reference) with- and without- pre-regulator, they were designed and simulated in 0.13 μm CMOS process with 2.5 V power supply voltage.

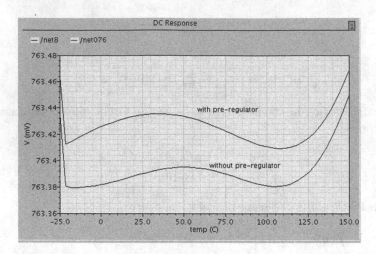

Fig. 3. Simulated output voltage of BGR with- and without- pre-regulator versus temperature.

Figure 3 showed that BGR without- and with- pre-regulator had, respectively, an output voltage variation about 581.6 μV and 576 μV when temperature ranging from -25 °C to 150 °C.

As was shown in Fig. 4, BGR without pre-regulator achieved −70.6 dB, −70.6 dB, −70.6 dB, −70.5 dB and −65 dB at 10 Hz, 100 Hz, 1 kHz, 10 kHz and 100 kHz respectively, and BGR with pre-regulator achieved −107.4 dB, −107.3 dB, −106.6 dB, −94.7 dB and −75 dB at 10 Hz, 100 Hz, 1 kHz, 10 kHz and 100 kHz respectively.

When power supply voltage Vdd ranging from 2.8 V to 6.3 V, the output voltage of BGR with pre-regulator had a variation of 0.1 mV in Fig. 5.

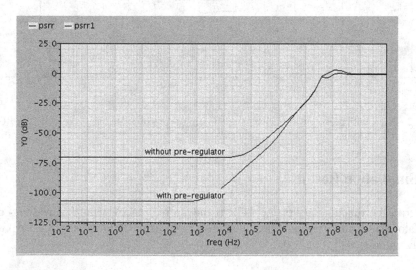

Fig. 4. Simulated PSRR (power supply rejection ratio) of BGR with- and without- pre-regulator versus frequency.

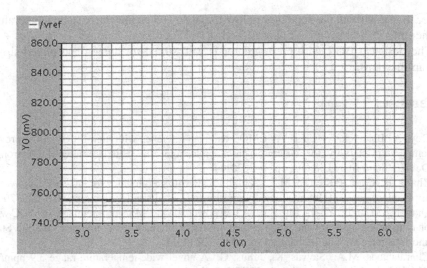

Fig. 5. Simulated output voltage of BGR (Bandgap reference) with pre-regulator versus power supply voltage

Finally, the performances of BGR with- and without- pre-regulator were summarized in Table 1. Simulation results showed that the designed BGR with pre-regulator achieved a better PSRR by adopting pre-regulator circuits.

Table 1. Performances of BGR with- and without- pre-regulator

		BGR with pre-regulator	BGR without pre-regulator
Power supply voltage (V)		2.5	2.5
Temperature coefficient (ppm/°C)		0.55	0.44
PSRR@25°C (dB)	10 Hz	−107.4	−70.6
	100 Hz	−107.3	−70.6
	1 kHz	−106.6	−70.6
	10 kHz	−94.7	−70.5
	100 kHz	−75	−65

5   Conclusions

CMOS bandgap references with- and without- pre-regulator was designed and analyzed in this paper. The topology with pre-regular achieves a theoretical and simulated superior performance than the topology without pre-regular. Simulation results show that the BGR with pre-regulator achieves excellent stability, relatively small temperature dependency and relatively well PSRR. The PSRR of BGR with pre-regulator is 37 dB higher than it without pre-regulator in low frequency when they have same temperature coefficient.

The designed BGR with pre-regulator is well suited for analog and mixed-signal SoC applications.

References

1. Dey, A., Bhattacharyya, T.K.: A CMOS bandgap reference with high PSRR and improved temperature stability for system-on-chip applications. In: IEEE Conference Electronics Devices Solid-State Circuits, pp. 1–2 (2011)
2. Zhang, H., Chen, P.K., Tan, M.T.: A high PSRR voltage reference for DC-to-DC converter applications. In: IEEE International Symposium on Circuits and Systems, pp. 816–819 (2009)
3. Qiao, N.S., Liu, L., Yu, F., Liu, Z.L.: A low power 14-bit 1 MS/s differential SAR ADC with on chip multi-segment bandgap reference. In: IEEE International Conference on Solid-State and Integrated Circuit Technology, pp. 205–207 (2011)
4. Charalambos, M.A., Savvas, K., Julius, G.: A novel wide-temperature-range 3.9 ppm/°C CMOS bandgap reference Circuit. IEEE J. Solid-State Circuits 27(2), 574–581 (2012)
5. Banba, H., Shiga, H., Umezawa, A., Miyaba, T., Tanzawa, T., Atsumi, S., Sakui, K.: A CMOS bandgap reference circuit with sub-1-V operation. IEEE J. Solid-State Circ. 34(5), 670–674 (1999)
6. Xu, X., Yuan, H.H., Chen, S.J., Liu, Q.: Design of super performance CMOS bandgap voltage reference and current refence. Semicond. Technol. 36(3), 229–233 (2011). (in chinese)
7. Tham, K.M., Nagaraj, K.: A low supply voltage high PSRR voltage reference in CMOS process. IEEE J. Solid-State Circ. 30(5), 586–590 (1995)
8. Mohieldin, A.N., Elbahr, H., Hegazi, E., Mostafa, M.: A low-voltage CMOS bandgap reference circuit with improved power supply rejection. In: International Conference on Microelectronics, pp. 343–346 (2010)
9. Kang, X.Z., Tang, Z.W.: A novel high PSRR bandgap over a wide frequency range. In: International Conference on Solid-State and Integrated Circuit Technology, pp. 418–420 (2010)
10. Yu, Q., Zhang, W.D., Chen, H., Ning, N.: High PSRR and high-order curvature-compensated bandgap voltage reference. In: Asia Pacific Conference on Postgraduate Research in Microelectronics and Electronics, pp. 154–157 (2010)
11. Tsividis, Y.: Accurate analyzes of temperature effects in Ie-Vbe characteristics with application to bandgap reference sources. IEEE J. Solid-State Circ. 15(12), 1076–1084 (1980)
12. Gunawan, M., Meijer, G., Fonderie, J., Huijsing, H.: A curvature-corrected low-voltage bandgap reference. IEEE J. Solid-State Circ. 34(5), 670–674 (1999)
13. Rincon-Mora, G.A., Allen, P.E.: 1.1-V current-mode and piece-wise-linear curvature-corrected bandgap reference. IEEE J. Solid-State Circ. 33(10), 1551–1554 (1998)
14. Lee, I., Kim, G., Kim, W.: Exponential curvature-compensated BiCMOS bandgap references. IEEE J. Solid-State Circ. 29(11), 1396–1403 (1994)
15. Razavi, B.: Design of Analog CMOS Integrated Circuits, p. 309. Xi'An Jiaotong University Press, Xi'An (2002). Chen Guican, tran. (in Chinese)
16. Tao, C., Fayed. A.: Spurious-noise-free buck regulator for direct powering of analog/RF loads using PWM control with random frequency hopping and random phase chopping. In: Proceedings of the IEEE Solid State Circuits Conference (ISSCC), pp. 396–398 (2011)
17. Holman, T.: A new temperature compensation technique for bandgap voltage references. In: IEEE International Symposium on Circuits and Systems, pp. 767–770 (1996)

Computer Application and Software
Optimization

Detection and Analysis of Water Army Groups on Virtual Community

Guirong Chen[1,2(✉)], Wandong Cai[1], Jiuming Huang[3], Huijie Xu[1], Rong Wang[2], Hua Jiang[2], and Fengqin Zhang[2]

[1] Department of Computer Science, Northwestern Polytechnical University, Xi'an 710029, China
guirongchen315@163.com, caiwd@nwpu.edu.cn, xhj004@gmail.com
[2] School of Information and Navigation, Air Force Engineering University of PL,
Xi'an 710077, China·
rongwang66@163.com, dzc_djjh@tom.com, fengqin_zhang@126.com
[3] College of Computer, National University of Defense Technology, Changsha 410073, China
jiuming.huang@qq.com

Abstract. Water army is prevalent in social networks and it causes harmful effect to the public opinion and security of cyberspace. This paper proposes a novel water army groups detection method which consists of 4 steps. Firstly, we break the virtual community into a series of time windows and find the suspicious periods when water army groups are active. Then we build the user cooperative networks of suspicious periods according to user's reply behaviors and cluster them based on their Cosine similarity. After that, we prune the cooperative networks by just remaining the edges whose weight is larger than some threshold and get some suspicious user clusters. Finally, we conduct deeper analysis to the behaviors of the cluster users to determine whether they are water army groups or not. The experiment results show that our method can identify water army groups on virtual community efficiently and it has a high accuracy.

Keywords: Social networks · Detection of water army groups · Empirical analysis of water army activities · Virtual community

1 Introduction

With the maturity and popularization of Web2.0 technology, kinds of interactive networks such as online forums, blogs, microblogs and other social networks have become more and more popular. According to the report of China Internet Network Information Center (CNNIC), there are around 618 million Internet users in China, which is approximately 45.8 % of its total population [1]. Not only does the Internet become the platform in which people communicate with each other, but also it has been the window through which people observe and supervise the management of the social and the country.

However, the inherent characteristics of Internet such as freedom, openness and anonymity and the immature of the laws and supervision mechanisms for Internet management make it possible for some malicious people to abuse it. Water army is one

© Springer-Verlag Berlin Heidelberg 2016
W. Xu et al. (Eds.): NCCET 2015, CCIS 592, pp. 105–117, 2016.
DOI: 10.1007/978-3-662-49283-3_11

typical example. To attract public attention towards their products or enhance their reputation or attack their competitor's, companies may hire many people to 'flood' the Internet with huge number of purposeful comments and articles. The Internet users who make money by posting comments and articles on different online communities or websites are called 'water army' in China.

Sometimes water army can be used as an efficient way in business marketing. For example, before a new movie or TV serial is released, the host company may hire water army to submit articles, posts and comments about the movie or TV serial, the actors or actress of it on kinds of online communities to attract people's attention and trigger their curiosity. But sometimes water army can be used in malicious ways. For example, some people or companies may hire water army to spread negative, false and concoctive information about their competitors. By initiating and taking part in discussions on Internet and submitting a great number of comments, water army can influence the opinions of other people towards some product or social event. Further more, some people or organizations who have an ulterior motive even might hire water army to slander the government and our country. In a word, water army is not only harmful to the benefits of ordinary internet users, normal companies, but also affects the social stability. Hence, detection of water army becomes one of the most important scientific issues today.

However, study on detection and analysis of water army is still in the initial stage and few papers about this problem has been published. There are 3 reasons for this: (1) water army is a new phenomenon of the Internet, and studies on this problem have just begun; (2) there is no public datasets in which users have been labeled as water army or not, and it is very difficult to recognize water army accounts by manually reading the comments they submit; (3) it is hard to verify the accuracy of the detection algorithm. Despite the difficulties, researchers at home and abroad have begun to conduct studies on this problem and obtained some achievements. Chen et al. conduct empirical research on the behavior patterns of water army by analyzing the '3Q conflict' real data which they get from several online communities and news websites. They get some meaningful conclusions: (1) water army prefers to submit new topics than replies; (2) the posting time intervals of water army are small; (3) water army would like to use different temporary accounts to log in virtual communities and most of them will discard the accounts when the task is completed; (4) in order to finish the task as quickly as they can, water army incline to submit duplicate or nearly duplicate comments [3]. Fan et al. analyze a real dataset of one online forum manually and find that there are many water army accounts on that online forum and they are well organized [4]. Li et al. try to use text sentiment analysis technology to identify network cheaters who are similar to water army [5].

Review spammer refers to people who submit spam reviews or spam opinions on social network or electronic commerce websites. As water army and review spammers exist similarity in many aspects such as purpose, behavior patterns, organization and so on, so the achievements on review spammer detection have important significance to water army detection. Mo et al. present an overview of spammer detection technologies and give some suggestions for possible extensions [6]. Professor Liu Bing and his research team conduct deep research on detection of review spam and spammers on electronic commerce websites [7–11]. Paper [7] takes advantage of text classification and pattern matching technology to detect review spam. By analyzing the product or brand rating behaviors of different users, paper [8] finds some abnormal rating patterns and detects some review spammers via mining abnormal rating behaviors. Paper [9] presents a novel review graph to describe the relationship of all the reviews, reviewers and stores, and proposes an iterative computation model to identify suspicious reviewers on the electronic commerce website. In view of the fact that spammers on electronic commerce websites usually appear in groups or twists, paper [10] constructs a dataset including spammer groups manually, and analyzes the spammers' behaviors on individual and population levels, and then proposes a new spammer group detection algorithm. The research findings of Professor Liu Bing and his team have great implications for the paper.

Spam and spammer detection problem has also attracted the attention of other researchers at home and abroad. Husn et al. conduct empirical analysis on the behavior characteristics of spam botnets [12]. Brendel et al. construct a social network of online users and detect spammers on that network through computing and analyzing the network properties [15]. Inspired by the PageRank algorithm, zhou et al. propose a novel ranking algorithm which can distinguish malicious users from normal ones. Like paper [8, 9], this algorithm is also based on the rating results of different users. Xu et al. analyze the collaborative behaviors of spammers [15], Lu et al. propose a spam and spammer detection algorithm using graph models [16]. Lin et al. present a new method to identify spam using social network analysis technology [17].

To cheat online, some internet users may use fake identities to create the illusion of support to some product or people pretending to be a totally different person. The different identities of the same person online is called 'sock puppet'. Recently, the problem of sock puppet detection attracts researchers' attention. Bu et al. present a novel sock puppet detection algorithm which combines link analysis and authorship identification techniques [18]. Based on the fact that sock puppets appear in pairs, Zheng et al. propose a simple method which detects sock puppets by analyzing the relationship of users [19]. Jiang et al. consider water army accounts as outliers and use the outlier detection algorithm to detect them [20]. In a word, the problem of malicious user detection has attracted wide attention [21].

Although researchers have carried on beneficial exploration on the problem of water army detection, there are still many problems to be solved. The findings of Chen et al. can detect water army whose purpose is to spread some specific information wildly [3], but they can't identify other type of water army. The method proposed by Li et al. can find water army whose comments have intense and consistent emotion or attitude [5], but most of the time, in order to create hot online topics, attract people's attention, trigger their curious, water army might release many comments whose emotion are ambiguous or contradictory with each other. The existing methods can't detect this type of water army.

The research findings about spammer and sock puppet detection are of great significance to the study of water army detection, while the methods can't be used to detect water army accounts on online forums directly. There are 3 reasons. Firstly, there is no rating mechanism on forums, so we can't identify water army accounts via analyzing users' rating behaviors. Secondly, the contents submitted by forum users are very complex, very difficult to describe, that the detection algorithm based on text analysis can't get a good accuracy when they are used to detect water army accounts on forums. Thirdly, most of the current spammer detection algorithms are based on supervised learning methods, and they all need labeled dataset while it is very difficult to determine whether a user is water army or not by hand. To avoid their comments or articles being deleted by the website managers, water army would pretend to be normal users, which makes it hard to identify water army accounts just by reading their comments.

To 'flood' the Internet with huge number of comments or articles in a short period of time, water army always works collaboratively. We call the water army accounts who write and submit comments collusively a water army group. Intuitively, water army has obvious community characteristics. This paper proposes a novel water army group detection method based on user behavior analysis. Our method consists of 4 steps. Firstly, we identify suspicious periods by doing some statistical analysis. Secondly, we find highly collaborative user pairs through comparing their reply objects based on the fact that users who have similar interests may reply to similar topics. Then we construct user collaboration network according to their reply behaviors and cluster the users to detect suspicious user groups. Finally, we carry on deep analysis to the suspicious user groups with some aspects such as reply time, reply intervals, burst and memory to confirm water army groups.

2   Problem Description

2.1   Analysis of the Working Mechanism of Water Army

In order to enhance the reputation of themselves or damage their competitors' on Internet, a common trick is to hire water army to make hot topics creating the illusion of supporting for it, or on the contrary, slandering it.

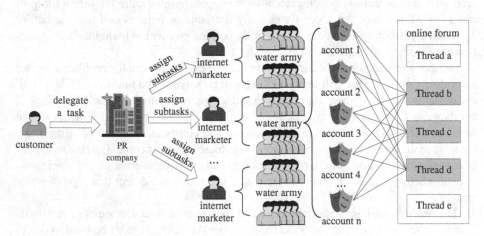

Fig. 1. The work flow of water army activities

As has been stated above, water army refers to internet users who make money by posting comments or articles online. Usually, there are 3 types of entities in water army activities: customer, public relationship (PR) company and water army. As we can see in Fig. 1, PR companies are the intermediary between customer and water army. They get tasks from customers, then break the tasks into a series of subtasks and assign them to internet marketers who are called water army leaders too. Internet marketers organize water army to finish the tasks, check their work and give out payoffs to them.

As Fig. 1 shows, to finish the tasks effectively, water army may register many accounts on the same website such as online forum, and pretend to be different people to release a huge number of comments or articles deliberately in a very short period of time. So when water army is active on some website, there must be hot topics there.

2.2   The Characteristics of Water Army on Online Forum

Online forum is an excellent virtual community for people to communicate and share information. Compared with other social networks on which people must use real names to register, online forum has greater openness and concealment. People can register new identification (ID for short) freely and arbitrarily without revealing their real information. Once log on a forum, people can browse all the articles submitted by all the other people but not limited to his/her friends. Therefore, online forum has become one the most important platforms for ordinary people to share information, discuss problems and express their views in China. On the other hand, the openness and freedom of online forum has resulted in some problems, it also facilitates criminals to swindle and scam. As Fan et al. say water army is popular on online forums [4].

On online forums, users discuss with each other by submitting new posts or replying to other's posts. We call a post and all its replies a thread. Threads about the same thing form a topic. Because water army fabricates hot topics by submitting huge number of replies, so this paper focuses on their reply behaviors.

Online forum is a dynamic system. New posts and replies are submitted almost every second. We divide the online forum into a series of time windows in time dimension and analyze the reply behavior in each time window. We choose 1 day as the size of the time window, because people work and rest in 1 day cycle.

Suppose on some day, there are 6 users submit replies on 8 different threads, as shown in Table 1. Here a user means a different ID but not a real person, which means if some person registers several IDs on the same website, each ID represents a different user. RNET in Table 1 represents the total reply number submitted to each thread, and RNEU represents the total reply number of each user.

From Table 1, we can see that user a, c and d are active on that day who submit 14,14 and 17 replies, respectively (bold). After further analysis, we find that this 3 users reply and just reply to thread 1,2,3,7, and the total reply numbers of these 4 threads are close. Their reply behaviors exhibit a high degree of similarity. It is reasonable to suspect that these replies are not submitted by normal users spontaneously, but by water army premeditatedly. We suspect it is done by 1 physical person with 3 different IDs, and he/she wants others to pay attention to thread 1, 2, 3 and 7. If there are many users show similar reply characteristics like user a, c or d, replying many times to some special

Table 1. Example of the reply number of one user on one day

thread / user	1	2	3	4	5	6	7	8	RNEU
a	3	2	4	0	0	0	5	0	14
b	0	0	0	1	1	0	0	0	2
c	3	3	4	0	0	0	4	0	14
d	4	4	4	0	0	0	5	0	17
e	0	0	0	0	1	2	0	0	3
f	0	0	0	0	1	1	0	1	3
RNET	10	9	12	1	3	3	14	1	

threads in a short period, it is reasonable to doubt they are water army groups. How to identify these user groups?

We use a user-thread bipartite network $G = (U, P, E)$ to represent the reply relationship of users, which consists of 2 types of nodes: user and thread, and U represents the user set, P represents the thread set, and E represents the edge set. For any user $u \in U$, if he/she replies to thread $p \in P$, add an edge between user u and thread p, let the total reply number of user u to thread p be the weight of the edge, noted as w_{up}. Let $m = |U|$ represent the number of users in user set U, $n = |P|$ represent the number of threads in thread set P. Define user reply matrix $W_{m \times n} = (w_{up})$, which has m rows and n columns. As stated above, w_{up} is the total number of replies of user u to thread p, which represents the strength user u take part in the discussion of thread p. The uth row of the matrix $W_{m \times n}$ record the numbers of replies of user u to the n threads, noted as w_u, which we call it reply vector of user u.

As most users are inactive and they seldom reply [22], the matrix is sparse. Because users' reply behaviors are affected by several factors and users' interests are very wide, the reply matrix is asymmetric. Cosine similarity is suit to the comparison of sparse vectors, so this paper chooses Cosine similarity to compare the similarity of two users' reply behaviors, which mainly focuses on which threads users take part in and how the intense is.

Suppose $w_u = (w_{u1}, w_{u2}, \dots w_{ui} \dots w_{un})$ and $w_v = (w_{v1}, w_{v2}, \dots w_{vj} \dots w_{vn})$ are the reply vectors of user u and user v, respectively. Define the reply similarity of the two users is the Cosine similarity of their reply vectors, that is $S_{(u,v)} = \frac{w_u \cdot w_v}{||w_u|| \ ||w_v||}$, in which $w_u \cdot w_v$ means the dot product of vector w_u and vector w_v, $||w_u||$ means the Euclidean norm of w_u, and $||w_u|| \neq 0, ||w_v|| \neq 0$.

Here we just consider users who at least reply one time on that day, that means if some user does not reply to any thread on that day, we will ignore he/she when we analyze the data of that day. So to any user u, it is always true $||w_u|| \neq 0$.

Obviously, $S_{(u,v)} = S_{(v,u)}$ and $S_{(u,u)} = 1$, which means the similarity is symmetry. Higher the similarity is, more similar the two users' reply behaviors are. We use a $n \times n$ triangular matrix $Sim_{n \times n}$ to represent the reply similarities of n users. Here, $S_{(i,j)}$ is the reply similarity of user i and user j.

$$Sim_{n \times n} = \begin{bmatrix} 1 & & & & \\ S_{(2,1)} & 1 & & & \\ S_{(3,1)} & S_{(3,2)} & 1 & & \\ \cdots & \cdots & \cdots & 1 & \\ S_{(n,1)} & S_{(n,2)} & \cdots & \cdots & 1 \end{bmatrix}$$

3 Water Army Group Detection and Analysis

3.1 Dataset

Sina is one of the most famous websites in China and Sina Forum which is an important part of this website is very popular. Our data is collected from Sina Entertainment Forum which is a sub forum of Sina Forum using our crawler [23]. The dataset covers all the post, reply and user information of 2010, containing 4407 threads, 80990 replies and 13099 users. Note that the users who didn't submit any post or reply in that year are ignored.

We use 3 tables to save the data and their names are post, reply and user, respectively. Table post keeps the basic information of all the threads of that year. Each record of the table includes 7 elements: post ID, post time, post user ID, headline, content, clicked counts, reply counts, which show the ID of the post, the time when the post is submitted, the user's ID who submits the post, the title of the post, the content of the post, the number that the post has been clicked or browsed, the number that the post has been replied, respectively. The reply table saves all the information of all the replies of that year. Each record of table reply has 5 elements: reply ID, reply user ID, reply time, content, post ID, which show the reply's ID, the user's ID who submits the reply, the time when the reply is submitted, the content of the reply, and the root post's ID of the reply, respectively. Here, the reply ID of a reply means the ID of the reply itself and the post ID means the thread to which this reply is submitted to.

3.2 Water Army Group Detection Method

The water army detection algorithm proposed by this paper combining human dynamics, statistical analysis, complex network and data mining techniques, reduces the calculation range for 3 times by excluding normal users constantly, and detect water army groups finally. So its computational complexity is small and it is fast.

3.2.1 Determine the Suspicious Period

The previous research results [22] show that the one-day reply number of a forum follows heavy tailed distribution, that means on most date the one-day reply number is small, while on some date, the reply number is very large. To attract attention or create hot topics, water army would release huge number of replies using different IDs in a very short period, which will change the activity of that day, leading a sudden increase in some indexes such as the total number of replies, the average number of replies of all the users, the average number of replies of all the threads and so on. We define 5 indexes to describe the activity of one day and the meanings of the indexes are shown in Table 2.

Table 2. The meaning of the indexes

Index	Meaning
RN	The total reply number of that day
RNPU	The average reply number of all the users on that day
RNPT	The average reply number of all the threads on that day
MRNPT	The maximum of RNPT
VRNPT	The variance of RNPT

We compute the values of each day and then get the values of the indexes. If the 5 indexes of some day are all bigger than their average, we think it is suspicious and we call them suspicious days. In this step, we can reduce the compute range through filtering the normal periods which cover most of the time.

Table 3 is the statistical data of 5 suspicious days. We can see that, the 5 indexes are much bigger than normal periods [22]. Deeper analysis shows that the one-post reply numbers of the 5 days are heterogeneous and most of the replies are all concentrated on a few of special active threads. They are hot threads.

Table 3. The statistical data of 5 suspicious days

INDEX DATE	RN	RNPU	RNPT	MRNPT	VRNPT
DAY 1	235	4.80	12.37	196	44.50
DAY 2	2803	6.34	96.66	674	200.59
DAY 3	18824	29.41	896.38	4687	1879.33
DAY 4	3513	7.05	70.26	933	237.2
DAY 5	2253	8.31	112.65	2213	494.37

3.2.2 Similar User Twists Detection

Here we build the user-thread bipartite network of suspicious time periods, and construct the reply matrix according to the method stated in Sect. 2. Then compute the Cosine similarity of every two users, build the similarity triangular matrix and find out the user twists whose similarity is larger than the threshold.

Because users having similar interests may reply to similar threads, so their reply behavior may be similar. To enhance the accuracy of the algorithm, avoiding taking normal users having similar interests as suspicious user twists, we set the threshold to be a large number 0.9.

3.2.3 Suspicious User Groups Finding

In this step, we construct user cooperative network according to their reply similarity. If the reply similarity between two users is larger than the threshold, we add an edge between them letting the weight of the edge be the reply similarity of the two users.

Then cluster the users of this network into different user clusters using the clustering algorithm based on distance, and consider the cluster as suspicious user groups. Suppose the similarity threshold is 0.6, the suspicious user groups of users in Table 1 are cluster 1 and cluster 3, as shown in Fig. 2.

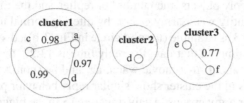

Fig. 2. The example of user cooperative network and forming of clusters of users

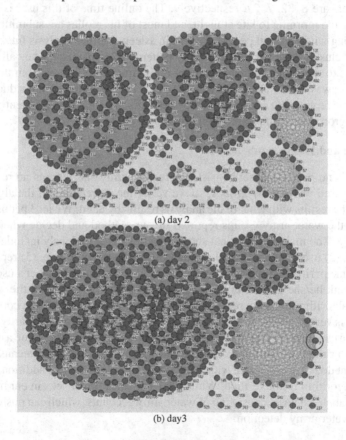

(a) day 2

(b) day3

Fig. 3. Users in suspicious time periods form clusters

Figure 3 is the user clusters of day 2 and day 3 when the user reply similarity threshold is 0.9. We can see that, the user cooperative network shows obvious community characteristics, and the network forms several clusters which are not connected with each other. The users in the same cluster show very high similarity, larger than 0.9. This is very suspicious. We consider them as suspicious user clusters.

3.2.4 Water Army Group Identification

After analyzing the reply objects, the number of replies and the time when the replies are submitted, we identify water army groups by filtering normal users.

Take user 7 in day 3 as example (in solid circle in Fig. 3(b)), deep analysis finds that he/she just reply one time on that day, the reply time is 13:27, the thread to which he submitted the reply is about 'free movie watching' and he submitted the reply to get a ticket. The other users in the cluster show similar reply behavior patterns. We confirm that they are not water army groups. Analyzing user 15 in the bigger cluster (in dashed circle in Fig. 3(b)), we can see that the user submit replies to 4 different threads, and the reply numbers are 8, 32, 7, 27, respectively. The online time of this user is very long, from early in the morning to late at night, and most of his replies are submitted on early in the morning when normal people are still in asleep. Further analysis finds that other users in that cluster have very similar reply patterns with that user. They all submitted many replies to the same 4 threads and the reply time are all on early in the morning which are far away from that of normal users and they all submitted many duplicate and near-duplicate replies. We confirm that they are water army groups. We identify all other water army groups using the same method.

3.3 Result and Discussion

Since there is no public dataset consisting of water army and there is no real answers for each reported water army groups, so we verify the correctness of the algorithm by comparing the results with what of the analysis results by hand. We let 3 people to check the users in the water army groups reported by our method and decide whether he/she is water army. The main factors what should be considered seriously include: (1) registration time, (2) user name, (3) total online time, (4) last log in time, (5) reply objects, (6) online time period of a day, (7) reply content. If 2 or 3 analysts label a user as water army, we think he/she is a water army user. The results show that all the water army groups our algorithm finds are real water army groups, which means the correctness of this method is very high. We think this is because we choose a high similarity threshold. Although we can detect water army groups effectively, there are still some aspects to be improved. Our method can't detect single water army account which means if a water army account does not cooperate with others, we can't identify it. In addition, the integrity of the algorithm is not verified. While there are some drawbacks in our method, we construct a labeled dataset consisting of water army accounts, which can push the development of water army detection.

3.4 Water Army Posting Patterns Analysis

In order to further understanding water army, we analyze the time characteristics of their reply behaviors. Figure 4 is the reply time distribution of 4 users in a water army group detected by our algorithm. The horizontal axis denotes time (0–24), each vertical line corresponding to a reply event.

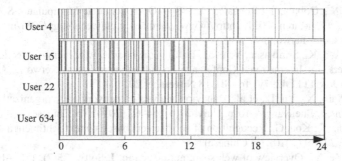

Fig. 4. The reply time distribution of water army's reply activity

We can see from Fig. 4 that the reply time of the 4 water army accounts are highly similar, including: (1) the online time are all very long, from early in the morning to late at night, (2) they would like to reply during the period early in the morning when normal user are still in asleep, (3) the reply time intervals show low burst and memory characteristics which is conflict with the pattern of normal internet users reported by Barabási [24].

4 Conclusion

Water army is a serious threat to the security of network space. Not only a sound legal system but also technical support is needed to supervise and manage the water army. The research of water army detection techniques has significant theory value and good application prospects. This paper proposes a novel method to detect water army groups in virtual community. Through computing the reply similarity of users, building user cooperative network, clustering users and analyzing their reply time distribution characteristics, we reduce the compute range constantly by filtering normal users for 3 times. Meantime, we constructed a dataset consisting of labeled water army accounts, which has significant meaning for the development of the study of water army detection. Future, we would like to improve our method by adding content analysis and user relationship analysis, and verify the new algorithm using the dataset we constructed in this paper.

Acknowledgement. This research is supported in part by the National Key Basic Research and Development Plan (Grant No. 2013CB329600), National Natural Science Foundation of China (Grant No. 71503260) and Natural Science Foundation of Shaanxi Province (Grant No. 2014JM8345).

References

1. Internet Network Information Center of China: The 33rd statistical report on Internet development of China [EB/OL]. http://www.eajcd.edu.cn/pub/wml.txt/980810-2.html, 2014-03-05/2014-05-06 (in Chinese)

2. Fielding, N., Cobain, I.: Revealed: US Spy Operation that Manipulates Social Media, Guardian, 17 March 2011. http://www.guardian.co.uk/technology/2011/mar/17/us-spy-operation-social-networks
3. Chen, C., Wu, K., Srinivasan, V., et al.: Battling the internet water army: detection of hidden paid posters. In: International Conference on Advances in Social Networks Analysis and Mining, arXiv:1111.4297v1 [cs.SI], 18 November 2011
4. Fan, C., Xaio, X., Yu, L., et al.: Behavior analysis of network navy organization based on web forums. J. Shenyang Aerosp. Univ. 29(5), 64–67 (2010). (in Chinese)
5. Li, G., Gan, T., Kou, G.: Recognition of net-cheaters based on text sentiment analysis. Libr. Inf. 54(8), 77–80 (2010). (in Chinese)
6. Qin, M., Ke, Y.: Overview of web spammer detection. J. Softw. 25(7), 1505–1526 (2014). (in Chinese)
7. Jindal, N., Liu, B., Lim, E.P.: Finding unusual review patterns using unexpected rules. In: Huang, J., Koudas, N., Jones, G. (eds.) Proceedings of the 19th ACM International Conference on Information and Knowledge Management (CIKM 2010), pp. 1549–1552. ACM Press, New York (2010)
8. Lim, E.P., Nguyen, V.A., Jindal, N., Liu, B., Lauw, H.W.: Detecting product review spammers using rating behaviors. In: Huang, J., Koudas, N., Jones, G., Wu, X., Collins-Thompson, K., An, A. (eds.) Proceedings of the 19th ACM International Conference on Information and Knowledge Management (CIKM 2010), pp. 939–948. ACM Press, New York (2010)
9. Wang, G., Xie, S., Liu, B., Yu, P.S.: Identify online store review spammers via social review graph. ACM Trans. Intell. Syst. Technol. (TIST) 3(4), 61 (2012)
10. Mukherjee, A., Liu, B., Glance, N.: Spotting fake reviewer groups in consumer reviews. In: Mille, A., Gandon, F., Misselis, J., Rabinovich, M., Staab, S. (eds.) Proceedings of the 21st International Conference on World Wide Web (WWW 2012), pp.191–200. ACM Press, New York (2012)
11. Liu, B.W., Yu, Y.T.: Web Data Mining. Tsinghua University Publication, Beijing (2013). (in Chinese)
12. Husna, H., Phithakkitnukoon, S., Palla, S., Dantu, R.: Behavior analysis of spam botnets. In: Proceedings of the 3rd International Conference on Communication Systems Software and Middleware and Workshops (COMSWARE 2008), pp. 246–253. IEEE Computer Society, Washington (2008)
13. Brendel, R., Krawczyk, H.: Application of social relation graphs for early detection of transient spammers. WSEAS Trans. Inf. Sci. Appl. 5(3), 267–276 (2008)
14. Zhou, Y.-B., Zhou, T.: A robust ranking algorithm to spamming. EPL (Europhys. Lett.) 94(4), 48002 (2011)
15. Xu, C., Zhang, J., Chang, K., Long, C.: Uncovering collusive spammers in Chinese review websites. In: He, Q., Iyengar, A., Nejdl, W. (eds.) Proceedings of the 22nd ACM Conference on Information and Knowledge Management (CIKM 2013), pp. 979–988. ACM Press, New York (2013)
16. Lu, Y., Zhang, L., Xiao, Y., Li, Y.: Simultaneously detecting fake reviews and review spammers using factor graph model. In: Davis, H.C., Halpin, H., Pentland, A. (eds.) Proceedings of the 5th Annual ACM Web Science Conference (WebSci 2013), pp. 225–233. ACM Press, New York (2013)
17. Lin, C., Zhou, Y., Chen, K., He, J., Yang, X., Song, L.: Analysis and identification of spamming behaviors in Sina Weibo microblog. In: Zhu, F., He, Q., Yan, R. (eds.) Proceedings of the 7th Workshop on Social Network Mining and Analysis (SNAKDD 2013), pp. 5–13. ACM Press, New York (2013)

18. Bu, Z., Xia, Z., Wang, J.: A sock puppet detection algorithm on virtual spaces. Knowledge Based Systems **37**, 366–377 (2013)
19. Zheng, X., Lai, Y.M., Chow, K.P., et al.: Sockpuppet detection in online discussion forums. In: 2011 Seventh International Conference on Intelligent Information Hiding and Multimedia Signal Processing, pp. 374–377 (2011)
20. Jiang, F., Du, J., Sui, Y., Cao, C.: Outlier detection based on boundary and distance. Acta Electronica Sinica **38**(3), 700–705 (2010). (in Chinese)
21. Lin, Y., Wang, X., Zhou, A.: Survey on quality evaluation and control of online reviews. J. Softw. **25**(3), 506–527 (2014). (in Chinese)
22. Chen, G., Cai, W., Xu, H., et al.: Empirical analysis on human behavior dynamics in online forum. J. Hunan Univ. **40**(11), 153–160 (2013). (in Chinese)
23. Peng, D., Cai, W.: The web forum crawling technology and system implementation. Comput. Eng. Sci. **44**(1), 157–160 (2011)
24. Barabási, A.L.: The origin of bursts and heavy tails in human dynamics [J]. Nature **435**(7039), 207–211 (2005)

Accelerating Molecular Dynamics Simulations on Heterogeneous Architecture

Yueqing Wang[✉], Yong Dou, Song Guo, Yuanwu Lei, Baofeng Li,
and Qiang Wang

National Laboratory for Parallel and Distributed Processing,
National University of Defense Technology, Changsha, China
yqwang2013@163.com,
{yongdou,songguo,yuanwulei,baofengli,qiangwang}@nudt.edu.cn

Abstract. Molecular dynamics (MD) is an important computational tool used to simulate chemical and physical processes at the molecular level. MD simulations focus on the motion of the interaction of numerous molecules or atoms. Most scholars focus on accelerating MD on multicore central processing units (CPUs) or other coprocessors, such as graphics processing unit (GPU) or many integrated cores [1]. However, most researchers disregard CPU resources and merely perceive a CPU as a controller when using coprocessors. Thus, hybrid computing cannot be achieved, thereby resulting in the waste of CPU computing resources. In this study, we propose three strategies to accelerate MD simulation. The first strategy uses Compute Unified Device Architecture [2] to rewrite the MD code and to run applications on a single-core CPU-GPU platform. This strategy can achieve satisfactory performance but does not make use of CPU resources to compute for most research activities. In the second strategy, the CPU is set to compute the pair force of a small part of molecules along with the GPU after accomplishing the task of starting the GPU computation. The third strategy is applicable under the condition that the GPU is shared by numerous MPI processes, each of which uses the GPU separately. In this situation, the performance can be improved.

Keywords: Molecular dynamics · GPU · Hybrid parallel · Accelerate

1 Introduction

Molecular dynamics (MD) simulation is a discrete simulation method that requires a large amount of computation to simulate molecular motion. Such simulation is achieved by calculating the force, position, and velocity of each molecule over a series of time steps. In practice, the computational demand of MD is large because of two features. First, the computing steps must be processed long enough to achieve reasonable computation accuracy. Second, the computation involved in each time step is intensive because the problem scales are always large. This condition leads to huge runtime requirements. Hence, identifying fast algorithms and designing parallel algorithms for MD are very

© Springer-Verlag Berlin Heidelberg 2016
W. Xu et al. (Eds.): NCCET 2015, CCIS 592, pp. 118–132, 2016.
DOI: 10.1007/978-3-662-49283-3_12

important. Moreover, MD is widely used in the fields of physical, chemical, and biological sciences, as well as materials, medicine, and new energy.

Graphics processing units (GPUs) provide a new platform for accelerating MD simulations. Compared with a central processing unit (CPU), a GPU is a highly parallel, multithreaded, multicore processor with tremendous computational horsepower and very large memory bandwidth. For example, the Tesla K40, NVidia's most recent GPU, performs up to 4.29 Tflops. However, a 3.08 GHz Xeon x5675 six-core CPU can only theoretically process approximately 140 Gflops. Thus, a GPU is more suitable for use in dealing with computation-intensive and highly parallel tasks. MD is a computation-intensive simulation that has natural parallelism because the required variables and constants do not depend on the calculation of other atoms when the acceleration of each atom is computed. Thus, performance can be improved by using the GPU acceleration program.

A GPU must be used as a coprocessor that is controlled by a CPU because the former cannot complete the computation without the latter. The CPU only has to be used for controlling, whereas the GPU has to be used for computing. In this way, multicore computing resources will not participate in the computation to prevent the wasting of resources.

Collaborative computing by the CPU-GPU may be confronted with numerous problems. First, tasks must be appropriately allocated to the CPU and GPU. Second, load balance between the CPU and the GPU must be ensured. Third, the number of CPU cores required to complete the tasks using the GPU must be properly chosen to achieve the best performance.

In this study, we show how MD simulations can benefit from the computing power of GPUs. We then present a strategy that explores both CPU and GPU computing potentials by efficiently allocating tasks between these devices to ensure load balance, which reduces CPU performance loss attributed to waiting for the GPU process.

The remainder of this paper is organized as follows: Section 2 describes the research on MD acceleration on different platforms and some programming models. Section 3 presents the main algorithms used in MD and the useful methods used for parallel MD simulation on a GPU. The CPU-GPU heterogeneous architecture is then introduced. Section 4 describes three strategies for accelerating MD simulations. Section 5 presents the experimental results and a simple analysis of these results. Section 6 provides the conclusion and contributions.

2 Related Work

We briefly review works related to the parallelization of MD simulations on the GPU platform before focusing on heterogeneous programming models.

Numerous commercial and academic MD software programs have been accelerated on GPUs. These programs include AMBER [3], CHARMM [4], GROMACS [5], and LAMMPS [6]. Christopher et al. [7], who designed algorithms that decompose atom data that result in low computation efficiency, examined the use of a GPU that is programmed to accelerate the calculation of cutoff pair potentials. They obtained 12 to 20 times speedup compared with the optimized CPU-only code.

Brown et al. [8] designed a framework for implementing MD for hybrid high-performance computers in LAMMPS. Their methods can be applied to many MD codes. Xu et al. [9] presented MD algorithms for macromolecular systems that run entirely on a GPU. They achieved approximately 10 times speedup on a single GPU.

Mark et al. [10] implemented an all-atom protein MD running on GPU, optimized the Compute Unified Device Architecture (CUDA) codes to take full advantage of GPU, and achieved more than 700 times speedup. Kylasa et al. [11] presented an efficient and highly accurate GPU implementation of PuReMD, which is a package for MD. Their experiments showed up to 16 improvement in runtime compared with a single-core CPU. Zhang et al. [14] introduced a method to identify the performance bottleneck and presented an approach to port the time-costly procedure to a GPU. They discussed how to decrease the memory usage in GPU and how to improve the maintenance of MD simulations.

Recent works proposed numerous programming models on the basis of heterogeneous architectures mixing CPUs and GPUs [12, 13]. Stratton [15] described a framework called M-CUDA, which enables CUDA programs to be executed efficiently on shared memory, multicore CPUs. Linderman et al. [16] proposed the Merge framework, which is a general purpose programming model for heterogeneous multicore systems. The Merge framework replaces current ad hoc approaches to parallel programming on heterogeneous platforms with a rigorous, library-based methodology that can automatically distribute computation across heterogeneous cores to enhance energy and performance efficiency. Pennycook et al. [17] presented an analysis of a port of the NASLU benchmark to CUDA, the most stable GPU programming model currently available. Jacobsen et al. [18] pursued mixed MPI-CUDA implementations and investigated three strategies to examine the efficiency and scalability of incompressible flow computations. Brown et al. [8] implemented the MD process on hybrid high performance computers and described an approach for dynamic load balancing of work between CPU and accelerator cores.

These work achieved impressive speedups on heterogeneous platforms compared with CPU. However, most of the aforementioned research activities failed to achieve CPU-GPU hybrid computing when only one large task exists in the task pool. This condition results in significant waste of CPU computing resources. Brown et al. [8] tried to assign some computational tasks to CPU, but they didn't figure out the theoretical allocating relationship between CPU and GPU. Moreover, previous works did not consider the relationship between GPU number and CPU core number. In this study, we propose a heterogeneous hybrid parallel strategy based on MD simulations. This strategy uses a process scheduling scheme to take advantage of the CPU computing power and thus improve overall performance.

3   Background

3.1   Molecule Dynamics Simulation

In MD simulations, each molecule is considered as a point mass. Given the interaction potential between molecules, the force acting on each molecule can be calculated. The motion of a large number of molecules can be easily described on the basis of Newtons second law. From the motion of molecules, some useful information can be extracted. Such information includes transport coefficients and structural properties.

In MD simulations, the time evolution of a molecular system is followed by integrating the equations of motion described by the following classical equations:

$$\begin{cases} F_i = m_i a_i \\ F_i = -\nabla_{r_i} P(r_1, \ldots, r_N) \end{cases} \tag{1}$$

In Eq. (1), the molecular system contains N molecules, m_i is the molecule mass, a_i is equal to $d^2 r_i / dt^2$ which is the acceleration, F_i is the force acting upon the system, and $P(r_1, \ldots, r_N)$ stands for the potential functions of the atoms in the system. In fact, f can be written as Eq. (2).

$$P(r_1, \ldots r_N) = \sum_{i,j} \phi_2(r_i, r_j) + \sum_{i,j,k} \phi_3(r_i, r_j, r_k) + \cdots \tag{2}$$

$P(r_1, \ldots, r_N)$ includes two or more molecule interactions. However, the occurrence of three or more molecular interactions is ignored. Hence, $P(r_1, \ldots, r_N)$ can be approximated as Eq. (3) in the system.

$$P(r_1, \ldots r_N) \approx \sum_{i,j} \phi_2(r_i, r_j) \tag{3}$$

In Eqs. (2) and (3), φ denotes the Lennard-Jones (L-J) potential which is used to describe the energy of interaction between two molecules. The L-J potential is defined as Eq. (4).

$$\phi_2(r_i, r_j) = 4\varepsilon [(\frac{\delta}{dis(r_i, r_j)})^{12} - (\frac{\delta}{dis(r_i, r_j)})^6] \tag{4}$$

$$dis(r_i, r_j) \leq r_c$$

In Eq. (4), r_{ij} is the distance between molecules i and j, δ is the diameter of one of the molecules, ε is the potential well, and r_c is the cutoff radius.

In MD simulations, the computation of interaction forces is one of the most time-consuming tasks, usually taking more than 90 % of the total simulation time because the force computation requires the calculation of interactions between each molecule in the system with every other molecule. This condition gives rise to $O(N^2)$ evaluations of the interaction in each time step. The interaction forces decreases rapidly with increasing distance between molecules. Thus, the forces between molecules separated by more than a cutoff distance r_c can be neglected, as shown in Eq. (4). This condition suggests that a molecule only has interaction forces with atoms that are in a sphere with a radius equal to r_c. The cutoff method is also called the neighbor list method. This approach reduces computational complexity to $O(N)$. We must determine whether the particles are adjacent when using the cutoff method. Thus, a good algorithm for searching neighbor molecules is important as this algorithm directly influences simulation performance. The cell-list method is one such efficient algorithm.

The cell-list method divides the simulation space into cubic cells. The length of the cell edge is sometime no smaller than the cut-off radius, r_c. Given a particle p (the black particle in Fig. 1) and its cell C5, all particles within the r_c of p must be adjacent to C5. Each particle and cell has its own ID to distinguish itself from others.

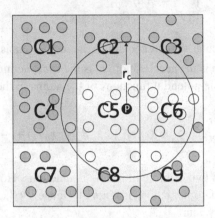

Fig. 1. 2-D cell-list structure.

Particle p only needs to check the distance with particles in neighbor cells. In fact, Newtons third law implies that only half of the neighbor cells are needed for the L-J force calculation, that is, only the white cells in Fig. 1 have to be checked.

Table 1 illustrates the pseudo code of the L-J force computation using the cell-list method. Cell neighbor lists must be updated before performing the computations.

Table 1. The cell-list method

1: *for each molecule i in cell c do*
2:    *for each cell d in c.neighbor_list do* 3:   *for each molecule j in cell d do* 4:   *i.force += Compute_force(i,j);* 5:   *j.force -= Compute_force(i,j);*
6:    *for each molecule k in cell c do* 7:   *if(k.id > i.id) do* 8:   *i.force += Compute_force(i,k);* 9:   *k.force -= Compute_force(i,k);*

3.2 CPU-GPU Heterogeneous Architecture

Quad-core (or more cores) CPU are the current mainstream. The availability of multiple core chips makes the CPU a powerful computing platform for general applications. With the increase in the number of cores, the CPU will have more powerful parallel computing capability. However, people gradually turn to GPU for support because isomorphic computers could not satisfy large-scale scientific computation requirements.

GPU was initially developed as a dedicated acceleration component to meet performance requirements for computer graphics and games. With the development of multicore CPU technology and the increasing requirement for graphics processing, GPU has become a multicore processing architecture for more general use and higher parallel computation, and its computing power and memory bandwidth simultaneously improved. For general GPU computations, the development and improvement of programming models or methods, such as NVidia's CUDA [2], Brook GPU [19], ATI Stream SDK [20], sh [21], and OpenCL [22], remarkably simplified GPU applications. For example, as an extension of the C language, CUDA, which represents programming models, enables users to develop it in ways similar to the C language and to control the interaction between CPU and GPU. This condition significantly improves the efficiency of the developed GPU application.

GPUs have two obvious characteristics. First is the exclusive use of computing resources. For example, if a computing task takes up a large amount of GPU resources, multiple computing tasks could not use the GPU at the same time, which results in a condition in which the GPU could only complete multiple tasks in a serial manner. Second is growing memory. All the data available to different kernels can be mapped to different locations of the memory, which makes parallel data distribution from different kernels possible. Figure 2 shows the CPU-GPU heterogeneous architecture with two CPUs and two GPUs. The CPUs and GPUs communicate via the I/O hub chipset and are connected to the I/O hub by Quick Path Interconnect Link and PCIE interface, respectively. Both CPUs and GPUs have their own memory.

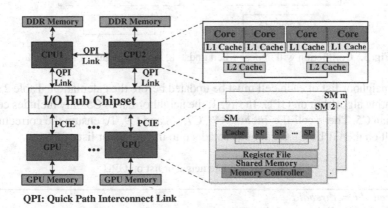

QPI: Quick Path Interconnect Link

Fig. 2. CPU–GPU heterogeneous architecture with two CPU chips and two GPUs.

4   MD Simulations on Heterogeneous Architecture

4.1   GPU-Based MD Simulation Algorithm

For Newton's third law, the force between two molecules i and j has to be calculated only once as shown in Table 1. Such force is commonly used in CPU implementation to minimize the computation by calculating the force between a pair of molecules once. However, on a GPU, the molecule i will be mapped to the ith thread, where as the molecule j will be mapped to the jth thread. If j is one of the neighbors of i, the ith and j^{th} threads may update molecule j's force at the same time as shown in Fig. 3. This condition results in write confliction. Therefore, the cell-list algorithm on the GPU should be modified.

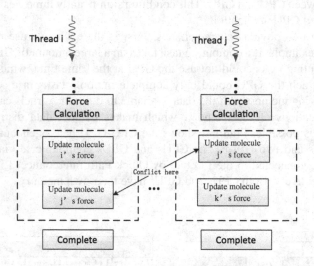

Fig. 3. Confliction will appear when updating the same value at the same time.

The neighbor list of each cell must be updated before the calculation. Table 2 shows the updating algorithm on GPU. In Fig. 1, the neighbor list of C5 only includes cell IDs larger than C5. These cell IDs include C6, C7, C8 and C9. To ensure the correctness of the result on the GPU, C1 C4 should be added to the neighbor list of C5.

Table 2.   Update neighbor list on GPU

1: *cell id c = threadId*
2: *for each cell d in c.neighbor_list do*
3:     *if d.id > c.id then do*
4:         *add c into d.neighbor_list*

The method will cause the neighbor list to become larger, such that more time will be consumed if the task is executed on a CPU, as shown in Table 3. The use of a GPU will result in improved performance and will yield a correct result.

Table 3. Cell-list method on GPU

1: *molecule id i = threadId*
2: *cell id c = i.parent_cell_id.*
3: *for each cell d in c.neighbor_list do*
4:     *for each molecule j in cell d do*
5:         *i.force += Compute_force(i,j);*
6: *for each molecule k in cell c do*
7:     *if k.id != i.id do*
8:         *i.force += Compute_force(i,k);*

4.2 CPU-GPU Hybrid Parallel Strategies

By taking advantage of the asynchronous feature of CUDA, the hybrid parallel strategy adopted the parallel intraprocess of the CPU and GPU for L-J force calculation. The characteristics of MPI process capability are likewise adopted to access the GPU serially to achieve the best performance by balancing the number of GPU processes.

For simplicity of discussion, MD simulation is divided into three parts, namely, preparation stage, L-J stage, and other calculation stage. Under actual conditions, the simulation is more complicated. After the L-J force calculation, the MPI processes have to perform synchronization operations because each process has to obtain the information on the molecules located in the other processes.

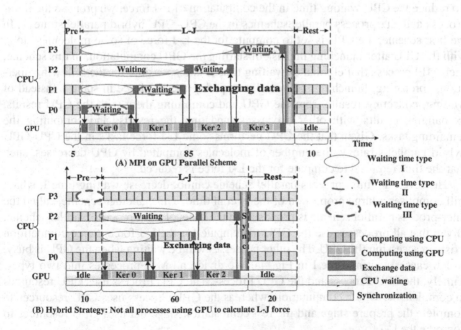

Fig. 4. Hybrid parallel scheme compared with general parallel scheme.

Three points have to be noted in the subsequent sections. First, MPI processes are generated by CPU cores, such that these processes are bound with these cores. Second, the computing tasks sent to the GPU by an MPI process are called kernels. Finally, the time noted in Fig. 4 is presented to explain the ratio of running time rather than the actual execution time.

4.3 General MPI-GPU Workload Assignment

The space-time diagram of the general MPI-GPU workload assignment is shown in Fig. 4a, where the x-axis represents the execution time of the application, and the y-axis stands for all MPI processes and GPU resources. In this work, the execution time of the L-J calculation based on the GPU is defined as 100 time units, and four MPI processes in the CPU are considered to operate in parallel as an example. Each MPI process is responsible for preparing the calculation, sending data and launching a kernel to the GPU, obtaining the results from the GPU, exchanging data with other MPI processes, and joining in the computations for the remaining tasks.

As shown in Fig. 4(a), CPUs and GPUs do not operate simultaneously. The CPUs only work in the first and third stages, whereas the GPUs only work in the second stage, during which all CPU cores are idle.

4.4 CPU-GPU Hybrid Workload Assignment

To reduce the CPU waiting time in the computation of L-J force, we propose the intra-process and interprocess parallel schemes in the CPU-GPU hybrid parallel strategy. In the first scheme, the CPU is set to compute for the L-J force of some molecules along with the GPU after launching the task of starting the GPU computation. In this scheme, each MPI process that eliminates waiting time II is responsible for the following operations: preparing, launching the kernel, computing the L-J force in stage 2 instead of waiting, collecting results from the GPU and combining them with the CPU results, exchanging results with other processes, updating the results, and computing the remaining tasks. Given that the CPU performs some L-J force tasks in the CPU-GPU hybrid parallel strategy, the number of molecules computed by GPU decreases, such that the time required to compute for the L-J force is reduced.

However, the intra-process parallel scheme cannot decrease waiting time I, which still comprises a large proportion of the overall time. Thus, another scheme, called the inter-process parallel scheme is proposed on the basis of intra-process parallel scheme. Given that all processes use the GPU to compute for the L-J force, fierce competition exists in accessing the GPU. The other processes will be waiting when the GPU is busy, which causes waiting time I in Fig. 4a. We divide all MPI processes into two types, namely, the CPU Process and the GPU Process. The CPU Process uses CPU resources to complete the whole computation, whereas the GPU Process uses CPU resources to complete the prepare stage and the rest computation stage but uses GPU resources to compute the L-J force.

Two aspects must be considered in reducing waiting time I in the inter-process parallel scheme. First, the process can slow down the competition for the GPU resource, thus reducing the competition time. Second, the number of CPU Processes increases, and the CPU processes share some computing tasks that originally belong to the GPU. Thus, the computing load of the GPU is reduced. Hence, the time required for the L-J force stage can be decreased. We will how much the time can be decreased in subsequent experiments. However, the reduction in the number of GPU Process also gives rise to some new problems. For example, given that the computing capability of GPU is stronger than that of CPU, we need to allocate more tasks to the GPU Process if we want . the CPU and GPU Process to complete the computing tasks concurrently in the L-J force stage. Thus, load imbalance will occur in the other two stages that do not need the GPU to participate in the computation, and the computing time of the GPU Processes in these two stages becomes greater than that of the CPU processes, thus producing new waiting time III.

Figure 4b shows that the performance will be optimized under three GPU Processes. Waiting time III is found to be larger than that shown in Fig. 4a, whereas waiting time I is smaller in the L-J force calculation. Overall, this strategy can achieve the best performance with the least waiting overhead.

Finally, the CPU Process will start the computation along with the GPU, which realizes a parallel heterogeneous architecture in two levels. The first level is the parallel inter-process between CPU and GPU processes, whereas the second level is the parallel heterogeneous GPU intra-process.

The difficulty of the process is that too few GPU processes will result in waiting overhead in the preparation stage and the remaining computations stage, whereas too many GPU processes can result in waiting overhead in the L-J force computation stage. Therefore, the number of GPU processes has to be justified to achieve the best overall GPU performance.

We consider the following information: the number of particles is N, the time spent in the L-J force computation (GPU acceleration part) is M times that in the other stages, and the number of MPI processes is Np. We suppose that x MPI processes will access the GPU with number L and computing capability that is k times that of the CPU. The following formula, which shows the relationship between the number of GPU processes x and the overall running time by derivation, can be obtained.

$$T(x, L) = \begin{cases} \frac{1+M}{Np}, & x = 0 \\ \frac{M*x+x*k}{x*(x*k+Np-x)}, & 0 < x \le L \\ \frac{\lceil \frac{x}{L} \rceil *(L*M)+L*k}{x*(L*k+Np-x)}, & x > L \end{cases} \tag{5}$$

The corresponding curve between the number of GPU Processes and the time when the number of GPUs L changes can be determined, as shown in Fig. 5.

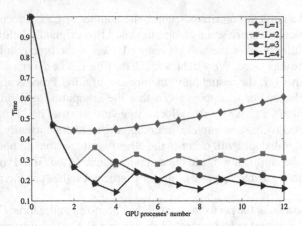

Fig. 5. The curves of execution time with the number of GPU processes.

In Fig. 5, the abscissa stands for the number of GPU processes started, the vertical axis represents the running time of the application, and L represents the number of GPUs. The four curves are obtained according to Eq. (5) by using MATLAB. The curve is smoother when $L = 1$. The time reaches the minimum when the number of GPU processes is equal to two. Thereafter, the time gradually decreases with the increase in the number of GPU processes. The other curves exhibit a saw-tooth shape accompanied by some fluctuations when $L = 2, 3, 4$.

5   Experimental Results

To exploit GPU capabilities for high-performance MD simulation, we present an algorithm for nonbonded short-range interactions within the molecule system. The algorithm is implemented by using C++ and CUDA in OpenFOAM, an object-oriented library for computational fluid dynamics and structural analysis [23]. The platform, used to test the performance of our hybrid parallel strategy, is composed of two CPUs of Intel Xeon X5675 series and one GPU of NVidia GTX580. The CPU has 3.06 GHz main frequency and 96 GB memory, whereas the GPU has 1.3 GHz main frequency, 6 GB GDDR5 RAM memory, and 144 GB/s bandwidth, as well as 448 CUDA cores. The operating system adopted in our experiment is the LinuxRedhat5.5, and the compiler is gcc-4.1.2; the CUDA version is 4.0

5.1   GPU Performance

To test the performance of the GPU-based MD algorithm, we select a data set with 110,000 H_2O molecules. The speedups of GPU-based MD are compared with those of CPU-based MD in Table 4.

Table 4. The relationship of GPU processes' number and the total time of MD

	1	2	3	4	5	6	Average
1-core(ms)	44950.4	44316.8	44555.6	44361.0	44391.2	44063.6	44439.8
4-cores(ms)	12754.9	12959.3	12971.8	12691.3	12548.0	12614.0	12756.5
12-cores(ms)	3991.37	4103.86	3991.32	3834.25	3802.4	3699.12	3903.72
GPU with 1 CPU core(ms)	3257.86	3164.47	3125.64	3118.63	3158.49	3162.45	3164.59
speedup	13.7975	14.0044	14.2548	14.2245	14.0545	13.9333	14.0449

5.2 Hybrid Parallel Strategy Performance

In this section, we discuss the performance of our hybrid parallel strategies. The total time of MD simulation when the number of GPU processes takes different values. To compare the theoretical and measured curves, we normalize both curves and draw them as shown in Fig. 6.

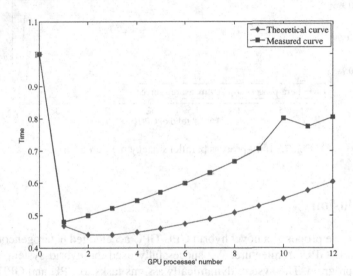

Fig. 6. The theoretical curve and the measured curve.

The measured and theoretical curves exhibit similar increasing and decreasing trends. The only difference is that the measured process will cause considerable uncertainty, which gives rise to some singular points. However, these points cannot affect the overall trend. The theoretical curve reaches the minimum point when the number of GPU processes is 2, whereas the measured curve reaches the minimum point when the number of GPU processes is equal to 1. This phenomenon can be attributed to the uncertainties in the experiment. Thus, a range of values, including a fixed value, is not recommended for use as the number of GPU processes. For example, when the theoretical minimum value is 2, we take the range from 1 to 3, which indicates that the curve may obtain the minimum value when the number of GPU processes falls into this range.

Figure 7 shows the result of intra-process parallel strategy. For simplicity, we fix the number of GPU processes to 12 and then use the intra-process parallel strategy. As can be seen from Fig. 7, the speedup of this strategy is only 1.0117 when the curve obtains the maximum value because waiting time II become short after processes launch a kernel to GPU, such that the ratio of tasks in the CPU becomes significantly smaller than that in the inter-process strategy.

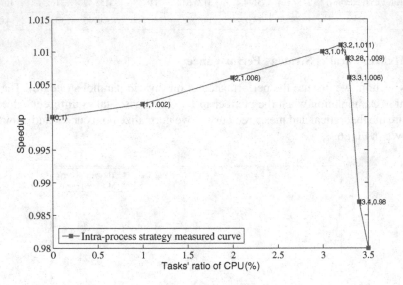

Fig. 7. Intra-process parallel strategy measured curve.

6   Conclusion

In this study, we proposed a novel hybrid CPU-GPU accelerated heterogeneous system based on CPU-GPU architecture. We successfully used the hybrid system in an MD simulation program. The system dynamically assigns tasks to CPU and GPU, realizes optimization on the basis of the version that has been accelerated on the GPU, and finally achieves efficient acceleration. The speedup of the hybrid parallel strategy reaches 15.24x when compared with a single-core CPU. Moreover, compared with that of the GPU process, performance is enhanced by 10.46 %. With the development of GPU and CPU technologies, the computing capability of CPUs and GPUs is significantly enhanced. Thus, the CPU-GPU hybrid system has become more popular for large-scale physical applications. Future research will focus on the acceleration advantages of the heterogeneous platform and will combine field programmable gate array and CPU with the GPU platform to explore further applications of the hybrid system to provide powerful support for performance improvement in physics.

Acknowledgement. This work is partially supported by NSFC (61125201).

References

1. Intel Xeon Phi Coprocessor. https://software.intel.com/zh-cn/mic-developer. Accessed March 2014
2. CUDATM 4.0 Programming Guide, NVIDIAR Corporation. http://www.nvidia.com (2011). Accessed November 2013
3. Salomon-Ferrer, R., Goetz, A.W., Poole, D., Le Grand, S., Walker, R.C.: Routine microsecond molecular dynamics simulations with AMBER - Part II: Particle Mesh Ewald (PME). J. Chem. Theory Comput. **9**, 3878–3888 (2013)
4. Brooks, B.R., Brooks III, C.L., Mackerell, A.D., Nilsson, L., Petrella, R.J., Roux, B., Won, Y., Archontis, G., Bartels, C., Boresch, S., Caflisch, A., Caves, L., Cui, Q., Dinner, A.R., Feig, M., Fischer, S., Gao, J., Hodoscek, M., Im, W., Kuczera, K., Lazaridis, T., Ma, J., Ovchinnikov, V., Paci, E., Pastor, R.W., Post, C.B., Pu, J.Z., Schaefer, M., Tidor, B., Venable, R.M., Woodcock, H.L., Wu, X., Yang, W., York, D.M., Karplus, M.: CHARMM: the biomolecular simulation program. J. Comp. Chem. **30**, 1545–1615 (2009)
5. Lindahl, E., van der Spoel, D., Hess, B., et. al.: http://www.gromacs.org/GPU_acceleration
6. LAMMPS Molecular Dynamics Simulator. http://lammps.sandia.gov/
7. Rodrigues, C.I., Hardy, D.J., Stone, J.E.: GPU acceleration of cutoff pair potentials for molecular modeling applications. In: CF 2008 Proceedings of the 5th Conference on Computing Frontiers, vol. 32, no. 4, pp. 273–282. ACM, New York, NY, USA (2008)
8. Brown, W.M., Wang, P., Plimpton, S.J., Tharrington, A.N.: Implementing molecular dynamics on hybrid high performance computers – short range forces. Comput. Phys. Commun. **182**(4), 898–911 (2011)
9. Xu, J., Ren, Y., Ge, W., Yu, X., Yang, X., Li, J.: Molecular dynamics simulation of macromolecules using graphics processing unit. Comput. Phys. Commun. **182**(4), 921–942 (2011)
10. Friedrichs, M.S., Eastman, P., Vaidyanathan, V., Houston, M.: Accelerating Molecular Dynamic Simulation on Graphics Processing Units, Wiley Inter Science. www.interscience.wiley.com (2009)
11. Kylasa, S.B., Aktulga, H.M., Grama, A.Y.: PuReMD-GPU: a reactive molecular dynamic simulation package for GPUs. J. Comput. Phys. **272**(1), 343–359 (2014)
12. Wu, Q., Yang, C., Tang, T., Xiao, L.: Exploiting hierarchy parallelism for molecular dynamics on a petascale heterogeneous system. J. Parallel Distrib. Comput. **73**(12), 1592–1604 (2013)
13. Yang, C., Wu, Q., Tang, T., Wang, F., Xue, J.: Programming for scientific computing on peta-scale heterogeneous parallel systems. J. Cent. South Univ. Technol. **20**, 1189–1203 (2013)
14. Zhang, X., Guo, W., Qin, X., Zhao, X.: A highly extensible frame- work for molecule dynamic simulation on GPUs. In: The 2013 International Conference on Parallel and Distributed, Processing Techniques and Applications (PDPTA 2013) (2013)
15. Hwu, W.W., Stratton, J.A., Stone, S.S.: MCUDA: an efficient implementation of CUDA kernels for multi-core CPUs. In: Amaral, J.N. (ed.) LCPC 2008. LNCS, vol. 5335, pp. 16–30. Springer, Heidelberg (2008)
16. Linderman, M.D., Collins, J.D., Wang, H., Meng, T.H.: Merge: a programming model for heterogeneous multi-core systems. ACM SIGARCH Comput. Archit. News- ASPLOS **36**, 287–296 (2008)
17. Pennycook, S.J., Hammond, S.D., Jarvis, S.A., Mudalige, G.R.: Performance analysis of a hybrid MPI/CUDA implementation of the NAS-LU benchmark. In: ACM SIG- METRICS Performance Evaluation Review Special Issue on the 1st International Workshop on Performance Modeling, Benchmarking and Simulation of High Performance Computing Systems (PMBS 2010), vol. 38, no. 4, pp. 23–29. ACM, New York, NY, USA (2011)

18. Jacobsen, D.A., Thibault, J.C., Senocak, I.: An MPI-CUDA implementation for massively parallel incompressible flow computations on multi-GPU clusters. In: 48th AIAA Aerospace Sciences Meeting and Exhibit, pp. 1–16, Orlando, Florida (2010)
19. Buck, I., Foley, T., Horn, D., Sugerman, J., Fatahalian, K., Houston, M., Hanrahan, P.: Brook for GPUs: stream computing on graphics hardware. ACM Trans. Graph. **23**, 777–786 (2004)
20. Technical Overview ATI Stream Computing. http://developer.amd.com/gpuassets/StreamComputingOverview.pdf (2009). Accessed November 2011
21. Cool, M.M., Toit, S.D.: Metaprogramming GPUs with Sh (2004)
22. Khronos Group. OpenCL. http://www.khronos.org/opencl/ (2008)
23. Openfoam: The Open Source CFD Toolbox, userguide. http://www.openfoam.org. Accessed August 2010

A Cloud Server Based on I/O Virtualization in Hardware

Yang You[1(✉)], Gongbo Li[2,3], Xiaojun Yang[4], Bowen Qi[5], and Bingzhang Wang[6]

[1] The PLA Information Engineering University, Zhengzhou 450002, People's Republic of China
bjyouyang@163.com
[2] Institute of Computing Technology, Chinese Academy of Sciences,
Beijing 100190, People's Republic of China
[3] University of Chinese Academy of Science, Beijing 100190, People's Republic of China
[4] Dawning Information Industry Co., Ltd., Beijing 100193, People's Republic of China
[5] School of Computer and Communication Engineering, University of Science and Technology
Beijing, Beijing 100083, People's Republic of China
[6] School of Electronics and Information, Northwestern Polytechnical University, Xi'an 710129,
People's Republic of China

Abstract. With the advent of Internet services and big data, cloud computing has generated much research interest, especially on cloud servers. In view of the development of lightweight server processors, i.e., x86 single-chip processors and ARM64 processors, and the high-performance interconnect fabric, an approach building a cloud server on top of virtualized I/O is presented in this paper. Its advantage is to provide high performance/cost, performance/Watt, high-density and high scalability compared with the existing method, to better meet the demands of cloud computing.

Keywords: Cloud server · Cloud computing · I/O virtualization · Virtualized storage · Virtualized network

1 Introduction

Cloud servers, also known as warehouse-scale computers and datacenter computers [1], are widely used for Internet services, big data applications and cloud computing, and are the target of increasing research interest. The workloads and performance requirements for cloud servers are often different from those of high-performance computing (HPC). The recent objective of the latter is to sustain exascale (10^{18}) floating-point operations per second (flops) on workloads such as large-scale matrix calculations [2].

A typical application scenario of a cloud server is illustrated in Fig. 1. Many user devices and/or physical object devices (PCs, smart phones, sensors nodes, etc.) interact with the cloud by issuing computing commands to the cloud. The cloud consists of various networks (e.g., the Internet, the mobile Web, Internet of Things) connecting the client devices to a cloud server. The commands reach the cloud server and are processed. Command processing forms the workloads of the cloud server.

© Springer-Verlag Berlin Heidelberg 2016
W. Xu et al. (Eds.): NCCET 2015, CCIS 592, pp. 133–144, 2016.
DOI: 10.1007/978-3-662-49283-3_13

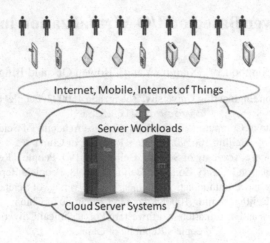

Fig. 1. A typical cloud server application scenario

The growth in cloud leads to growth in servers in datacenter and new requirements for servers. Cloud computing is redefining traditional servers. We are targeting the research and implementation of a new server to be used in datacenter in future, which can meet the above requirements coming from datacenter better, e.g. high density, high performance/cost and performance/Watt. Although much work has been done on processor and cloud server research and many cloud server systems are in production use, the basic high density, high performance/cost and high performance/Watt questions are still not satisfactorily answered.

The remainder of the paper is organized as follows. Section 2 briefly introduces the research background. Section 3 details the cloud server architecture. A prototype system and its performance evaluation are discussed in Sect. 4. Finally, Sect. 5 concludes the paper.

2 Background

In this section, the background technology and motivation are introduced.

2.1 Processor Technology Overview

In the cloud server market, Intel has introduced lower-powered versions of its traditional server chips, as well as a "server-grade" version of the Atom chip. However, the ARM-based chips that dominate mobile phones and tablets are also making a play for the datacenter, and workloads that are targeted at cloud servers seem perfect for ARM designs. No matter Atom or ARM, they are designed specifically for cloud server, with the common features such as low power, higher physical density, Single-chip BGA solution integrated I/O.

In December 2012, Intel launched the 64-bit Centerton family of Atom processors, designed specifically for use in servers. Centerton adds features previously unavailable in Atom processors, such as Intel VT virtualization technology and support for ECC memory. On 4 September 2013 Intel launched a 22 nm successor to Centerton, code-named Avoton. Moreover, Intel is developing the next-generation single-chip processor named Broadwell-DE for the future of cloud server systems.

ARM is a family of instruction set architectures for computer processors based on a reduced instruction set computing (RISC) architecture developed by British company ARM Holdings. A RISC-based computer design approach means ARM processors require significantly fewer transistors than typical CISC x86 processors in most personal computers. This approach reduces costs, heat and power use. A simpler design facilitates more efficient multi-core processors and higher core counts at lower cost, providing improved energy efficiency for servers. At present, 64-bit ARM Processors are ready for cloud server development today, and are working closely with ecosystem partners for OS, Hypervisor, JDK and application stacks.

Processors are playing an important role in the cloud server system as soon as high-performance processors for HPC systems. They can make cloud server more high density, high performance/cost and performance/Watt compared with the high-performance processors, i.e., AMD Opteron, Intel Xeon E5, and Intel Xeon E7. Of cause, some non single-chip processers also can be used into cloud server system to meet the needs of some special workloads better such as Intel Xeon E3, AMD APU, Nvidia GPU and Intel Xeon Phi coprocessor. Their own the best single threaded performance, integrated graphics, socket flexibility.

2.2 Cloud Server Technology Overview

The traditional server systems are cluster of server nodes the dedicated local storage and connected over an Ethernet network as Fig. 2 shown. These server nodes use their directed-attached-storage as scratch/swap space and use a storage server on the Ethernet network for primary storage.

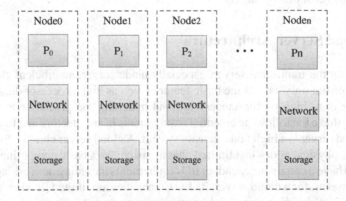

Fig. 2. The traditional server systems

In the cloud era, on one hand, optimized TCO, compute efficiency, and fastest growing server segment will grow to dominate the server. On the other hand, cloud deployment models, big data analytics, and datacenter virtualization are driving highly evolving paral-lelized workloads. The cloud server in large scale datacenter requires high performance/cost and high performance/Watt [3]. Furthermore, Rapid growth in dense compute shows dense compute clusters is future of volume servers for cloud computing [4].

Facebook and others have largely proven that a giant farm of cloud servers or a similar technology is the best way to handle millions of concurrent web requests. In 2013, cloud servers were widely hyped as the future of the datacenter. Increased demand for scalable computing led companies like HP to allocate resources to building servers for specific applications. HP announced their first Moonshot microserver with an Intel Atom processor in April 2013 [5]. AMD SeaMicro SM15000 Fabric Compute System brings together compute, networking, and storage in an energy efficient system with offering based on AMD Opteron, Intel Atom, and Intel Xeon E3 for unparalleled density and flexibility [6]. AMD SeaMicro SM15000 Fabric Compute System and HP Moonshot System are representative two cloud server systems for cloud computing.

2.3   Motivation

Our goal is to propose a SoC-based cloud server based on I/O virtualization for cloud computing to achieve high density, high performance/cost and high performance/Watt. The research focuses on the server inter-system interconnect fabric used to construct a resource pool, and hardware-based I/O virtualization used to share network and storage.

The cloud server will be a new density option for datacenters. It consists of many small, 1-socket nodes sharing a chassis, fans, power supplies and interconnection to achieve higher efficiency and density. Dedicated hosting, web serving, content delivery and gaming are the typical workloads of cloud computing. These workloads need a scale with physical nodes architecture, whose parallel software benefits most from more indi-vidual servers with sufficient I/O between nodes. For the field of scale with physical nodes, cloud servers have more opportunities. Cloud servers hit unique density, perform-ance, rack, and cost design targets.

3   A Cloud Server Architecture

Different from the traditional server, especially blade server, an efficient cloud server system should not only have some basic features such as high processor densities, high performance/cost, high performance/Watt, and matching the processor to workloads well, but also have the following essential requirements in architecture and functionality.

The cloud server is a high node-density system. A cloud server chassis, for example, houses more physical nodes in a limited chassis space. As a basic computing unit, each node should have a certain independent I/O requirements including networking and local storage. However, for a cloud server, its I/O capabilities are limited. In view of cost and chassis space, all inside nodes should share the server's network uplink resource and the limited local storage resource, rather than have exclusive uplink and HDD/SSD. Generally, for a typical cloud server, it only has one or two uplinks and several HDDs/SSDs.

Here, an I/O virtualization in hardware-level scheme is proposed to not only solve the above mentioned question, but also improve the utilization of server I/O resource because of the realization of shared network and shared storage. As Fig. 3 shown, the I/O resource distributed to each processor is logical I/O resource, not physical resource. The virtualization is done in hardware, so any processor is not aware enough of the fact that its I/O resource has been virtualized. I/O virtualization in hardware-level ensures the compatibility of OS, driver, and application software.

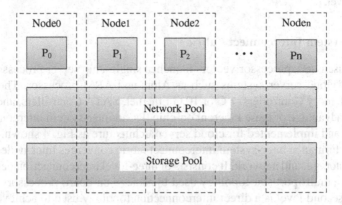

Fig. 3. I/O virtualization in hardware-level

According to the above discussion and proposal in cloud server architecture, some design schemes are detailed here, including distributed I/O sharing architecture, virtualized network and storage.

3.1   Distributed I/O Virtualization Architecture

Different from some existing cloud server architecture, i.e., the traditional cluster architecture as Fig. 2 shown, and the SeaMicro's centralized I/O virtualization architecture, Fig. 4 shows a distributed I/O virtualization architecture here.

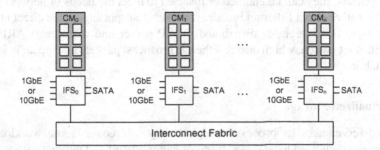

Fig. 4. A distributed I/O virtualization architecture

Cloud server I/O resource, i.e., network and storage, are distributed to inner nodes of the server. In other words, there are not independent network and storage units for the server. Processers can share their local I/O symmetrically, and also share the remote I/O through a cluster-wide extended bus. This cluster-wide extended bus is called an interconnect fabric, which has on each physical node an interconnect fabric switch (IFS). The high performance interconnect fabric strongly supports the share mechanism of cloud servers, and to improve the remote I/O access performance. The distributed I/O sharing architecture not only ensures cloud server maximum efficiency under minimal standard capacity, but also effectively breaks the I/O bottleneck under virtualization in hardware-level.

3.2   Inter-system Interconnect Fabric

As Sect. 2 discussed, processor vectors launched single-chip server processors to meet the needs of cloud server systems such as Atom and ARM processor. The processer integrates Memory Controllers, 1 G or 10 G Ethernet, SATA Controllers, and PCIe IPs. To take full advantage of these inherent on-chip IPs, an inter-system interconnect fabric is presented and implemented for cloud server architecture as Fig. 4 shown.

High-performance inter-system interconnect fabric converges inter-node communication, I/O, storage, and network. It consists of three-level interconnection network. The first level is a multi-port star topology used to achieve on-board processors communication. The second level is a direct interconnection topology used to achieve off-board processors communication. The third level is fat-tree topology used to achieve off-chassis processors communication. High-bandwidth fabric ensures the distributed I/O virtualization mechanism implementation for efficient cloud server systems.

3.3   Virtualized Network

Virtualized networking means Ethernet over a high-performance inter-system interconnect fabric based on a customized protocol, by which Ethernet packets can be efficiently transported from one node to another node, and each node can share the enabled Ethernet uplinks of cloud server to communicate with the outside Ethernet devices, e.g., server, switch or router. Ethernet uplinks are distributed in every IFS as Fig. 4 shown. According to the workloads, they can be enabled or disabled to meet the needs of networking.

To efficiently restrict Ethernet broadcast packets transporting on the direct interconnect topology, IFS integrates distributed DHCP server and distributed ARP proxy besides Ethernet switch, which ensure Ethernet broadcast packets not appear in its interconnect fabric.

3.4   Virtualized Storage

The cloud server asks its processors high-density. Moreover, some workloads ask processor own dedicated local disks. It seems more difficult and unpractical for a cloud server to configure one processor with one disk in a space-limited chassis [7]. In order to save disk space, share storage resource with multiple processors, a virtualized storage fabric in hardware-level is proposed as Fig. 4 shown. Virtualized storage means HDD/SSD as one storage pool of cloud server can be shared with all of processors in the cloud server system. Unlike legacy servers, in which a disk is unalterably bound to a processor, the virtualized storage architecture is far more flexible, allowing for much more efficient disk use. Any disk can mount any processor. Moreover, the virtualized storage architecture allows disks to be carved into slices called virtual disks. A virtual disk can be as large as a physical disk or it can be a slice of a physical disk. A single physical disk can be partitioned into multiple virtual disks, and each virtual disk can be allocated to a different processor. Conversely, a single virtual disk can be shared across multiple processors in read-only mode, providing a large shared data cache. Sharing of a virtual disk enables users to store or update common data, such as operating systems, application software, and data cache, once for an entire system.

4   Implementation and Evaluation

A prototyping cloud server system with 64 processors had been implemented to evaluate the architecture presented in this paper, and to validate some key technologies such as high-performance inter-system interconnect fabric and its IFS, virtualized storage, and virtualized network.

4.1   Cloud Server Prototyping System

Figure 5 shows the 64-processor cloud server prototyping system architecture, which is compatible with the features of distributed I/O virtualization architecture. The server hardware resource can be pooled and used according to the different workloads.

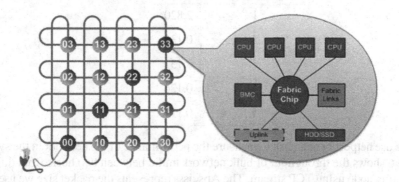

Fig. 5. A 64-processor cloud server prototyping system

The processor is Intel Pentium G2100T @ 2.6 GHz. The memory capacity of each processor is 8 GB. The FPGA used as IFS is Altera Stratix V S5GXMA7N40C2 [19]. The network is 1 G Ethernet, the uplink is 10 G Ethernet, and the SATA is compatible with SATAII spec. The inter-system interconnects is 2-lane. The link data rate is 10 Gbps per direction. The routing algorithm for the 4×4 2D torus Interconnects is the shortest path based adaptive routing algorithm.

4.2 Performance Evaluation

In this section, we evaluating the shared networking and shared storage performance for the developed cloud prototyping system.

(1) Shared Networking

We have built a prototype of the cloud server system as shown in Fig. 5. As it is just a prototype, we only choose IFS_00, IFS_11, IFS_22 and IFS_33 as shown in Fig. 10 to be full compute systems which contain processors, memory and hard disk drives. Others which only have FPGAs are just responsible for the routing of the 2D torus interconnect fabric. We configure IFS_00 to be an uplink whose bandwidth is 10 Gbps.

We have 16 hosts (processors) in the system and each IFS has 4 hosts. We number them from 0 to 15 and 0 to 3 belong to IFS_00, 4 to 7 belong to IFS_11 and so on. We can use host0 in IFS_00 to ping host15 in IFS_33. The Round-Trip Time (RTT) sequences of the ping command are shown in Table 1. From the Table we can see that the RTT of the first ICMP message is much longer than the subsequence. The reason is that the first RTT contains the time of the ARP request and reply from the ARP proxy in the IFS. The subsequent RTT just contain the time of the ICMP echo request and echo reply after the local ARP cached table being updated.

Table 1. The RTT of ping command

icmp_seq	RTT (ms)
1	2.820
2	0.135
3	0.151
4	0.136
5	0.115

We use netperf benchmark to measure the performance of the network in the system. Figure 6 shows the throughput of bulk network traffic between two hosts from different computing node using TCP stream. The Abscissa represents the packet size we used and the Ordinate is the throughput. When the two hosts communicate with each other, they need go across the 2D torus interconnection network, and the results using different packet size are approximately 109 MB/s. They are close to the theoretical peak of the Gigabit Ethernet.

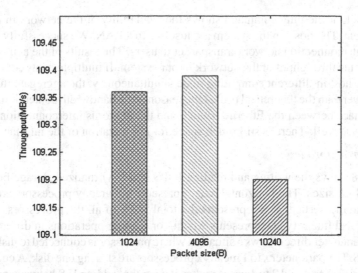

Fig. 6. The throughput between hosts in the different computing node across the 2D torus interconnection network

We also use 4 different hosts as clients to communicate with a host as a server simultaneously as shown in Fig. 7. The aggregate throughput of bulk network traffic using TCP stream of the 4 hosts is approximately 75 MB/s which is much lower than the theoretical peak of the Gigabit Ethernet.

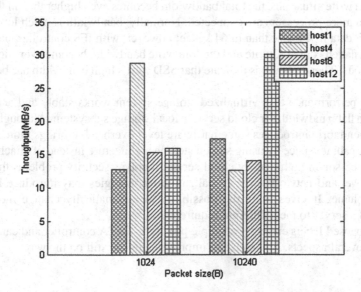

Fig. 7. The throughput of four different host communicate with another one simultaneously

The result of the ping command shows the availability of the network in the cloud server system. The hosts in the system are just like in a LAN. We successfully make the 2D torus interconnection network transparent to users. The results of the netperf benchmark show the throughput of the network in our system. If multiple hosts communicate in the same host in different computing node simultaneously, the aggregate throughput is much lower than the theoretical peak. One reason is the bandwidth contention. Another is the interface between the Ethernet switch and the 2D torus interconnection network works not that well. There is still much space for optimization of the interface.

(2) Shared Storage

Figure 8 shows the writing and reading IOPS of this virtualized storage fabric with different block sizes. The horizontal axis represents how many processors are sharing the disk and the vertical axis represents the total IOPS of all the processors. Different line colour and linear types represents writing or reading operations in different block size. The parameter direct shows a situation where processor is connected to disk directly without IFS. The parameter x to 1 means x processors are sharing one disk. A comparison between direct, 1 to 1 and 2 to 1 cases makes it clear that adding IFS between processors and disk introduces latency and results in an IOPS decrease. But when two processors share one SSD at the same time, the total IOPS almost doubled in 4 k rand read, 4 k rand write and 4 k write cases. When three or more processors share one SSD, IOPS trend lines increase gently because of the bottleneck of SSD and IFS latency.

Moreover, Fig. 8 reports the total access bandwidth of this virtualized storage fabric. From this figure we can see: for 4 k read and random read cases the bandwidth doesn't change much whether IFS is used. The bandwidth of 64 K reading and writing only decreases in the 1 to 1 occasion because of the latency introduced by IFS. In 4 k write and random write situations, the total bandwidth becomes even higher than in the direct mode when more processors are connected. Normally, bandwidth is much lower when we transmit data in 4 k size than in 64 k size; however, with IFS controller, bandwidth fluctuation flattens out. 4 K write and random write bandwidth become even higher than in direct mode. These situations indicate that SSD card's high bandwidth has been fully used.

During performance test, virtualized storage system works stably and accurately, providing a flat bandwidth for cloud server's local storage subsystem. Although storage virtualization fabric introduces some hardware level overhead, it brings more benefits. It saves the cabinet space by using shared storage architecture instead of attaching disk to each processor in high-density cloud server. It solves security problems that many software level and network level virtualization technologies may introduce by using Private Volume. It gives users the possibility to automatically change the storage capacity of a server to meet different requirements.

The proposed IFS is currently a simple prototype SATA controller and can be optimized in several aspects. Research and improvements are still on the way.

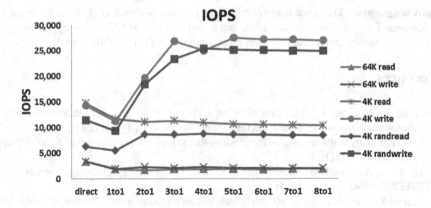

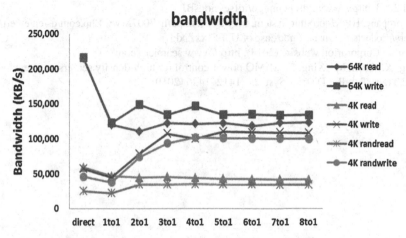

Fig. 8. Shared storage fabric's IOPS and bandwidth

5   Conclusion

To better meet the demands of cloud computing, a distributed I/O virtualization cloud server architecture is proposed here. A FPGA-based system controller integrated shared network, shared storage, and IFS is designed and implemented to connect a set of lightweight processors for building a high-density cloud server. All the processors can share the networking and storage resources through the interconnect fabric. On the 64-processer prototyping system, the result of evaluation experiments shows the cloud server not only keeps traditional cluster advantages such as the compatibility with OS and SW, but also gives the better scalability and performance for workloads.

Acknowledgments. The work is supported in part by the National High-Tech Research and Development Plan of China under grant numbered 2013AA01A209, and by Beijing City Committee of science and technology plan project numbered D141100003414001.

References

1. Barroso, L., Hoelzle, U.: The datacenter as a computer: an introduction to the design of warehouse-scale machines. Synth. Lect. Comput. Archit. **4**(1), 1–108 (2009)
2. Xu, Z.: How many watts are needed for a billion-thread high-throughput server. Front. Comput. Sci. **6**, 339–346 (2012)
3. Raza, M.A., Azeemuddin, S.: Multiprocessing on FPGA using light weight processor. In: CONECCT 2014, pp. 1–6 (2014)
4. Kulkarni, R.: Microservers: target workloads and architecture trends. Technical report, Intel, April 2013. http://www.intel.com/go/idfsessionsBJ
5. HP Company. HP MoonShot System, May 2014. http://h17007.www1.hp.com/us/en/enterprise/servers/products/moonshot/index.aspx#.U3F51xxZpdg
6. Seamicro Corporation website (2014). http://www.seamicro.com
7. Wang, X., Chen, M., Xing, F.: MIMO power control for high-density servers in an enclosure. IEEE Trans. Parallel Distrib. Syst. **21**, 1412–1426 (2010)

The Evolution of Supercomputer Architecture: A Historical Perspective

Bao Li[✉] and Pingjing Lu

School of Computer, National University of Defense Technology,
Changsha 410073, China
{baoli,pingjinglu}@nudt.edu.cn

Abstract. Approaches to supercomputer architecture have taken dramatic turns since the earliest supercomputer systems were introduced in the 1960s. Massively Parallel Processor keeps losing its rank in the fastest computer list. Cluster's rank and share in the TOP500 list has been steadily rising at a tremendous speed. Perspectives are given on how supercomputers have evolved thru time. The architectures are presented in chronological order. And finally, the trend of current supercomputer architecture design is analyzed.

Keywords: Supercomputer architecture · Cluster · MPP · SMP

1 Introduction

Since the advent of CDC6600, a computer designed by Seymour Cray at Control Data Corporation (CDC) and released in 1964 to be the first supercomputer, supercomputers have developed rapidly. Supercomputers of today are the general purpose computers of tomorrow. Supercomputer architecture is constantly evolving as well. According to TOP500 [1] classification, the current architectures of supercomputers include: cluster, Massively Parallel Processor (MPP), Constellations, Symmetric Multiprocessor, (SMP), Single-Instruction Multiple-Data (SIMD), and Parallel Vector Processor (PVP). Among them, cluster has gradually become the mainstream supercomputer architecture. In the high-performance computer TOP500 rankings, both the system share and performance share of supercomputers with cluster architecture are steadily rising at a tremendous speed.

Most SIMD computers are dedicated, and the others belong to Multiple Instruction Multiple Data (MIMD) computer. The vast majority of modern supercomputers use commodity hardware configuration, but many components of PVP supercomputers are custom designed.

This literature survey report explores and compares the architecture of these top-performance supercomputers, Perspectives are given on how supercomputers have evolved thru time. The architectures are presented in chronological order. And finally, the trend of current supercomputer architecture design is analyzed.

© Springer-Verlag Berlin Heidelberg 2016
W. Xu et al. (Eds.): NCCET 2015, CCIS 592, pp. 145–153, 2016.
DOI: 10.1007/978-3-662-49283-3_14

2   A Brief History of Supercomputer Architecture Evolution

2.1   Embryonic Stage of Supercomputers (1964–1975)

Representative supercomputers of embryonic stage include CDC6000 [2] invented in 1964, ASC and STAR-100 vector machines during early 1970s, Illiac- parallel machine in 1974 [3]. CDC6600 invented in 1964 with computing speed of 1Mflops is recognized as the world's first supercomputer. CDC6600 provides a non-symmetrical shared storage configuration, the central processor is connected to a plurality of external processors, but also uses dual CPUs. STAR-100 is the world's first vector machine, due to the long development cycle, the techniques adopted by STAR-100 such as magnetic core memory, have been lagging behind the development of techniques. Therefore, STAR-100 was not put to the market when it was completed. Although Amdahl's law [4] presented in 1967 questioned the theory that achieve performance accelerated through increasing the processor, but in 1972 the University of Illinois and Burroughs undertook the task to jointly developed Illiac- SIMD computers based on earlier work of Solomon 64 processor, and finally completed the world's first SIMD array system–Illiac- in 1974 [4]. Illiac- originally planned to include four quadrants of 256 arithmetic units, however, it only installed a quadrant and cut back to 64 arithmetic units in fact, due to its programming mode is quite different from state-of-art supercomputers, the programmer have to consider how to accommodate the problem scale to the scale of computers, and its stability was poor, so Illiac- has not been promoted [3].

2.2   Development and Peak Stage of Vector Processors (1976–1990)

In 1976, Cray Company produced the first vector processors: Cray-1 [5], which uses vector instructions and the vector registers and fast CPU and main memory are closely coupled, their performance was higher than the scalar system an order of magnitude [6]. Moreover, although Illiac- had been successfully developed in 1972, which is today the undisputed MPP ancestors, the international community generally named 1976 when Cray-1 was invented as "supercomputing first year", and "supercomputer" connotes a Cray-1.

The Cray-1 was the fastest computer from 1976 to 1981. After the advent of Cray-1, vector computers have firmly controlled the entire high-performance computer market for 15 years. By the 1980s, the emergence of parallel vector processor (PVP), further improve the processing speed through parallel processing. PVP inherit the advantages of vector computers with mature technique and high efficiency, and the interconnection network routers can easily inserted in PVP, which fertilizes the combination optimization of various designs. PVP system contains a small amount of custom designed high performance vector processors (VP), each having at least 1Gflops processing capabilities. The system uses a specially designed high-bandwidth crossbar network which connects VP to the shared memory modules, and therefore memory can provide data to the processor with the speed of several megabytes per second. Such PVP machines typically do not use Cache, but use a large number of vector registers and the instruction buffer.

People continue to introduce new PVP vector computers, including the CDC's Cyber205, Fujitsu's VP1000/VP2000, NEC's SX1/SX2 and China's YH-1 and so on. PVP has almost become synonymous with supercomputer. The development trends of PVP include increasing the speed of a single processor and researching multi-processor systems (such as Cray X-MP). By the late 1980s, Cray 2/Cray 3 launched one after the other, and with the emergence of standard UNIX operating systems and vector compilers, more and more software vendors can port their applications to Cray systems, making Cray vector series PVP machines have been successful almost in many fields of applications [6]. PVP which were typically represented by Cray vector machines, dominated the supercomputer industry more than ten years.

Vector processors are very favorable to increase computing speed, to help make full use of the pipeline and multi-functional components, but because of the clock cycle is close to the physical limit, the further development of vector processors is already impossible. By the early 1990s, due to the speed limitations of physical devices of PVP vector processors, Cray-3 has been difficult to produce until the company merged SGI, Cray, from then PVP vector computers were no longer mainstream supercomputers [6].

2.3 The Emergence and Rising Stage of MPP (1990–1995)

Since 1990s, MPP system get rid of the stagnant situation over the years, and gradually revealed the trend to replace and transcend PVP system.

MPP generally refers Very Large-Scale computer system. MPP supercomputer is evolved from SIMD array machine, which followed the network topology of SIMD array machines, but made fundamental improvements on the control mode, communication mode, communication mechanisms, communication bandwidth, communication speed and operating system, and etc. MPP uses many processors with its own memory, running in parallel and linked with high-speed buses in the motherboard. All MPP systems use physically distributed memory, and many use the distributed I/O. The main application of MPP is to calculate the computing-dominated fields of scientific computing, engineering simulation and signal processing. Intel Paragon, IBM SP2, Intel TFLOPS and Dawning 1000, are all MPP systems [7].

Now MPP systems constructed using cluster method are usually classified as a separate category, and are generally named as Cluster supercomputers, such as IBM SP2, Dawning 1000 A system, and Dawning 2000 system.

2.4 The Coexisting Phase of a Variety of Architectures (PVP, MPP, SMP, Constellation, Cluster) (1995–2002)

From 1995 onwards, MPP system continues to see solid growth in the possession of the world's top 500 fastest computers; and its performance has been further improved, for example, the theoretical peak speed of ASCI Red has reached

1Tflops; meanwhile PVP vector computers manufacturers introduced the SX-4 and VPP700 and their theoretical peak speed have reached 1Tflops [6].

At the same time, since 1994, symmetric multi-processor (SMP) has been widely welcomed by industry users, due to the relatively mature development and excellent cost/performance ratio. SMP system uses commodity microprocessor (with on-chip or an external cache), which is connected to the shared memory via a high-speed bus (or crossbar). SMP architecture has the following characteristics: symmetry, a single address space, and cache coherence, and low communication latency. This machine is mainly used in business, such as databases, online transaction processing systems and data warehouses. What is the most important is that the system is symmetrical, and each processor can equivalently access shared memory, I/O devices and the operating system services. Because it is symmetrical, it can develop a high degree of parallelism; and also its shared memory restrict that the SMP system can't compose too many processors (typically less than 64), and meanwhile the bus and crossbar interconnect is also difficult to expand once finalized. IBM R5O, SGI Power Challenge, and DEC Alpha Server 8400 are all SMP systems. During mid-1990s, due to better cost/performance ratio, SMP replaced MPP in the medium and low supercomputer market.

NUMA (Non-Uniform Memory Access) machine is a natural extension of the SMP system, CC-NUMA (Coherent Cache NUMA) is actually a Distributed Shared Memory (DSM) system by connecting together some SMP as a single node. The most significant advantage of CC-NUMA architecture is that the programmer does not need to explicitly allocate data on the node, hardware and software of systems automatically assign data at each node in the beginning, while the application is running, and cache coherency hardware automatically transfer the data to the place where it is required. In October 1996, SGI launched Origin 2000 supercomputer system, which uses a CC-NUMA architecture.

Since 1998, there has been a trend of the combination of SMP systems and MPP system, which is actually DSM. DSM is a natural combination of SMP and MPP, the building blocks of a single SMP system connected to each other to form a new cluster system, and cache directory DIR can support distributed cache coherency. The main difference between DSM and SMP are: DSM have physically distributed local memory in each node which forms a shared memory. For the users, system hardware and software provides a programing space with a single address. The superiority of DSM relative to MPP is that programming on DSM is easier. Stanford's DASH is the world's first true DSM system. Cray T3D and SGI/Cray Origin2000 are all DSM systems.

In the late 1990s, with the emergence of Intel chips and other low-cost micro-computer components, and the rapid development of network technologies, ordinary microcomputer or workstation being used as a compute node and high-speed interconnection of parallel computing systems has become possible, Cluster of Workstation (COW) came into being. COW system interconnected a group of high-performance workstations or high-end computer with interconnect network, and parallel programming and visual development environment supports interactive inheritance, which make full use of the workstation's resource in order to achieve efficient parallel computing. Berkeley NOW, Alpha Farm, Digital Trucluster and China's Dawning 3000 are all COW structure.

After 2000, Cluster emerged, which was cluster system using commercial processor as node, and Constellation also emerged which use SMP parallel machines as compute nodes [7]. Cluster computers are a group of loosely-coupled computers that work together and act as a single computer to solve a particular problem. The biggest thing that happened to supercomputing is the advent of cluster computers, companies such as Dell, IBM and HP are now supplying cluster packages. Cluster and MPP are all distributed memory architecture, therefore they have strong scalability. Specifically, Cluster consists of node computers, high-speed interconnection network, operating system, a single system image and other middleware, parallel programming environments and applications. Judging from memory access method, Cluster and MPP use the same distributed memory (DM) structure, which has high scalability. Representative Cluster computers have the Los Alamos National Laboratory Avalon Cluster, ASCI Blue Mountain, DeepComp 1800/6800 and Dawning 2000.

Constellations refer to the Cluster that use the large-scale SMP (the number of processors is less than 16) as nodes. The nodes of constellations are interconnected by high-speed private network, therefore constellations are also called Cluster-SMP or CSMP. IBM ASCI White system uses constellations structure, consisting of 512 nodes, and each node contains 16 Power3 processors, shared memory within a node, and nodes are interconnected by the crossbar.

To sum up, the supercomputer architecture in the 1990s, were mainly MPP and SMP, with a small amount of Single Processor and SIMD machines. Over time, Single Processor, SMP and SIMD machines are gone, and the architecture of Cluster began scenery together.

2.5 Cluster, Constellations and MPP coexist, and cluster's dominance continues to expand (2003–2011)

Since 2003, SMP supercomputer architecture completely get out of the historical stage from the TOP500 list; Cluster, Constellations and MPP coexist on TOP500. With the rapid development of Cluster, it gradually occupied the absolute dominance in the market, and dominance is still expanding. Constellations and MPP's market share continue to be squeezed, especially Constellations, was out of TOP500 in 2012.

2.6 Cluster is More and More Popular, but MPP Cannot be Ignored (2012-Present)

Till now, glancing at the machine on the TOP500, supercomputer architecture composes 80% of the cluster plus 20% of the MPP. Cluster is more and more popular, but MPP cannot be ignored. Cluster system with industrial standardization occupy TOP500 HPC monopoly, meanwhile MPP architecture systems for the high-end market should not be overlooked. The basic difference between these two types of systems are components of the system. Clusters usually use commodity hardware, software, and networking components. The MPP use customized compute nodes, plug-ins, modules and chassis, and the interconnection between them is a specific package. MPP require high bandwidth, low latency, better energy efficiency and high reliability. Considering the cost, clusters allow system growing modularly to meet performance. Due to high cost, MPP systems are less. In general, each country only have a few MPP supercomputers.

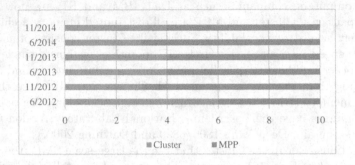

Fig. 1. The system share of architecture during recent three years on TOP10 list

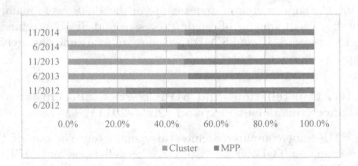

Fig. 2. The performance share of architecture during recent three years on TOP10 list

According to November 2014 TOP500 statistics, Cluster supercomputer architecture dominant advantage, its market share is up to 85.8%. Cluster architecture supercomputing system, especially the so-called "Beowulf Cluster" system which is composed by ordinary commercial chip and inline technology become the mainstream of supercomputer system [7]. It is popular mainly due to its cost-effectiveness and openness. The difference between MPP and Cluster is that Cluster generally uses inexpensive general IA server computing node, and small-scale systems generally use Ethernet interconnect, large-scale systems or systems of higher performance requirements mostly use InfiniBand, QsNET or

Myrinet as the interconnect networks, plus free, open, general-purpose operating system (Linux) and parallel programming interface (MPI), so the cost of super-computers is no longer astronomical, so the company with a general size can afford [8]. Cluster-based system can vary in size. Cluster supercomputer system has a flexible structure, versatility, safety, easy to expand, high availability, high cost/performance ratio and many other advantages, so now most of the new supercomputers use Cluster.

Although the supercomputers using MPP (including CC-NUMA) architecture is less than those using Clusters in the TOP500 supercomputers, but MPP can get higher performance, therefore they are often used in high-end high-performance computing. According to November 2014 TOP500 supercomputer ranking, MPP architecture machines occupy 14.2% system share with 32.99% performance share. Among TOP10 machine, there are 4 Cluster architecture machines and 6 MPP architecture machines; IBM's four BlueGene/Q, Cray's XK7 and XC30 are MPP architecture, Tianhe 2, Japan's K, Dell's PowerEdge and Cray's CS-Storm are Cluster architecture. Since 2012, there are only Cluster and MPP supercomputer architecture on the TOP500 list. Figures 1 and 2 demonstrate the system share and performance share distribution of Cluster and MPP architecture of recent three years on the TOP10 list. It can be seen that high-end high-performance supercomputers are evenly divided by MPP and Cluster. Although Cluster is popular in HPC, but MPP cannot be ignored.

3   Conclusions and Prospects

Figures 3 and 4 shows the architecture trend of system share and performance share on the TOP500 list since 1993. It can be seen on the TOP500 list, the super-computer architecture in the 1990s were mainly MPP and SMP, with a small amount of Single Processor and SIMD machines. Over time, Single Processor, SMP and SIMD machines are gone, and the architecture of Cluster began scenery together. Since 2003, SMP supercomputer architecture completely get out of the historical stage from the TOP500 list; Cluster, Constellations and MPP coexist on TOP500. With the rapid development of Cluster, it gradually occupied the

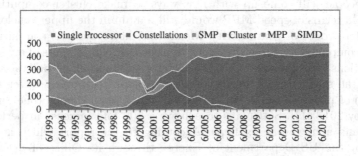

Fig. 3. The system share of architecture during 1993–2014 on TOP500 list

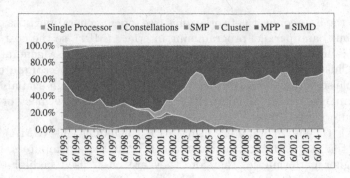

Fig. 4. The performance share of architecture during 1993–2014 on TOP500 list

absolute dominance in the market, and dominance is still expanding. Constellations and MPP's market share continue to be squeezed, especially Constellations, was out of TOP500 in 2012. In 1993, 250 systems among TOP500 supercomputers are SMP, and these SMP systems are no longer in use after June 2002. Most SMP architecture uses shared memory and I/O devices. In 1993 there are 120 MPP systems, and the number of MPP systems reached the peak of 350 systems in 2000. However, the number of MPP systems among TOP500 reduce to less than 100 systems in 2014. Till now, glancing at the machine on the TOP500 list, supercomputer architecture composes 80% of the cluster plus 20% of the MPP.

In summary, the supercomputer architecture evolves to constant pursue convenience and flexibility. The mainstream architecture of supercomputers evolves from vector machine to SMP, then MPP, and finally on the TOP500 list there are only two types of architectures–Cluster and MPP. Cluster becomes the mainstream for its high availability and high scalability, meanwhile, MPP architecture are also used in high-end high-performance computing due to its high performance.

In the future, parallelism (MPP or Cluster) would still remain a mainstream among supercomputers [9]. Parallelism is one of the few ways to cope up with Moore's Law and increase the overall performance of a computer. Performance would be derived by increasing the number of processors in a design. In terms of numbers, cluster computing would dominate over MPP since it is cheaper and software people will come up with new ways to make cluster computing more desirable. In terms of speed MPP would still remain in the upper echelon due to its fast inter-processor connectivity. Meanwhile, heterogeneous computing is an emerging computing architectures now, to meet the requirements of a wide range of applications [10]. Pairwise CPU/accelerator or stand-alone bulk accelerators is among the major issues in developing new supercomputers. Given the current speed of progress, supercomputers will reach one exaflops (one quintillion FLOPS) by 2018 [11]. SGI plans to achieve a 500 fold increase in performance by 2018, and achieve one exaflops. According to the report which is recently released by the US Department of Energy through its Office of Science [12], co-design and integration framework is necessary for exascale.

Acknowledgement. This work was partially supported by the National Natural Science Foundation of China under Grant No. 61202334 and No. 61103014, the National Research Foundation for the Doctoral Program of Higher Education of China under Grant No.20134307120031, and the National High Technology Development 863 Program of China under Grant No. 2013AA01A208.

References

1. Meuer, H., Simon, H., Strohmaier, E., Dongarra, J.: TOP500 Supercomputer Sites. http://www.top500.org
2. Kolodzey, J.S.: CRAY-1 computer technology. IEEE Trans. Compon. Hybrids Manuf. Technol. **CHMT–4**(2), 181–186 (1981)
3. Jin, Y., Huang, Y., Chen, Z., Gui, Y., Qi, F.: Key techniques and development trend of High Performance computers. Chinese Eng. Sci. **3**(6), 1–8 (2001)
4. Amdahl, Gene: Validity of the single processor approach to achieving large-scale computing capabilities. AFIPS Conf. Proc. **30**, 483–485 (1967)
5. Chen, G.: Parallel Computer Architecture. Higher Education Press, Beijing (2002)
6. Zeng, Q., Chen, T.: Scalable parallel computers: system architecture and up-to-date development. Comput. Sci. **30**(9), 158–161 (2003)
7. Tango, S.: Review of high performance computer system structure. Computer CD Soft. and Appl. **15**, 51–52 (2010)
8. Graham, S.L., Snir, M., Patterson, C.A.: Getting Up to Speed: The Future of Supercomputing. National Academies Press, Washington, DC (2004)
9. Ancajas, D.M.B.: Trends in Supercomputing. www-inst.eecs.berkeley.edu/~n252/su06/dean_trends.pdf
10. Qian, D.: HPC R&D in China-A Brief Review and Prospects. IHPCF talks, Tianjin (2015)
11. Bell, G.: The Supercomputer Class Evolution: A personal perspective (2013). http://research.microsoft.com/en-us/um/people/gbell/supers/bell,g_history_of_supercomputers_talk_at_20llnl2013-04-24.pdf
12. Lucas, R. and et. al.: Top Ten Exascale Research Challenges. ASCAC Subcommittee Report, DOE (2014)

Technology on the Horizon

Simulation of Six DOF Vibration Isolator System for Electronic Equipment

Yufeng Luo[✉], Jinwen Li, Yuanshan Li, and Xu Chen

School of Computer, National University of Defense Technology,
Changsha 410073, China
yufengluo73@126.com, lijinwen@sina.com,
{liyuanshan0528, chenxufree}@163.com

Abstract. Electronic equipment system is always manufactured as a super precision system. However, it will be used in harsh environment. For example, the computer in moving carriers will acted by vibrations. The objective of this paper is to provide a systematic investigation to computer-aided design of the vibration isolator for protection of electronic equipment in harsh vibration environment. This papers deal with fast solving method of natural frequency and system response of six DOF (Degree of Freedom) vibration isolator system. In the foundation of a mathematical model of vibration motion differential equation, the state space method is derived and presented. Through transforming the vibration isolation differential equations into the state space equations, it is convenient to facilitate the solution of vibration isolation coefficient of vibration isolation system of six DOF of freedom, by using the state space method and the MATLAB/Simulink model. Comparisons with reality data, Simulation results showed the result is consistent with the reality result. The state space method can find further applications on the selection of vibration isolation system and the evaluation of vibration isolation efficiency.

Keywords: Vibration isolator · Electronic equipment · Natural frequency · State space method

1 Introduction

Research on the design of vibration isolators to improve the characteristics of electronic in moving carrier has rapidly increased in recent years. Most designs of electronic equipment include some vibration isolators to attenuate vibrations so as to improve vibration safety [6]. An accurate characterization of the vibration isolator is of paramount importance for sufficiently precise mathematical models of the vibration isolator for design purposes. Some literatures have discussed the relevant investigate of vibration isolator before [1, 2]. Narimani researched the frequency response of a linear vibration isolator [3]. Li researched the dynamics motion equation which single rigid body is installed in the elastics board [4]. Arkadiusz study the dynamic analysis of vibration device [5]. But all the method can't provides simulation of six DOF vibration isolation system.

© Springer-Verlag Berlin Heidelberg 2016
W. Xu et al. (Eds.): NCCET 2015, CCIS 592, pp. 157–163, 2016.
DOI: 10.1007/978-3-662-49283-3_15

The objective of this paper is to provide a systematic investigation to test and computer-aided design for protection of electronic equipments system in harsh vibration environment. Electronic equipment in vibration environment usually requires the vibration isolators for vibration isolation [7]. Analysis of such problems, the electronic equipment is generally regarded as a rigid body. Electronic equipment and vibration isolators is composed of six DOF vibration system. There are six natural frequency, which are three translational vibration along the coordinate axis and three rotary vibration around the coordinate axis. The six DOF of electronic equipment couple mutually, which the natural frequency of six DOF disperses broadly. It is difficult to calculate the natural frequency, and it is complex to design the vibration isolator system.

Figure 1a shows a system scheme for electronic equipments system in moving carriers. There are some vibrations in moving processing, so electronic equipment system must be designed for safety [8]. In general, the straight direction vibrations and impact are the leading vibration direction. It must be considered chiefly in reinforcement design for the system. In fact, the reinforcement design is the most economic measure when applying the general electronic equipments to work in harsh environment.

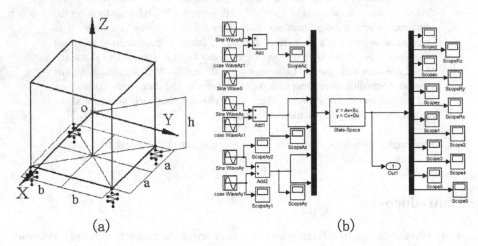

(a)   (b)

Fig. 1. (a) The installation of Vibration isolation system. (b) The system frequency response simulation model established by MATLAB/Simulink.

In the presented work, four vibration isolators are installed at the bottom of the electronic equipment. A single rigid body and six DOF vibration isolation system is established by using MATLAB/Simulink module. The natural frequencies and vibration isolation coefficient of three directions is calculated quickly, which provides a theoretical basis for the design of vibration isolation. The vibration isolator is the key factor for the dynamics of the reinforcement system. Therefore, the natural frequency of the electronic equipment must be designed well-connected.

2 Mathematical Model of Bottom-Mounted Vibration Isolator

It is the most common situation to install the vibration isolators at the bottom of the equipment in electronic equipment. A equipment with vibration isolation system is shown in Fig. 1a. Given the center of the device gravity is along with the geometric center line, and the configuration of the shock absorber is symmetrical with two inertia axis plane, which the installed position is symmetrical with two vertical planes through the center of gravity (xoz and yoz plane). Given the stiffness of the vibration absorber at X, Y, Z direction is the same. Namely: kx1 = kx2 = kx3 = kx4 = kx; ky1 = ky2 = ky3 = ky4 = ky; kz1 = kz2 = kz3 = kz4 = kz.

Where, kx, ky, kz are the spring stiffness of the shock absorber along the x, y, z axis.

Defining a generalize displacement array, refer with Eq. 1:

$$X = \begin{bmatrix} z & \phi_z & x & \phi_y & y & \phi_x \end{bmatrix}. \tag{1}$$

Then, the system motion differential equations without the damped vibration refer with Eq. 2:

$$M\ddot{X} + KX = U \tag{2}$$

Where, M is the mass matrix, K is the stiffness matrix, refer with Eq. 3. Each elements of K is as follow: $k11 = 4k_z$, $k_{22} = 4(b^2k_x + a^2k_y)$, $k_{33} = 4k_x$, $k_{44} = 4(h^2k_x + a^2k_z)$, $k_{55} = 4k_y$, $k_{66} = 4(h^2k_y + b^2k_z)$, $k_{34} = k_{43} = 4hk_x$, $k_{56} = k_{65} = 4hk_y$.

$$M = \begin{bmatrix} m & & & & & \\ & I_z & & & & 0 \\ & & m & & & \\ & & & I_y & & \\ & 0 & & & m & \\ & & & & & I_x \end{bmatrix}, \quad K = \begin{bmatrix} k_{11} & 0 & 0 & 0 & 0 & 0 \\ 0 & k_{22} & 0 & 0 & 0 & 0 \\ 0 & 0 & k_{33} & k_{34} & 0 & 0 \\ 0 & 0 & k_{43} & k_{44} & 0 & 0 \\ 0 & 0 & 0 & 0 & k_{55} & k_{56} \\ 0 & 0 & 0 & 0 & k_{65} & k_{66} \end{bmatrix} \tag{3}$$

Assumed that the vibration isolation system employs three vibration value along the x, y, z axis, the three vibration value is as follow: $a_x = A_x*\sin(pt + \alpha_x)$, $a_y = A_y*\sin(pt + \alpha_y)$, $a_z = A_z*\sin(pt + \alpha_z)$. Then, we can get the input array of U, refer with: Eq. 4.

$$U = \begin{bmatrix} 4k_zA_z \sin(pt + \alpha_z) \\ 0 \\ 4k_xA_x \sin(pt + \alpha_x) \\ 4k_xhA_x \sin(pt + \alpha_x) \\ 4k_yA_y \sin(pt + \alpha_y) \\ 4k_yhA_y \sin(pt + \alpha_y) \end{bmatrix} \tag{4}$$

Knowing from Eq. 4, there are two coupled degrees of freedom, which are both the x direction of translation and rotation about the y-axis with the y direction of translation and rotation about the x-axis. Solving the differential equation is very difficult, and the calculation workloads are very great.

3   MATLAB/Simulink Model

For undamped vibration motion differential equation, refer with Eq. 2. Given there is a particular solution, refer with Eq. 5

$$x = \phi e^{j\omega t} \tag{5}$$

Assumed the input array U is equal to zero, and putting the Eq. 5 into Eq. 2, we can get the Eq. 6.

$$(K - \omega^2 M)\phi = 0 \tag{6}$$

This is a question about generalized eigenvalue, which ω^2 is the eigenvalue and φ is the feature vector. By solving the Matrix KM^{-1}, the eigenvalue can be obtained. From calculating the radical sign of the eigenvalue, each rank natural frequency of the system is available [6–8].

Using MATLAB M-files to make a program [9], and inputting the initial date into the program, we can get the natural frequency of system.

If we want to obtain the response of the multiple DOF forced vibration, it is essential to solve the differential equation, refer with Eq. 2. Because this is a six DOF differential equation, which are coupled each other, it is very complex to solve directly. It is necessary to adopt numerical method to solve the differential equations. To arrive at the system response curve under various excitation frequency, it is required to transform differential equations into state-space equation, refer with Eq. 7.

$$\begin{cases} \dot{Z} = AZ + BU \\ Y = CZ + DU \end{cases} \tag{7}$$

Where, Z is the state vector. U is the input vector. Y is the output vector. A is the state coefficient matrix. B is the input coefficient matrix. C is the output coefficient matrix. D is the coefficient matrix. Refer with Eq. 8.

$$Z = \begin{bmatrix} X \\ \dot{X} \end{bmatrix}_{12 \times 6} . A = \begin{bmatrix} 0 & 1 \\ -M^{-1}K & -M^{-1}C \end{bmatrix}_{12 \times 12} . B = \begin{bmatrix} 0 \\ M^{-1} \end{bmatrix}_{12 \times 6} . C = I_{12 \times 12}. D$$
$$= 0_{12 \times 12} \tag{8}$$

By using the state space module in the MATLAB/Simulink, the system frequency response simulation model is established, and the model is shown below in Fig. 1b. Six sinusoidal signal source modules is the input vector of U. By crossing the mixing modules, the input vector is imported into the state space module, and the state space model can be solved. The result is stored in the MATLAB workspace, and the results can be shared with M-file.

In order to obtain the system response curve at each excitation frequency and amplitude, recycling need to be established in the MATLAB M-files. The largest system response of each direction under every response frequency are calculated by using Simulink modelule. The results is stored in the MATLAB workspace, and The response curve is drawn by way of MATLAB M-files.

4 Case Study

Vibration isolator is mounted in an electronic equipment as shown in Fig. 1a. There are four vibration isolators that are installed at bottom of the electronic equipment. The system parameter is shown as follow. m = 87.7 kg, Ix = 2.57 kg * m^2, Iy = 4.94 kg * m^2, Iz = 3.04 kg * m^2. a = 0.2 m, b = 0.15 m, h = 0.30 m. the stiffness of each shock absorber is shown as follow. kx = 1.5 × 105 N/m, ky = 8.75 × 105 N/m, kz = 1 × 105 N/m.

Inputting the above data into MATLAB/Simulink model, six natural frequency of the system are obtained. The comparison between the MATLAB solution and reality solution is shown in Table 1. They natural frequency curve drawing of three directions from MATLAB solution are shown in Fig. 2.

Table 1. The natural frequency of vibration isolation system.

Natural frequency [Hz]	Z-axis direction	Rotation around the Z-axis	X-axis direction	Rotation around the Y-axis	Y-axis direction	Rotation around the X-axis
MATLAB solution	10.75	15.13	5.31	22.45	4.31	21.95
Theory solution	10.75	15.76	5.44	22.77	4.25	21.66

From above table, it can be seen that it is feasible to solve the feature of six DOF vibration isolation system with MATLAB program. Compared to theory resolution method, the MATLAB method is simple and quick, which take advantage of the computer numeral method. In the early stage of the design, it can help us to quickly select a vibration isolator.

Referring military computer universal norms, sinusoidal vibration condition of from 5 to 80 Hz is applied in the three directions. Making use of the MATLAB method, the vibration isolation coefficient curve in the x.y.z direction can be obtained. From the drawing of Fig. 2a, in the x direction, the resonance phenomenon is occurred in the 5.31 Hz and 22.45 Hz, respectively. In y direction, the resonance phenomenon is occurred in the 4.31 Hz and 22.15 Hz, as refer with Fig. 2b. Because the excitation frequency is from 5 to 80 Hz, the resonance point in 4.31 Hz isn't in the Fig. 2b. In z direction, the resonance phenomenon is occurred in the 10.75 Hz, as refer with Fig. 2c.

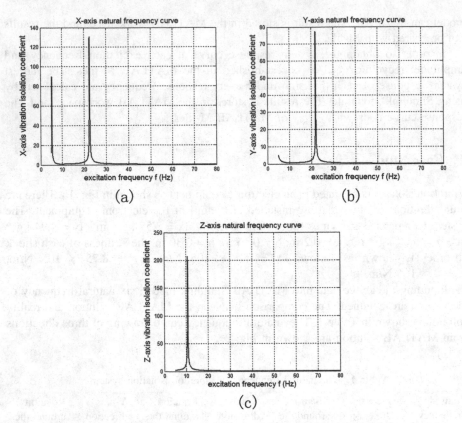

Fig. 2. The natural frequency curve of MATLAB solution. (a) X-axis natural frequency curve. (b) Y-axis natural frequency curve. (c) Z-axis natural frequency curve.

5 Conclusions

(1) A mathematical model of six DOF vibration isolation system of electronic equipment has been investigated, and a new method of state space method has been put forward to simulate the mathematical model.

(2) Through transforming the vibration isolation differential equations into the state space equations, it is convenient to facilitate the solution of vibration isolation coefficient of vibration isolation system of six DOF of freedom, by using the state space method and the MATLAB/Simulink model, and the state space method has good practical value.

(3) From the simulation results it is showed the result is conformable with the theory result. State space method can be used to carry on the selection of vibration isolation system and the evaluation of vibration isolation efficiency. The state space method can find further applications on the selection of vibration isolation system and the evaluation of vibration isolation efficiency.

(4) Without considering the effect of damping, it cannot accurately reflect the system response of the excitation frequency, which needs to be deeply researched in the future.

Acknowledgement. This work was supported by the National High Technology Development 863 Program of China under Grant NO. 2012AA01A301.

References

1. Harris, C.W., Crede, C.E.: Harris Shock and Vibration, 5th edn. McGraw-Hill Publications, New York (2009)
2. Guo, P.F., Lang, Z.Q., Peng, Z.K.: Analysis and design of the force and displacement transmissibility of nonlinear viscous damper based vibration isolation systems. Nonlinear Dyn. **67**(4), 2671–2687 (2012)
3. Narimani, A., Golnaraghi, M.E., Jazar, G.N.: Frequency response of a piecewise linear vibration isolator. J. Vib. Control **10**(12), 1775–1794 (2004)
4. Li, W.L., Lavrich, P.: Prediction of power flows through machine vibration isolators. J. Sound Vib. **224**(4), 757–774 (1999)
5. Trabka, A., Majewski, L., Klosinski, J.: Dynamic analysis of vibrating device. J. Solid State Phenom. **164**, 327–332 (2010)
6. Li, Y.T., Meng, G., Ding, H.: Adaptive switching control method for active vibration isolation. In: 9th IEEE International Workshop on Advanced Motion Control, pp. 462–467 (2006)
7. Park, K., Kim, S., Choi, D., Sohn, B.: An active vibration isolation system using a loop shaping control technique. In: IEEE/ASME International Conference on Mechatronics and Embedded Systems and Applications, pp. 586–590 (2008)
8. Hanieh, A.A.: Frequency variation for the purpose of vibration isolation. In: IEEE International Conference on Mechatronics, pp. 176–180 (2006)
9. Huang, Y., Ma, L., Li, H.: MATLAB7.0/Simulink6.0 Modeling with Simulation Development and Advanced Engineering Applications. TSinghua University Publications, Beijing (2005)

Impact of Heavy Ion Species and Energy on SEE Characteristics of Three-Dimensional Integrated Circuit

Peng Li$^{(\boxtimes)}$, Wei Guo, Zhenyu Zhao, and Minxuan Zhang

College of Computer, National University of Defense Technology,
Changsha 410073, China
li1986p@163.com

Abstract. Via Geant4 simulations, SEEs are characterized for each die of 3DIC with different heavy ion species and energy in this paper. It is found that the incident ions with high atomic number make the SEE more serious for each die and there are obvious differences on SEE characteristics between each die after the low energy heavy ions striking 3DIC. Our research also indicates that SEE sensitivity of inner dies is no less than that of the outer ones unless the heavy ions stop above the inner dies. It is because the secondary particles induced by nuclear reaction and the scattered heavy ions caused by low energy incident can trigger severe multi-SEEs. It concludes that the inner dies of 3DIC also need to be hardened, and the technologies restraining severe multi-SEEs should be taken for them, if the higher reliability is required.

Keywords: Three-dimensional integration circuit (3DIC) · Heavy ions · Single event effects (SEEs) · Deposited charge

1 Introduction

Three-dimensional integrated circuit (3DIC) stacks multi dies and solves the severe problems two-dimensional integrated circuit (2DIC) faced [1]. Because of high density and small delay, 3DIC keeps the Moore's law still holding in the nano era [2]. However, 3DIC used in the space environments also suffers soft errors brought by single event effects (SEEs), such as single event transition (SET) and single event upset (SEU) [3,4]. Although 3DIC has been researched for several years, the study about SEE characteristics of 3DIC evolves slowly and its response to the incident heavy ions is unclear.

Zhang et al. made the first attempt to characterize the soft error of 3DIC [5]. Utilizing semiconductor physics formulas, they found that alpha particles induced by package material only affect the top die, and less than 0.4 % of incident particles can reach to the inner dies. They termed this phenomenon as

P. Li—The research is supported by Specialized Research Fund for the Doctor Program of Higher Education of China with Grant No. 20124307110016, and by National Natural Science Foundation of China with Grant No. 61176030.

© Springer-Verlag Berlin Heidelberg 2016
W. Xu et al. (Eds.): NCCET 2015, CCIS 592, pp. 164–172, 2016.
DOI: 10.1007/978-3-662-49283-3_16

shielding effect, and proposed that the circuits in inner dies need not to be hardened. However, they did not consider the heavy ions with stronger striking ability in the space environments. Gouker et al. studied SEU and SET characteristics of 3DIC fabricated in SOI technology [6,7]. In their terrestrial radiation test results, both SET and SEU exist in each die of 3DIC. They also used the Geant4 Monte Carlo simulations, which applies a lot of random simulations to get the statistical characteristics of research object, to confirm that SEE characteristics are nearly the same for each die of 3DIC. But only one kind of heavy ion was calculated in their simulations, which made their conclusion incomprehensive in the space environments with abundance radiation particles.

In this work, we build a refined 3DIC model in Geant4 simulations, and get the deposited charge in sensitive detector to study SEE characteristics of each die. We find that SEE characteristics of each die seriously rely on the incident heavy ion species and energy, and the secondary ion induced by nuclear reaction can affect the SEE characteristics. The best disadvantage of 3DIC is that the heavy ions with low energy can bring multi-SEEs (e.g., multi-cell upset (MCU)) simultaneously in the inner dies. It makes the hardened design for 3DIC more difficult. The conclusions got in this work can provide reference for 3DIC radiation research, and guide the hardened design for 3DIC.

2   Simulation Setup

We construct a complex 3DIC model using Geant4, which refers to Ref. [6]. The 3DIC model is 'shown in Fig. 1, which is a cube at the size of $10\,\mu m \times 10\,\mu m \times 33.4\,\mu m$ including 3 dies. Since only the deposited charge in the device layers can trigger SEE, the device layers in 3DIC model are regard as the sensitive volume (SV) for radiation.

The heavy ion species and energy are referred the one used at Brookhaven National Laboratory (BNL) and Texas A&M University (TAMU). In each Geant4 simulation, there are 10^7 mono-energetic heavy ions vertically striking at the center of the surface of 3DIC model. The list of the physical processes, which describes the reaction between particles and material, is based on the standard package of physics lists QGSP_BIC [8].

The deposited charge in SV is treated as analysis object for studying SEE Characteristics of 3DIC. Thus, the deposited energy obtained in Geant4 simulation need to be converted to charge according to Eq. (1):

$$Q = \frac{E_{dep}}{3.6eV/pair} \times 1.6 \times 10^{-19} C/pair \tag{1}$$

where Q is the charge converted by deposited energy E_{dep}. The data analysis tool ROOT is used to record the deposited charge in each event for all of 3 sensitive detectors. Since the secondary particles produced by nuclear reaction can influence SEE cross section, their details are also recorded in ROOT.

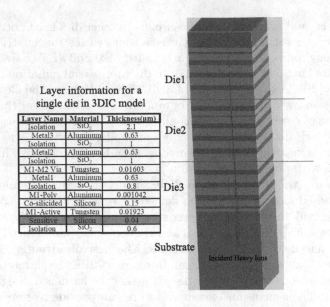

Layer information for a
single die in 3DIC model

Layer Name	Material	Thickness(μm)
Isolation	SiO₂	2.1
Metal3	Aluminum	0.63
Isolation	SiO₂	1
Metal2	Aluminum	0.63
Isolation	SiO₂	1
M1-M2 Via	Tungsten	0.01603
Metal1	Aluminum	0.63
Isolation	SiO₂	0.8
M1-Poly	Aluminum	0.001042
Co-silicided	Silicon	0.15
M1-Active	Tungsten	0.01923
Sensitive	Silicon	0.04
Isolation	SiO₂	0.6

Fig. 1. 3D-IC Geant4 model referred to Ref. [6].

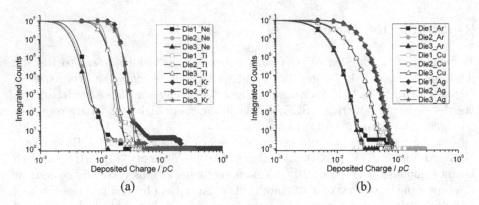

Fig. 2. Integrated counts spectrum of deposited charge for different heavy ion species at nearly the same energy, about (a) $4.50\,\mathrm{MeV/u}$ and (b) $12\,\mathrm{MeV/u}$.

3   Simulation Results

The plots of integrated counts versus deposited charge in SV of Die1, 2 and 3 for the Ne($4.50\,\mathrm{MeV/u}$), Ti($4.03\,\mathrm{MeV/u}$) and Kr($4.50\,\mathrm{MeV/u}$) are shown in Fig. 2(a), and for the Ar($12.35\,\mathrm{MeV/u}$), Cu($11.57\,\mathrm{MeV/u}$) and Ag($11.01\,\mathrm{MeV/u}$) are shown in Fig. 2(b). It demonstrates that the deposited charge in each die of 3DIC is increased with the atomic number (Z) when the heavy ions have the similar energy. When the heavy ion energy is about 4 MeV/u, there are obviously differences for each die on the integrated counts plots. For the heavy ion energy

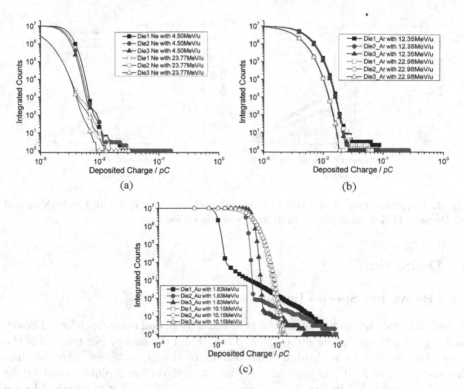

Fig. 3. Integrated counts spectrum of deposited charge for the (a) Ne, (b) Ar, (c) Au at different energy.

arriving at about 12MeV/u, the differences nearly disappear in low deposited charge region, but it is also evident in high deposited charge region as shown in Fig. 2(b). Compared with Fig. 2(b), the high-energy tails of the integrated counts plots in Fig. 2(a) are more markedly. These interesting phenomena will be discussed in depth in next section.

Figure 3 shows the comparison of the integrated counts versus deposited charge for the Ne(4.50 MeV/u and 23.77 MeV/u), Ar(12.35 MeV/u and 22.98 MeV/u) and Au(1.83 MeV/u and 10.15 MeV/u), respectively. These simulation results further indicate that there are great differences in deposited charge between each die in low energy heavy ion striking, especially in Fig. 3(a) and (c). In Fig. 3(a) and (b), the integrated counts plots come to left while the heavy ion energy increasing. It seems that the higher the energy, the lower SEE sensitivity for each die of 3DIC. The most abnormal simulation results are existed in Fig. 3(c). For the Au at 1.83 MeV/u, there are great differences in the integrated counts plots between Die1, 2 and 3, and the count of deposited charge more than 0.2 pC is very huge. Whereas, the largest deposited charge for Au at 10.15 MeV/u is no more than 0.2 pC. It is concluded that 3DIC are more sensitive for the high atomic number (high Z) heavy ions at low energy.

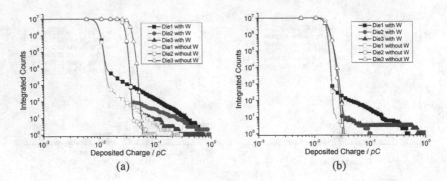

Fig. 4. Integrated counts spectrum of deposited charge for (a) Au at 1.83 MeV/u and (b) Br at 3.44 MeV/u in the normal and contrast cases.

4 Discussion

4.1 Heavy Ion Species Impact

As well-known, the heavy ion species is indexed by Z, and the energy loss of heavy ions is proportional to the square of Z. Thus, when the energy per nucleon is the same, the heavy ions with high Z deposit more charge in target material than the one with low Z. It can explain why the integrated counts plots come to right with the increased Z in Fig. 2. Furthermore, we conclude that the high Z heavy ions produce higher SEE susceptibility in each die of 3DIC if they can come to the bottom of 3DIC.

4.2 Heavy Ion Energy Impact

As a heavy ion enters the semiconductor lattice, it may undergo collision with nucleus, which leads to a nuclear reaction and releasing one or multi secondary particles. Many studies have concluded that the secondary particles increase the SEE cross section for ICs [9]. According to Ref. [6], the secondary particles make the SEE susceptibility of the bottom die higher than other dies while the Kr at 16 MeV/u striking the 3DIC model. The same phenomena are also caught in our simulation results as shown in Figs. 2 and 3.

A contrast case is hold to analyze the influence of the nuclear reaction on SEE characteristics of 3DIC. In the contrast case, all of the tungsten layers are replaced by SiO_2 layers. The simulation results in Fig. 4(a) give the plots of integrated counts versus deposited charge for the Au at 1.83 MeV/u. The difference between the normal and contrast case is obviously, especially in the high deposited charge region. Although the maximum deposited charge is more than 1 pC in the normal case, there is none secondary ion produced in 10^7 simulations through examining the record information. It shows that the high deposited charge for Au at 1.83 MeV/u is not produced by secondary particles. However, it also relates to the tungsten layers because of the obvious differences on integrated

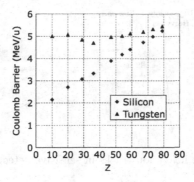

Fig. 5. The Coulomb barrier computed in [10]

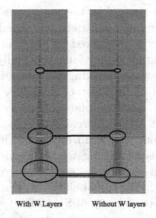

With W Layers   Without W layers

Fig. 6. The tracks of the Au at 1.83 MeV/u in 3DIC model with and without tungsten layers.

count plots for normal and contrast case. The same abnormity also appears in the simulations for Br at 3.44 MeV/u as shown in Fig. 4(b).

The Coulomb barrier is an important metric to establish the potential relationship for nuclear reactions between the incident particles and the target nucleus. Only if the incident energy of particle is more than the corresponding Coulomb barrier, it would react with target nucleus to release secondary particles. In Ref. [10], Reed et al. computed the Coulomb barrier between the typical heavy ions available at SEE test facilities and 2 different targets, silicon and tungsten, as shown in Fig. 5. It is obvious that the Coulomb barriers for the Au (Z = 79) and Br (Z = 35) are much more than 1.83 and 3.44 MeV/u, respectively. Thus, none nuclear reaction happened in simulations for Au and Br at low energy is coincident with the theoretical derivation. The reasons for these abnormities will be further studied in the following part of this paper.

Figure 6 shows the profile of 3DIC model with and without tungsten layers, containing the tracks of Au at 1.83 MeV. The scattering scope of the Au with tungsten layers is much larger than that without tungsten layers, because the

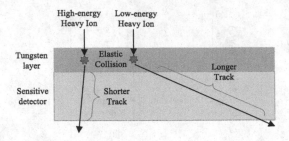

Fig. 7. Illustration of the heavy ion tracks in sensitive detector for different energy.

incident heavy ions are easier to scatter in the high-Z material. In addition, we can infer that the speed of Au in 3DIC model is low, especially in Die1, from the phenomena that the Au stops in the substrate of 3DIC model. The low speed makes the Au scatter more diffusely after striking into tungsten layers. The incident range of heavy ions showed in Fig. 6 indicates that the tungsten layers increase the scattering for heavy ions, especially at low energy.

After the low speed heavy ions striking the tungsten layer, an extreme event would be happened: the motion direction of the heavy ion is changed largely and the angle between the track and the plane of the layers is decreased. Figure 7 illustrates the extreme event, which increases the track of scattered heavy ion in sensitive detector overly. Thus, the abnormities in Fig. 4 can be explained. The higher deposited charge tails with tungsten layers are due to the long track of the low energy Au and Br in sensitive detectors. Moreover, both in Fig. 4(a) and (b), the highest deposited charge tails belongs to Die1. There are 2 reasons for this: (1) a tungsten layer is on the top of SV in Die1, increasing the probability for the long track of heavy ion in sensitive detector; (2) the low speed of the heavy ions in tungsten layer makes the severe scattering and increases the track in SV of Die1.

Since LET is defined as the energy loss per unit path length of the particle, the average deposited charge generated by indirect ionization can be calculated according to the Eq. (2):

$$Q = LET \times \frac{1.6 \times 10^{-19} C/pair}{3.6 eV/pair} \times \rho \times l \qquad (2)$$

where Q is the deposited charge, ρ is the density of the target material (the density of Si is $2321 \, mg/cm^3$ for SV) and l is the track length. For the Au at $1.83 \, MeV/u$, LET is $82.7 \, MeV \cdot cm^2/mg$, and the deposited charge reaches the $0.8 \, pC$ in Fig. 4(a). Under these conditions, the track length is $0.98 \, \mu m$ calculated by Eq. (2). The ratio of the transverse and longitudinal for the track in SV is 24.5:1 as the thickness of SV is $0.04 \, \mu m$ in Geant4 3DIC model. It is inferred that the higher SV, the longer the track length of the heavy ions in it. For the bulk process, the height of SV is about $0.5 \sim 1 \, \mu m$, and the transverse track length of the heavy ion can reach to $12.3 \sim 24.5 \, \mu m$ calculated by the ratio above, which may lead serious multi-SEEs. For example, the cell size in the commercial 40 nm

SRAMs is $0.36\,\mu\text{m} \times 1.04\,\mu\text{m}$ while the diagonal is $1.10\,\mu\text{m}$, and the transverse track length $12.3\,\mu\text{m}$ may trigger around 12 SEUs.

In previous researching, 3DIC has the shielding effect for its inner dies, and the hardened design in inside dies can be neglected or general adopted. But, in our researching, multi-SEEs in inner dies can be triggered while the low energy heavy ion striking 3DIC, which makes it difficult to harden the circuit to restrain multi-SEEs. Moreover, the probability of multi-SEEs happened in inner dies is relevant to the number of dies. It is because the more the stacked dies, the lower the energy and speed of the heavy ions become, and then the probability of serious scattering in tungsten layers is increased.

In conclusion, for the heavy ions which can reach to the bottom of 3DIC, the SEE susceptibility of inner dies is no less infirm than that of the outer dies. Also, the inner dies would produce serious multi-SEEs for the low energy heavy ion striking, and it needs to get specialized attention on the hardened design for the inner dies in 3DIC.

5   Conclusion

In this paper, we study the impact of heavy ion species and energy on SEE characteristics of 3DIC. Geant4 simulations are conducted to study SEE characteristics for each die of 3DIC via the charge deposited in SVs of a complex 3DIC model. It is found that the differences between SEE characteristics of different dies are great for the low energy heavy ions striking, but are small or even disappear for the high energy heavy ions striking. In addition, SEE characteristics of each die increases as Z with the same energy. Although the low energy heavy ion can not react with tungsten layers to produce secondary particles, it may be scattered much by tungsten and leaves a long track in sensitive detector. Moreover, these serious multi-SEEs always happen in the inner dies due to the lowest energy and speed during the whole track in 3DIC. Thus, the inner dies need to be specially hardened to restrain multi-SEEs. This work is a good guidance for researching the radiation sensitivity and hardened design of 3DIC.

References

1. Burns, J.A., Aull, B.F., Chen, C.K., et al.: A wafer-scale 3-D circuit integration technology. IEEE Trans. Electron Devices **53**, 2507–2516 (2006)
2. Puttaswamy, K., Loh, G.H.: 3D-integrated SRAM components for high-performance microprocessors. IEEE Trans. Comput. **58**, 1369–1381 (2009)
3. Chen, J., Chen, S., He, Y., et al.: Novel layout technique for single-event transient mitigation using dummy transistor. IEEE Trans. Dev. Mater. Rel. **13**, 177–184 (2013)
4. Chen, J., Chen, S., He, Y., et al.: Novel layout techniques for n-hit single-event transient mitigation via the source-extension. IEEE Trans. Nucl. Sci. **59**, 2859–2866 (2012)

5. Zhang, W., Li, T.: Microarchitecture soft error vulnerability characterization and mitigation under 3D integration technology. In: Proceedings of 41st IEEE/ACM International Symposium on Microarchitecture, pp. 435–446, Lake Como (2008)
6. Gouker, P.M., Tyrrell, B., Renzi, M., et al.: SET characterization in logic circuits fabricated in a 3DIC technology. IEEE Trans. Nucl. Sci. **58**, 2555–2562 (2011)
7. Gouker, P.M., Tyrrell, B., D'Onofrio, R., et al.: Radiation effects in 3D integrated SOI SRAM circuits. IEEE Trans. Nucl. Sci. **58**, 2845–2854 (2011)
8. Huang, P., Chen, S., Chen, J., et al.: Single event pulse broadening after narrowing effect in nano CMOS logic circuits. IEEE Trans. Device Mater. Reliab. **14**, 849–856 (2014)
9. Dodd, P.E., Schwank, J.R., Shaneyfelt, M.R., et al.: Impact of heavy ion energy and nuclear interactions on single-event upset and latchup in integrated circuits. IEEE Trans. Nucl. Sci. **54**, 2303–2311 (2007)
10. Reed, R.A., Weller, R.A., Schrimpf, R.D., et al.: Implications of nuclear reactions for single event effects test methods and analysis. IEEE Trans. Nucl. Sci. **53**, 3356–3362 (2006)

Analysis and Simulation of Temperature Characteristic of Sensitivity for SOI Lateral PIN Photodiode Gated by Transparent Electrode

Bin Wang, Yun Zeng$^{(\boxtimes)}$, Guoli Li, Yu Xia, Hui Xu, and Caixia Huang

School of Physics and Electronics Science, Hunan University,
Changsha 410082, China
yunzeng@hnu.edu.cn

Abstract. This paper performs the structure and principle of SOI Lateral PIN photodiode Gated by Transparent Electrode. The temperature models of photocurrent and dark current are presented and validated by 2D ATLAS simulation. The variation of temperature on sensitivity is addressed when the LPIN PD-GTE is fully depleted. In contrast, the same work is presented on SOI Lateral PIN photo diode. The simulated results indicate the internal quantum efficiency of SOI LPIN PD-GTE remains about (95 %) with illumination of 400 nm wavelength as the temperature rises while the signal-noise-ratio decreases. SNR achieves 10^7 at 300 K and decreases to 10^3 at 473 K. FHWM is almost unchanged varing the temperatures. Thus, the sensitivity decreases when the temperature rises. Still, considering the fact that the operating temperature of the device generally cannot be 473 K or higher, SOI Lateral PD-GTE can be used at high temperature with good sensitivity.

Keywords: SOI · Lateral PIN PD-GTE · Temperature · Sensitivity

1 Introduction

In recent years, there is a great need for responsive photo detectors with high sensitivity and low dark photocurrent for the emerging market of optical storage systems [1] and optical communication systems [2]. In that case, thanks to the silicon-on-insulator (SOI) technology, SOI lateral PIN photodiode (SOI LPIN PD) has been proposed and analyzed in [3]. However, the intrinsic region (I-region) of SOI LPIN PD is not necessary fully depleted. Other phenomena have to be considered like surface and volume recombinations [4]. In such cases, the ultimate performances are limited.

Considering the shortcomings of the SOI LPIN PD, a novel SOI Lateral PIN Photodiode Gated by Transparent Electrode (SOI LPIN PD-GTE) is firstly proposed and analyzed in [5,6]. Based on typical SOI CMOS process [7], SOI

Y. Zeng—This work has been supported by the National Natural Science Foudation of China (NO.6350007).

W. Xu et al. (Eds.): NCCET 2015, CCIS 592, pp. 173–181, 2016.
DOI: 10.1007/978-3-662-49283-3_17

LPIN PD and BJMOSFET [8], the structure of the photo detector is similar to that of SOI LPIN PD, but with Indium Tin Oxide (ITO) fabricated on the topside as transparent gate electrode. When the photo detector is in working status, gate voltage is applied to make the I-region fully depleted, the transverse electric field caused by cathode voltage separates the photo generated carriers. Finally, the photocurrent is formed. The characteristics of SOI LPIN PD-GTE are analyzed at room temperature (T = 300 K) in [9].

The photo detectors are used frequently in different environments. However, few researchers focus on temperature characteristics of SOI LPIN PD-GTE. Temperature vehemently influences the photocurrent, dark current, quantum efficiency and therefore sensitivity of the detector. In this paper we present the current physical model with different operating temperatures and validate it by two dimensional (2D) ATLAS numerical measurements. Electrical simulations are performed by changing the temperatures in order to point out the sensitivity at higher temperature of the device. Besides, we have performed the same work on SOI LPIN PD for contrast.

2   Structure and Principle

In our model, SOI CMOS technology is applied to fabricate SOI LPIN PD-GTE and the device parameters are depicted in Fig. 1. d_{ox1}, d_{si} and d_{ox2} are, respectively, the thickness of silicon film, the topside oxide, and the buried oxide which equal to 30 nm, 600 nm, and 600 nm. The length of the I-region (L_i) is equal to 8 μm. The length of contact P^+ and N^+ region is equal to 1.6 μm. P^+ and N^+ doping are both about $10^{20}\,cm^{-3}$ while P^- doping is about $10^{15}\,cm^{-3}$.

The operation of the device can be simply divided into three steps: photo generated carriers generation, carriers transport and photocurrent output. Once the light falls on the surface of device vertically, light absorption in the channel (i.e. I-region) generates electron-hole pairs. When the silicon film is fully depleted, the electron-hole pairs produced by the light are separated by the lateral electrical field. The current is formed by carriers drift while diffusion is neglected because of FD. Then, the external signal can be detected.

3   Physical Models

3.1   Temperature Characteristic of Photocurrent for SOI LPIN PD-GTE

Once a steady single beam of light incidents on the surface of the detector, we assume that the quantum efficiency equals to 1 in I-region which means every photon produces a pair of electron and hole. The pair generation rate [10] along the y-direction is:

$$G(y) = \frac{P_{opt} \cdot (1 - R) \cdot \lambda}{A \cdot h \cdot c} \alpha e^{-\alpha y} \tag{1}$$

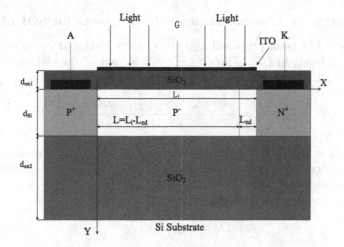

Fig. 1. Schematic view of SOI LPIN PD-GTE under study.

where P_{opt}, R, λ, A, α represent, respectively, incident optical power, reflectance of gate, wavelength of light, device area and optical absorbance. Then the available photocurrent can be given by:

$$I_A = -q \cdot W \cdot \int_0^{Li} \int_0^{d_{si}} G(y) dy dx \qquad (2)$$

When the detector works in a stable condition at room temperature, gate voltage makes the I-region fully depleted vertically. The total current of the device is:

$$I_{tot} = I_{dr}(L_{zd}) + I_{diff}(L) \qquad (3)$$

Where the $I_{dr}(L_{zd})$ is the drift current due to photo carriers within the lateral depletion region and $I_{diff}(L)$ represents the diffusion current outside the lateral depletion region. The output current from cathode electrode is the total current of the detector [11] ($I_k = I_{tot}$).

Ignoring the current from carriers recombination, the diffusion current is negligible. The total current depends on the drift current which can be obtained by available current approximately. In such case, the output photocurrent at room temperature [12] is given by:

$$I_K \approx I_A = -q \cdot W \cdot \int_0^{Li} \int_0^{d_{si}} G(y) dy dx \qquad (4)$$

Here, we take the derivative of I_k with respect to temperature (T)

$$\frac{dI_k}{dT} \approx \frac{d[-q \cdot W \cdot \int_0^{Li} \int_0^{d_{si}} G(y) dy dx]}{dT} = 0 \qquad (5)$$

From Eq. (5), the photocurrent is almost unchanged varying the temperatures. It means the temperature characteristic of SOI LPIN PD-GTE photocurrent is excellent.

3.2   Temperature Characteristic of Photocurrent for SOI LPIN PD

SOI LPIN PD has been proposed and the characteristics at room temperature have been analyzed in [13]. The operation principal of the detector resembles that of SOI LPIN PD-GTE. The photocurrent density is given by

$$J_{phn}(x) = -\frac{q \cdot D_n \cdot G_0 \cdot \tau_{eff} \cdot sinh(\frac{x}{L_{Dni}})}{L_{Dni} \cdot cosh(\frac{L}{L_{Dni}})} \tag{6}$$

Where D_n is the electron diffusion coefficient, G_0 is the average generation rate of photo carriers, τ_{eff} is the electron equivalent lifetime, L_{Dni} is the diffusion length of the elections in the I-region.

These parameters can be obtained by:

$$D_n = \mu_{ni} \cdot K \cdot T/q \tag{7}$$

$$G_0 = K[1 - exp(-\alpha d_{si})] \tag{8}$$

$$\tau_{eff} = \frac{d_{si} \cdot \tau}{d_{si} + s \cdot \tau} \tag{9}$$

$$L_{Dni} = \sqrt{\tau_{eff} \cdot \mu_{ni} \cdot K \cdot T/q} \tag{10}$$

Where G_0, D_n, L_{Dni} are functions of temperature, they will change if the temperature is changed. Clearly, $J_{phn}(x)$ will change in accord with the variation of operating temperature. In that case, the photocurrent of SOI LPIN PD will be different along with the changes of working temperature.

3.3   Temperature Characteristic of Dark Current for Both Detectors

Dark current is the cathode current without light illumination. It determines the minimum light detection power.SOI LPIN PD and SOI LPIN PD-GTE are both working in condition of PN reverse biased. Reverse saturation current of PN junction can be approximated as dark current. Considering the same process, the dark current of the two detectors can be given by:

$$I_R = (\frac{q \cdot D_p \cdot p_n}{L_p} + \frac{q \cdot D_n \cdot n_p}{L_n})[exp(-V_K /K \cdot T) - 1] \tag{11}$$

Where V_K is the voltage of cathode electrode. If V_K is much larger than $K \cdot T$, we can rewrite the equation of (11) as:

$$I_R = -(\frac{q \cdot D_p \cdot p_n}{L_p} + \frac{q \cdot D_n \cdot n_p}{L_n}) \tag{12}$$

Where D_p, p_n, n_p, L_p, L_n are sensitive to temperature. Combining the basic characteristics of common diode, it can be obviously predicted that the dark current will increase as the temperature rises.

4   Simulation and Analysis

4.1   Temperature Characteristics of Photocurrent

We use 2D ATLAS of SILVACO software [14] to validate the physical model of SOI LPIN PD-GTE above. Thermal simulation and photocurrent simulation are combined to perform numerical measurements. The parameters set in ATLAS is given as follows: The optical reflection coefficient(R) equals to 1, Single beam light is applied and the optical power (P_{opt}) is 5 W/cm2, the cathode voltage (V_K) equals to 1 V. When the wavelength of incident light is about 400 nm, the responsibility of both detectors reaches the peak. So 400 nm is set in ATLAS for better simulation results. In order to perform the temperature characteristic of photocurrent, we set different working temperatures (T = 273 K, 300 K, 323 K, 423 K, 473 K). Besides, in contrast, we repeat the same simulation on SOI LPIN PD. The parameters in ATLAS of the device are the same with the simulation of SOI LPIN PD-GTE except that the cathode voltage varies from 0 V to 5 V. The result is shown in Fig. 2.

As is shown in Fig. 2(a), with the temperature increasing from 273 K to 373 K, the photocurrent is almost constant when the SOI LPIN PD-GTE is fully depleted. Until the temperature becomes higher such as 473 K, the photocurrent increases a little because the intrinsic excitation carriers cannot be neglected. The intrinsic excitation carriers make contributions to the output current as well. Significantly, the photocurrent of SOI LPIN PD-GTE is very close to the available photocurrent. From Fig. 2(b), it can be clearly seen that the photocurrent of SOI LPIN PD decreases as the temperature increases from 273 K to 473 K.

Combing the simulation results and model analysis of the two photo detectors, the temperature characteristic of SOI LPIN PD-GTE photocurrent is great and better than that of SOI LPIN PD.

4.2   Temperature Characteristics of Dark Current

We simulate the dark current in the same way. No light illumination is set in ATLAS and two different temperatures(T = 300 K, 473 K) are applied considering the little influence on dark current caused by temperature lower than 300 K. The results of SOI LPIN PD-GTE and SOI LPIN PD are shown in Fig. 3.

As shown in Fig. 3, the dark current of both detectors increases as the temperature rises. The simulation results are consistent with the physical model analysis. It can be seen from the simulation results of SOI LPIN PD-GTE, there always exist a peak in every curves of I-V characteristic, the phenomena is mainly caused by the accumulation of carriers on the surface. The values become steady after the peaks with the gate voltage rising. Results show a very low value (10^{-14} magnitude) of dark current at room temperature (T = 300 K). If the temperature reaches 473 K, the dark current of SOI LPIN PD-GTE increases to 10^{-10} magnitude. Thanks to the totally fully depleted I-region, the value of dark current of SOI LPIN PD-GTE is much lower than that of SOI LPIN PD in Fig. 3.

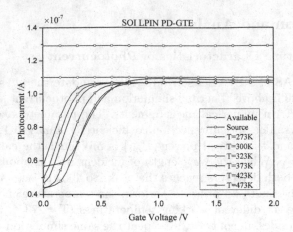

(a) Temperature characteristic of photocurrent for SOI LPIN PD-GTE.

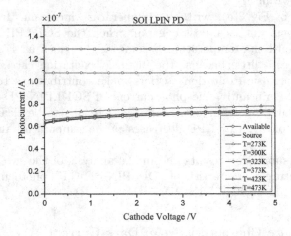

(b) Temperature characteristic of photocurrent for SOI LPIN PD

Fig. 2. Temperature characteristics of photocurrent for SOI LPIN PD-GTE and SOI LPIN PD.

4.3   Temperature Characteristics of Sensitivity

Signal-to-noise ratio (SNR), quantum efficiency and FHWM are significant parameters to measure the sensitivity of photo detectors. SNR is the ratio of photocurrent to dark current. According to Figs. 2 and 3, the SNR of SOI LPIN PD-GTE achieves 10^7 at 300 K while the SNR of SOI LPIN PD is 10^6. As the temperature rises, SNR of both the detectors decreases mainly due to the rapid increases of dark current. At temperature of 473 K, the SNR of SOI LPIN PD-GTE reduces to 10^3 while the SNR of the other is 10^2. According to the Eqs. (4) and (12), SNR of SOI LPIN PD-GTE is mainly affected by the length of the

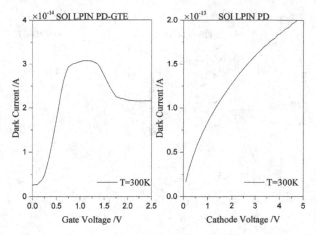

(a) T=300K, the dark current of SOI LPIN PD-GTE and SOI LPIN PD.

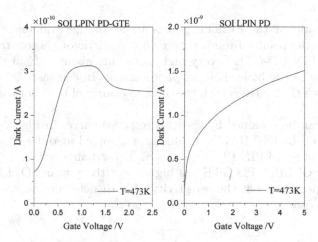

(b) T=473K, the dark current of SOI LPIN PD-GTE and SOI LPIN PD

Fig. 3. Temperature characteristics of the dark current for SOI LPIN PD-GTE and SOI LPIN PD.

channel (Li). Longer channel will increase SNR to some extent. However, increasing the length of the channel will lower other performances, such as frequency characteristic.

Quantum efficiency (QE) mainly depends on the value of photocurrent, it can be obtained by:

$$QE = QI \cdot \frac{P_{abs}}{P_{opt}} \tag{13}$$

Where P_{abs} is the optical power absorbed by silicon film, P_{opt} is the incident optical power of the gate electrode, QI is the internal quantum efficiency.

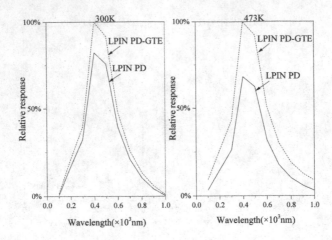

Fig. 4. Spectral response of the detectors at different temperatures.

QI the ratio of the cathode photocurrent to the available photocurrent. According to the result of temperature characteristic of photocurrent in Fig. 2, QI of SOI LPIN PD-GTE is very high, achieving about 95 % at different temperatures due to the little changed photocurrent. In contrast, QI of SOI LPIN PD is lower which decreases with the obvious change of the photocurrent at high temperature.

FHWM can be obtained by spectral response curves in Fig. 4. We find that FHWM of SOI LPIN PD-GTE is almost unchanged at different temperatures and FHWM of SOI LPIN PD decreases at higher temperature.

Overall, SOI LPIN PD-GTE has higher sensitivity than SOI LPIN PD does at high temperature, but the sensitivity of both detectors decreases while the temperature rises.

5   Conclusion

In this paper, we analyzed the operation principle of thin-film SOI Lateral PIN diode with gated transparent electrode, presented the temperature characteristics of photocurrent and dark current, then validated by ATLAS simulation. On the basis of such works, we analyzed the temperature characteristic of sensitivity of SOI LPIN PD GTE. In contrast, we performed the same works on the SOI LPIN PD.

The final results show the temperature characteristic of sensitivity for SOI LPIN PD-GTE is better than that of SOI LPIN PD. The QI yields about 95 % and the SNR is 10^7 at 300 K. As the temperature rises to 473 K, QI remains stable and SNR becomes 10^3 which means the sensitivity decreases with the rising of temperature. Besides, FHWM of SOI LPIN PD-GTE is hardly affected by temperature but FHWM of SOI LPIN PD decreases while the temperature rises. However, photo detectors rarely work in condition of such high temperature environment like 473 K. We can draw a conclusion that the SOI LPIN PD-GTE is capable of working at high temperature with high sensitivity.

References

1. Abid, K., Rahman, F.: Gated lateral p-i-n junction device for light sensing. IEEE Photo. Tech. Lett. **23**, 911–913 (2011)
2. Mueller, T., Xia, F.N., Avouris, P.: Graphene photodetectors for high-speed optical communications. Nat. Photo **4**, 297–301 (2010)
3. Afzalian, A., Flandre, D.: Measurements, modeling and electrical simulations of lateral PIN photodiodes in thin film-SOI for high quantum efficiency and high selectivity in the UV range. In: Proceedings of ESSDERC Conference, 16–18 Sep 2003, pp. 55–58. Portugal (2003)
4. Afzalian, A., Flander, D.: Characterization of quantum efficiency, effective lifetime and mobility in thin film ungated SOI lateral PIN photodiodes. Solid State Electron. **51**, 337–342 (2007)
5. Zeng, Y., Xie, H.Q., Huang, W.Q., Zhang, G.L.: Physical model of lateral PIN photodiode gated by a transparent electrode fabricated on SOI film. Opt. Photon. Lett. **2**, 15–20 (2009)
6. Li, G.L., Zeng, Y., Hu, W.H., Zou, Y., Xia, Y.: Operation of thin-film gated SOI lateral PIN photodetectors with gate voltage applied and intrinsic length variation. Optik **125**, 6483–6487 (2014)
7. Csutak, S., Schaub, J., Wu, W., Campbell, J.: CMOS-compatible high speed planar silicon photodiodes fabricated on SOI substrates. IEEE J. Quantum Electron. **38**(2), 193–196 (2002)
8. Zeng, Y., et al.: Threshold voltage in short-channel SOI BJMOSFET. J. Funct. Mater. Devices **14**(4), 831–834 (2008)
9. Xie, H.Q., Zeng, Y., Zeng, J.P., Wang, T.H.: Analysis and simulation of lateral PIN photodiode gated by transparent electrode fabricated on fully-depleted SOI film. J. Cent. South Univ. Technol. **18**, 744–748 (2011)
10. Sze, S.M., Ng, K.K.: Physics of Semiconductor Device. Wiley Interscience, Hoboken (2007)
11. Zeng, Y., Xia, Y., Hu, W., Li, G., Peng, W.: Modeling and electrical simulations of thin-film gated SOI lateral PIN photodetectors for high sensitivity and speed performances. In: Xu, W., Xiao, L., Zhang, C., Li, J., Yu, L. (eds.) NCCET 2013. CCIS, vol. 396, pp. 235–243. Springer, Heidelberg (2013)
12. Li, G.L., Zeng, Y., Hu, W., Xia, Y.: Analysis and simulation for current-voltage models of thin-film gated SOI lateral PIN photodetectors. Optik **125**, 540–544 (2014)
13. Afzalian, A., Flandre, D.: Physical modeling and design of thin-film SOI lateral PIN photodetectors. IEEE Trans. Electron Devices **52**, 1116–1122 (2005)
14. Atlas Users Manual Device Simulation Software. SILVACO Inc. (2010)

Mitigation Techniques Against TSV-to-TSV Coupling in 3DIC

Quan Deng[✉], Minxuan Zhang, Zhenyu Zhao, and Peng Li

School of Computer Science, National University of Defense Technology, Changsha, China
dengq_nudt@126.com

Abstract. TSV in 3DIC introduces a large and fickle parasitic capacitance inevitably, causing serious problems on Power/Signal Integrity (P/SI). In this paper, we give two methods to mitigate TSV-to-TSV coupling, which are buffer insertion and shield insertion. The effect of the buffer insertion and shield insertion are studied by comparison experiment, and the experiment results have proved that these two methods can reduce the coupling capacitance effectively. Factors as location, number and drive capability of buffers in this course are also discussed. TSV-to-TSV coupling reduces by 99 % at maximum. Through combining the two method, we can get a low cost and effective optimization for reduction of TSV-to-TSV coupling in consideration of actual design restrain, which can also be utilized in EDA tools.

Keywords: 3DIC · TSV-to-TSV coupling · Shield insertion · Buffer insertion

1   Introduction

Three Dimension Integrated Circuit (3DIC) is a promising way for the future of Very Large Scale Integrated Circuit (VLSI). Through Silicon Via (TSV) plays an important role in 3D IC designs. TSVs are critical signal passes as vertical connection in 3D IC, which effectively decrease the length of wires. However, there are parasitic capacitances between TSVs because of their array structure. In TSV array, TSV-to-TSV coupling influences both the output and the input. It does not only degrades the standard of signal, but also delivers coupling noise to near dies [1].

Recognizing the harm of TSV-to-TSV coupling, a series of researches have been done. In [2, 3], the electronic model of single TSV and TSV array are modeled, which provide basis for further research. To our knowledge, these literatures have not discussed the correlation of substrate capacitances of multi TSVs. In [4] Peng analysis the TSV-induced silicon and field effect and give a noise analysis flow for full-chip. Moreover, the optimized manufacturability and optimization method in system level are also put forward in [5, 6], respectively. However, the methods are either too expensive or lack

The research is supported by Specialized Research Fund for the Doctor Program of Higher Education of China with Grant No. 20124307110016, and by National Natural Science Foundation of China with Grant No. 61176030.

W. Xu et al. (Eds.): NCCET 2015, CCIS 592, pp. 182–190, 2016.
DOI: 10.1007/978-3-662-49283-3_18

of deep analysis. Therefore, a research on effective optimizations with low cost is essential based on accurate models which consider the correlation of substrate capacitances of multi TSVs.

In this paper, we provide an accurate model and propose two optimization methods to reduce TSV-to-TSV coupling. Both of the two proposed methods do not need any change in manufacture of TSV. Through sacrificing few area or power, they reduce TSV-to-TSV coupling by 99 % at maximum. The relation between the optimization effect and factors as location, numbers and drive capability are given. Depending on different design restrain, we can offer an optimization flexibly.

2   TSV-to-TSV Coupling

TSV-to-TSV coupling degrades the quality of signal. The parasitic network of double TSVs is shown as Fig. 1. And the parasitic capacitance of substrate and TSV are two main parameters of coupling, which connect adjacent TSVs. The parasitic capacitance of TSV is determined by the physical size of TSV, while the parasitic capacitance of substrate is determined by the relative position of TSVs. It is given by the following expressions [7]:

$$C_{si,\max} = \frac{2\pi \in_0 \in_{si} L}{In(P/r)} \tag{1}$$

$$L_{si,ii} = \frac{\mu_{si} L}{\pi} \ln\left[\frac{P_{i0}}{r + t_{ox}}\right] \tag{2}$$

$$L_{si,ij} = \frac{\mu_{si} L}{2\pi} \ln[\frac{P_{i0} P_{j0}}{P_{ij}(r + t_{ox})}] \tag{3}$$

$$[C_{si}] = \mu_0 \in_0 \in_{si} L^2 [L_{si}]^{-1} \tag{4}$$

$$C_{si,ii} = \sum_{k=1}^{N} C_{si,ik} \tag{5}$$

The test circuit for experiment is set as Fig. 2, which have two adjacent signal TSV passes. The buffers behind the inputs are used to adjust the drive capability of input in the course of simulation. And the diameter and length of TSV is 2 μm, 20 μm respectively. The thickness of oxide barrier is 0.03 μm; the pitch between TSVs is 4 μm. The parasitic capacitance of TSV in this size can be 146fF as maximum and 22.8fF as minimum. To reflect the worst situation, we use the max parasitic capacitance of TSV during the simulations.

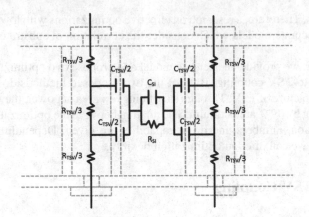

184   Q. Deng et al.

Fig. 1. Parasitic network of double TSV

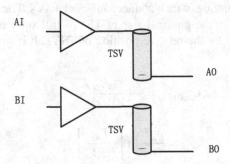

Fig. 2. Test circuit for experiment

The output of path A and path B is shown in Fig. 3 using the parasitic network as Fig. 1. TSV-to-TSV coupling makes that the rise time of path A becomes longer. And the coupling noise of path B comes into being in the form of pulse spike with a peak value of 273 mV. The transition of signal on path A becomes very large, and the coupling noise in path B may cause inaccurate upset in the next functional unit.

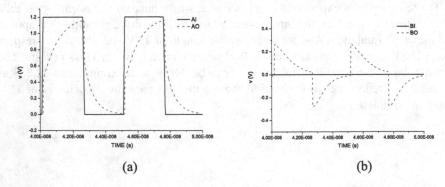

Fig. 3. The output without optimization (a) the output of path A (b) the output of path B

3   Buffer Insertion

Buffer insertion is an easy and effective way to reduce TSV-to-TSV coupling. The effect of buffer insertion depends on the factors as position, number and drive capability. In considering of that, we firstly analyze pro-insertion and then post-insertion.

3.1   Buffer Pro-insertion

The effect of buffer insertion differs with the location of the inserted buffer. Here we discuss the pro-insertion. Using D0-16 of standard cells in 45 nm as the pro-insertion, the output of path A and path B are shown in Fig. 4. On one hand, pro-insertion helps reduce TSV-to-TSV coupling. If the drive capability of the new one is the same as the old one, there is no difference between the output of path A and path B. The transition and the peak value of signal remain unchanged. Increasing the drive capability of the new one helps reduce the transition of the output on path A. And the peak value of the output on path B reduces, while decreasing the drive capability makes the quality of signal worse. On the other hand, when the drive capability increase, the benefit become smaller and smaller. The relation between the drive capability and the peak value on path B is shown in Fig. 5.

Buffer insertion need extra area for extra buffers. Table 1 lists the area of D0-16 in 45 nm standard cells. High drive capability of buffer helps reduce TSV-to-TSV coupling, while the extra area of those buffers is bigger and bigger. How to balance the extra area and the signal quality depends on the actual design constrain and the request of design.

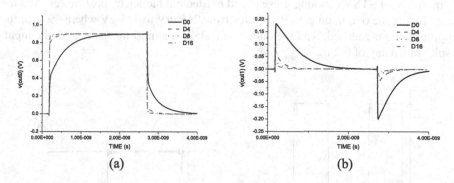

Fig. 4. The output with buffer pre-insertion at different drive capability (a) the output of path A (b) the output of path B

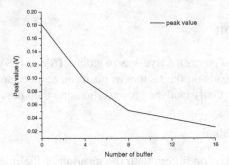

Fig. 5. The relation between the drive capability and the variation of peak value on path B

Table 1. Parameters of buffers in 45 nm with different drive capability

Drive capability of buffer	Width (μm)	Area (μm^2)
D0	0.56	0.9408
D4	1.26	2.1168
D8	2.24	3.7632
D16	4.06	6.8208

3.2 Buffer Post-insertion

When inserting the buffer behind the TSV, the outputs of path A and path B are shown in Fig. 6. TSV-to-TSV coupling noise is still existed but hidden by post-buffer. And the peak value of the output on path B changes from 266 mV to 715 μV where 99 % of the coupling noise is reduced. And the output of path A is almost the same with the input, in spite of a delay of 0.2 ns.

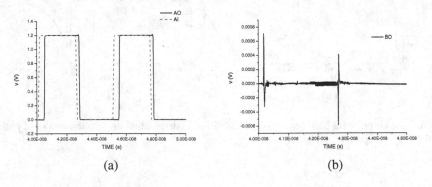

(a)   (b)

Fig. 6. The output with buffer post-insertion (a) the output of path A (b) the output of path B

Buffer post-insertion is an effective way to improve signal quality. But it changes according to the number of insertion. Here we add two buffers behind TSV in Fig. 2. And the output of path B is shown in Fig. 7 where the peak value becomes 20.6 μV. Compared with the former experiment, the peak value decreases by 97 %. Consequently, increasing the number of post-insertion contributes to reduce coupling noise. However, along with the increase of the buffer number, more extra area are need. Usually inserting one buffer behind, we can get a satisfactory result.

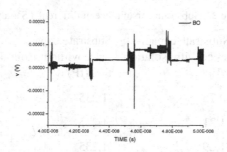

Fig. 7. The output of path B with double buffers

4   Shield Insertion

Shield insertion is another effective way to reduce TSV-to-TSV coupling. In consideration of the location of shield and attacker, it can be classified into two groups, which are direct isolation and indirect isolation. This is because the shield has an effect of protection for the near TSV around it.

Inserting an extra TSV between the attacker and the victim, the influence from attacker becomes weaker. As shown in Fig. 8, the TSV in the center is the victim, while there are six attackers and a shield around. The six attackers keep the same distance with the victim. And the shield is just in the middle of A0 and V. The pitch of TSV is 6um; the radius of TSV is 1 μm; the thickness of oxide is 0.05 μm; the length of TSV is 20 μm.

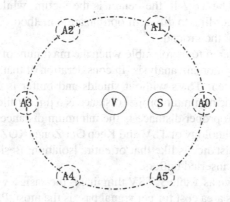

Fig. 8. Diagram of signal TSVs and isolation TSVs

According to the coupling model of TSV, the parasitic capacitances of substrate are shown in Table 2. Without any shield, the six attackers around victim carry the same parasitic capacitance. Comparing with the situation which has only one attacker, the substrate parasitic capacitance of each one is smaller. However, the total influence of six attackers is more serious than that of only one attacker. With a shield, the substrates parasitic capacitance decrease at different degree. While the angle of attacker-shield-victim increases, the effect of isolation for attacker is weaker.

Table 2. Substrate capacitance of different TSV array

Attacker	Substrate capacitance with isolation (fF)	Substrate capacitance without isolation (fF)	Substrate capacitance for only one attacker (fF)
1	0.75	1.235	3.69
2	1.21	1.235	3.69
3	1.29	1.235	3.69

The parasitic capacitance of substrate between two TSVs is related to the number and the shape of TSV array. Adjacent TSVs around referential TSV interact with each other. As the number increases, the substrate parasitic capacitance of each one decreases. While the total substrate parasitic of adjacent TSV increase. In consideration of that, it is proper to turn adjacent signal TSV pass into shield which can decrease the parasitic capacitance of other adjacent signal TSV. When the shield on the line made of attacker and victim, TSV-to-TSV coupling between signals is isolated by shield entirely. On the other hand, when the position of shield is between attacker and victim but not on the line of them, TSV-to-TSV coupling is attenuated.

5   Cost Comparison

To compare the cost of different optimization methods, we study the extension of triangle TSV array in Fig. 9. The TSV in the center is the victim, while the outer TSVs are attackers or shields according to different optimization methods. The shields generally connect to the power or the ground.

The noise is considered to be tolerable when the maximum of magnitude is smaller than -30db in frequency domain analysis. In consideration of that, the minimum proper distance between adjacent TSVs without shields and buffer is 6 μm. And in partial isolation as Fig. 9(a), the minimum proper distance is 3 μm. While in entire isolation as Fig. 9(b), the minimum proper distance is the minimum distance which is determined by the manufactory technology of TSV and Keep Out Zone (KOZ). To buffer insertion, the minimum proper distance is like that of entire isolation. Besides, it also cost extra area and power for the inserted buffers.

Cost of area is shown as Table 3. TSV thinning is the easiest way to reduce TSV-to-TSV coupling while its area cost for per signal pass is the most. Partial Shield insertion

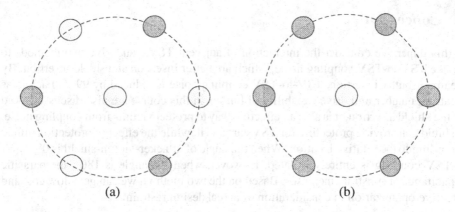

Fig. 9. Shield insertion (a) partial isolation (b) entire isolation

is a proper way to reduce coupling comparing with entire shield insertion. The area per signal of the former one is only 56.8 % as the later one. And the benefit of area is related to the relative location of TSVs and the shield number. For all of these, the cost of area for buffer insertion is the minimum. And we use the area of D8 to calculate in this course.

Table 3. Cost of area for different optimization methods

Optimization method	Area (μm^2)	Number of signal passes	Area per signal pass (μm^2)
TSV thinning	113.0	7	16.1
Partial shield insertion	28.3	4	7.1
Entire shield insertion	12.5	1	12.5
Buffer insertion	12.5 + 3.8*7	7	5.6

Only considering of area, buffer insertion is the best way to reduce TSV-to-TSV coupling. But compared to other methods, buffer insertion need more power to drive the extra inserted buffers. The number of the inserted buffers is the same as the number of signal TSVs. For now, as the size of TSV is much bigger than that of traditional wires, the number of TSVs is about tens of thousands. The extra power is not too much. But as the manufacturability of TSV develop fast, this situation will change. The more we used TSV, the more extra power for reducing TSV-to-TSV coupling it need.

It is difficult to judge which way is better to mitigate TSV-to-TSV coupling. But according to actual request and constrain of design, we can choose an optimal solution to mitigate TSV-to-TSV coupling for the area or power dissipation.

6 Conclusion

In this paper, we consider the interaction of adjacent TSVs, and give two methods to reduce TSV-to-TSV coupling noise, which are buffer insertion and shield insertion. By means of buffer insertion, TSV-to-TSV coupling noise is reduced by 99 %. Factors as location, number and drive capability of buffers in this course are also discussed. And by the shield insertion, it is also an effective way to protect victims from coupling noise. A shield can provide protection for TSVs around it, while the effect of protection differs according to the relative location. When the angle of attacker-victim-shield is 0°, TSV-to-TSV coupling is entirely isolated. However, when the angle is 180°, the parasitic capacitance of substrate increases. Based on the two method, we can get a low cost and effective optimization in consideration of actual design restrain.

References

1. Koo, K., Kim, M., Kim, J.J., Kim, J., Kim, J.: Vertical noise coupling from on-chip switching-mode power supply in a mixed-signal stacked 3-D-IC. IEEE Trans. Compon. Packag. Manuf. Technol. **3**, 476–488 (2013)
2. Katti, G., Stucchi, M., De Meyer, K., Dehaene, W.: Electrical modeling and characterization of through silicon via for three-dimensional ICs. IEEE Trans. Electron Devices **57**(1), 256–262 (2010)
3. Xie, B., Swaminathan, M., Han, K.J., Xie, J.: Coupling analysis of through-silicon via (TSV) arrays in silicon interposers for 3D systems. In: IEEE International Symposium on Electromagnetic Compatibility (EMC), vol. 1353, pp. 16–21 (2011)
4. Peng, Y., Song, T., Petranovic, D., Lim, S.K.: On accurate full-chip extraction and optimization of TSV-to-TSV coupling elements in 3D ICs. In: IEEE/ACM International Conference on Computer-Aided Design (ICCAD), pp. 281–288 (2013)
5. Gu, X., Jenkins, K.: Mitigation of TSV-substrate noise coupling in 3-D CMOS SOI technology. In: IEEE 22nd Conference on Electrical Performance of Electronic Packaging and Systems (EPEPS), pp. 73–76 (2013)
6. Serafy, C., Srivastava, A.: TSV replacement and shield insertion for TSV–TSV coupling reduction in 3-D global placement. IEEE Trans. Comput. Aided Des. Integr. Circuits Syst. **34**(4), 554–562 (2015)
7. Song, T., Liu, C., Peng, Y., Lim, S.K.: Full-chip multiple TSV-to-TSV coupling extraction and optimization in 3D ICs. In: 50th ACM/EDAC/IEEE Design Automation Conference (DAC), pp. 1–7 (2013)

Author Index

Printed in the United States
By Bookmasters